Praise for
THE PROFESSIONAL SIGN LANGUAGE INTERPRETER'S HANDBOOK

"Finally! A hands-on, no holds barred, resource book on the practical, everyday, experiential aspects of sign language interpreting. Having graduated from an ITP, taught interpreter training workshops and worked as an interpreter for 25+ years, I can see how this book will be a valuable resource to interpreters in our profession. Linda has bridged the gap between the academics taught in interpreter training programs and the reality of what it takes to develop a successful interpreting practice."

Tracy J. Pifer
CI, CSC, SC:L

"WOW! This **HANDBOOK** is an excellent resource! As a consumer of sign language interpreting services, I hope that professional interpreters, student interpreters, and anyone who is considering becoming an interpreter will read this book! It provides a thorough, fair, and well-balanced view of the profession.

Its extensive resources make Ms. Humphreys' **HANDBOOK** equally as valuable for both state and local government agencies as well as for all service providers and agencies that work with individuals who are deaf and hard-of-hearing and that utilize sign language interpreters. It is also an excellent tool for interpreting training programs.

I have worked with Ms. Humphreys for many years. She is an exceptional example of a sign language interpreter with a high level of business professionalism. It is my belief that everyone will benefit from following her practical and straight-forward advice."

Richard L. Ray
ADA Compliance Officer
Los Angeles, California

"Would that I had had a beginning resource guide 45 years ago, I would have known quicker and sooner what was involved. Anything that would have made my job more certain would have been much appreciated. Therefore I can recommend Linda Humphreys' *THE PROFESSIONAL SIGN LANGUAGE INTERPRETER'S HANDBOOK* as a basic resource for the interested and as a training and discussion guide for interpreter training programs. I see this work filling the gap of materials needed in this field.

Even for those currently working as professional interpreters, this **HANDBOOK** should be required reading! Ms. Humphreys' book provides an understanding of what true professionalism requires and be a catalyst to increase professionalism."

Lon Ramsel, MA
Sign Language Interpreter
NAD Level 5
CCASD Level 6

The
Professional
Sign Language
Interpreter's
Handbook

The complete, practical manual for the interpreting profession

LINDA HUMPHREYS, M.A., CSC, SC:L

Second Edition

Sign Language Interpreting Media

Brentwood, California

The Professional Sign Language Interpreter's Handbook

Linda Humphreys, M.A., CSC, SC:L

Published by Sign Language Interpreting Media
P.O. Box 491147
Brentwood, CA 90049-4521, USA
(310) 364-3938
www. InterpretingInfo.com

ATTENTION: SCHOOLS AND ASSOCIATIONS
Discounts on bulk quantities are available to corporations, professional associations, and educational or other organizations. For details and discount information, contact the Special Sales department at Sign Language Interpreting Media (310) 364-3938/ fax (310) 861-5959.

Publisher's Cataloging-in-Publication
(Provided by Quality Books, Inc.)
Humphreys, Linda
    The professional sign language interpreter's handbook
    / Linda Humphreys. --
    p.cm.
    Includes index.
    LCCN: 2002094064
    ISBN: 0-9724161-1-0
    1. Interpreters for the deaf--Handbooks, manuals,
    etc. I. Title.

HV2402.h86 2004   362.4'283
                         QBI02-200763

Printed in the United States of America

Book Interior Designer: Pamela Terry, Opus 1 Design, www.opus1design.com
Book Cover Designer: Alan Dale Enterprises, Inc. (Marcelle La Cour), ad@alan-dale.com
Book Cover Photographers: Miranda Alcott and Bob Parry
Editor: Janice M. Humphreys, humphreysonline@earthlink.net

0 9 8 7 6 5 4 3 2 1

Second Edition

THE PROFESSIONAL
SIGN LANGUAGE INTERPRETER'S HANDBOOK
by
Linda Humphreys, M.A., CSC, SC:L

Foreword by Virginia Hughes, MCSC, SC:L   xv

Introduction   xvii

What We Live By:

    Registry of Interpreters for the Deaf: Code of Ethics   xix

    National Association of the Deaf: Code of Ethics   xxi

PART I: INTRODUCTION TO THE FIELD   21

Informal Surveys Reveal...   23

Definition of an Interpreter   24

What We Do   25

Other Terms to Be Aware Of   25

Who We Are   26

Registry of Interpreters for the Deaf (RID)   26

    Interpreter Profile   27

    RID Certifications   28

    Degree Requirements For RID Test Candidates   29

    Certification Maintenance Program (CMP)   30

National Association of the Deaf (NAD)   30

    NAD Certifications   31

    NAD Certification Maintenance Requirements   31

National Council on Interpreting (NCI)   31

National Interpreter Certification (NIC)   32

Salary Ranges   32

    Some Things to Consider When Developing Your Fees   35

    Fee Schedule Worksheet   37

PART II: GETTING STARTED   39

Getting Out There   41

Federal Government Interpreting Positions   43

Identification   43

    Birth Certificate   44

Social Security Number	44
Passport	44
Business Cards	45
Getting Organized	45
Resumes	46
Sample Resume	48
Resume Worksheet With Explanations	49
Letters of Introduction	51
Explanation of Letter of Introduction	53
Assignment Intake Forms	55
Assignment Intake Information	56
Travel/Mileage Records	57
Billing and Filing	57
Invoices	58
Sample Invoice	59
Taxes	60
Sample Estimated Quarterly Taxes Worksheet	62
Planning for Today/Planning for Tomorrow	63
Health Insurance	63
Workers' Compensation Insurance	64
Disability Insurance	65
Professional Liability/Errors and Omissions Insurance	66
Life Insurance	66
Financial Planning	66
"Tool Kit" for Interpreters	67

PART III: INTERPRETING SITUATIONS AND CIRCUMSTANCES — 71

AIDS-Related Interpreting	74
Agency or "Staff" Interpreting	75
Business/Corporate Interpreting	76
Community Services Interpreting	78
Deaf-Blind Interpreting	79
Educational/Academic Interpreting	82
Emergency Interpreting	84

Public Emergency Situations 84

"911" Situations 85

Government Interpreting Position 86

Legal Interpreting 89

Medical Interpreting 91

Mental Health Interpreting 94

Platform/Performing Arts Interpreting 96

Religious Interpreting 98

Spiritual/Metaphysical/"Alternative" Interpreting 99

Social Interpreting 101

Support Groups Interpreting 103

Technical Interpreting 105

Video Relay Service (VRS) Interpreting 106

PART IV: PROFESSIONAL CHALLENGES 109

Your Role? Follow the Code of Ethics 111

Preparation 112

Taking Precautions Prior to the Assignment 114

Workers' Compensation 117

Carpal Tunnel Syndrome/Repetitive Motion Disorder 118

Stress 120

Sometimes, You May Have to Just Say "No" 123

Personal Safety Considerations 125

PART V: WORKING WITH OTHERS 129

Professional Presentation 131

Professional Courtesy 133

Giving Back to the Community 135

APPENDIX 139

Conventions/Conferences/Workshops 141

Course Training Record 142

Networking Information 143

Applying for a Federal Job 144

Application for Federal Employment – SF 171   146

General Information   150

Optional Application for Federal Employment –OF 612   151

Birth Certification Location Information   153

Social Security Application   167

Request for Earnings and Benefit Estimate Statement   172

United States Passport Application   174

United States Passport Application by Mail (Renewals Only)   178

Resume Worksheets   182

References Worksheet   184

Assignment Intake Information   185

Travel/Mileage Record Form   186

Estimated Quarterly Taxes Worksheet   187

Internal Revenue Service Centers   188

State Tax Information   190

"Tool Kit" for Interpreters Worksheet   193

Emergency Essentials   194

Alcoholics Anonymous Preamble/Serenity Prayer/   195
   Twelve Steps/Twelve Traditions   196

"SIGNER-CISES"   198

Carpal Tunnel Syndrome/Repetitive Motion Disorder References   199

Donations Sample Worksheet   200

RESOURCES   201

Directory of National Organizations of and for Deaf and Hard of
   Hearing People   203

Workers' Compensation Administrators Directory   227
   (United States, Other U.S. Areas and Canada)

Registry of Interpreters for the Deaf (RID) Information: 251

   Associate, Certification, and Continuing Education Programs   251
     (U.S. and Canada)

   Bachelor's and Graduate Degree Programs   265

   Annual Membership Application (SAMPLE)   273

   NAD Certified Interpreter Special Membership Application   274
     (SAMPLE)

Explanation of Certificates   275

National Testing System Computer-Based Testing Application (SAMPLE)   280

National Testing System Comprehensive Application (SAMPLE)   281

    Certification Maintenance Program (CMP)   283

    Associate Continuing Education Tracking (ACET) Program   288

    Approved CMP and ACET Sponsors   291

    RID Affiliate Chapters and Regions   298

National Association of the Deaf (NAD) Membership Application   299

National Association of the Deaf (NAD) Certifications   300

RID Certification Updates   301

    NCI Test Question Development   301

    Overview of the NCI Performance and Interview Examinations   302

    Performance Test Procedures   304

    NAD/RID National Interpreter Certification Knowledge (Written) Test Application   305

    NAD/RID National Interpreter Certification (NIC) Knowledge Examination Suggested Reference Materials   306

Americans With Disabilities Act (ADA) Handbook Information   307

INDEX   **308**

Acknowledgments

Special Thanks:

To Divine Guidance, who helped me find the field of sign language interpreting;

To the Deaf community for enriching my life and life's experiences;

To my fellow interpreters who taught me, inspired me, and helped to make the work more fun;

To the National Association of the Deaf (NAD) for their kind permission to reproduce materials;

To everyone at the Registry of Interpreters for the Deaf (RID) for their assistance and kind permission to reproduce materials;

To Dr. Roger Beach: a true "brother," friend and "guardian angel";

To Virginia Hughes for her enthusiastic support;

To Lon Ramsel for his wisdom and humor;

To Janice Humphreys, the best sister-in-law a girl could have, for the long talks, cups of tea and hours spent editing;

To my family and true friends, the ones who encouraged and supported me through the arduous process of writing and publishing a book. You know who you are. I am grateful for your love and support.

To my Dad, Robert L. Humphreys, who showed me the power of having a gentle spirit and unconditional love. I will always love you.

NAMASTE !

Our deepest fear is not that we are inadequate. Our deepest fear is that we are powerful beyond measure. It is our light, not our darkness, that frightens us. We ask ourselves, Who am I to be brilliant, gorgeous, talented, and fabulous? Actually, who are you *not* to be? You are a child of God. Your playing small doesn't serve the world. There's nothing enlightened about shrinking so that other people won't feel insecure around you. We are all meant to shine, as children do. We were born to manifest the glory of God that is within us; it's in everyone. And as we let our own light shine, we unconsciously give other people permission to do the same. As we are liberated from our own fear, our presence automatically liberates others.

Marianne Williamson

To laugh often and love much; to win the respect of intelligent persons and the affection of children; to earn the approbation of honest critics and to endure the betrayal of false friends; to appreciate beauty; to find the best in others; to give of oneself; to leave the world a little better, whether by a healthy child, a garden patch or a redeemed social condition; to have played and laughed with enthusiasm and sung with exultation; to know that if even one life has breathed easier because you have lived. This is to have succeeded.

Ralph Waldo Emerson

Life is a daring adventure - or it is nothing.

Helen Keller

FOREWORD

As a working interpreter and interpreter instructor, I am pleased to be invited to write the foreword to this manual. We have a plethora of sign language books but a lack of books that focus on the essential ancillary information for the sign language interpreter. This handbook addresses the necessary preparation new and seasoned interpreters must follow to have success in this profession. This approach assumes a practitioner has the Sign and English ability to interpret and just needs assistance with all the nuts and bolts that make this such a great task. This manual will suggest answers to every query and in such a palatable manner that leaves the final action in the hands of an educated interpreter.

Carry this HANDBOOK with you. Read, reread, and digest every page and allow Linda Humphreys' positive attitude toward this very democratic task to influence you as you set off on your assignments.

Virginia Hughes, MCSC, SC:L

INTRODUCTION

I graduated as a member of the second "hearing" class to be awarded an undergraduate degree from Gallaudet University.

Although I was taught many things during my time at Gallaudet, after my graduation, on my own as a freelance interpreter, I realized that there was a deficit in my education. I was taught the "how-tos" of interpreting. I was not, however, exposed to other aspects of the interpreting profession such as preparation techniques for specific assignments, operation of a small business, organizational skills and maximizing availability and productivity.

This is a workbook designed for people who are curious about the actual experiences of a sign language interpreter, for the "Interpreting 101" student, and for those new to the profession. It is also a valuable resource for career counselors, vocational rehabilitation counselors, advocates and agencies that serve the D/deaf and hire sign language interpreters, or anyone associated with a related field. THE PROFESSIONAL SIGN LANGUAGE INTERPRETER'S HANDBOOK provides awareness of and exposure to the non-manual aspects of the sign language interpreting profession. Here you will find a compilation of information and resources that are significant and useful. My experiences as a government interpreter, staff interpreter for an advocacy/interpreting agency, and independent contractor will benefit you. Everything, except the "how-to" sign aspects of sign language interpreting is included.

This book has six parts. PART ONE is an introduction to the field. PART TWO is "nuts and bolts" i.e., how to get started and how to get yourself out there. PART THREE explains what you may find "out there" by describing the kinds of work we do, where we do it, what interpreter attributes best suit the specific kind of work, and what we can do to better prepare ourselves. PARTS FOUR and FIVE are discourses on various topics, including professional issues and working with other interpreters. Personal anecdotes are used to illustrate concepts and practices. Here you will see just how difficult some of the non-manual aspects of interpreting can be. You can learn from my experiences. Additionally there are APPENDIX and RESOURCES sections which offer extensive support information related to the field of sign language interpreting.

My hope is that this book will lead to greater awareness of and respect for interpreting and for those we call the "professional sign language interpreter." Use it to prepare yourself for a fulfilling and challenging career.

This book is my contribution to the field of sign language interpreting. At times it deals with difficult issues. This is my attempt to help you deal with these issues and how they relate to us as interpreters. The text was written to encourage stimulating dialogue, questioning, and thinking. I challenge you to learn by exposing yourself to different perspectives. Challenge yourself to think anew, or perhaps, to discover certain information for the first time. Use this book as a tool to become proactive rather than reactive; take action.

I intend to make a positive contribution to the field of sign language interpreting. If, through this book, I have made life a bit easier for even one interpreter, then I have accomplished my goal.

Linda Humphreys M.A., CSC, SC:L

WHAT WE LIVE BY

REGISTRY OF INTERPRETERS FOR THE DEAF, INC.

CODE OF ETHICS

1. Interpreters/transliterators shall keep all assignment-related information strictly confidential.

2. Interpreters/transliterators shall render the message faithfully, always conveying the content and spirit of the speaker using language most readily understood by the person(s) whom they serve.

3. Interpreters/transliterators shall not counsel, advise or interject personal opinions.

4. Interpreters/transliterators shall accept assignments using discretion with regard to skill, setting, and the consumers involved.

5. Interpreters/transliterators shall request compensation for services in a professional and judicious manner.

6. Interpreters/transliterators shall function in a manner appropriate to the situation.

7. Interpreters/transliterators shall strive to further knowledge and skills through participation in work-shops, professional meetings, interaction with professional colleagues, and reading of current literature in the field.

8. Interpreters/transliterators, by virtue of membership or certification by the RID, Inc., shall strive to maintain high professional standards in compliance with the Code of Ethics.

Reprinted with permission from RID

NATIONAL ASSOCIATION OF THE DEAF

INTERPRETER CODE OF ETHICS

1. All information in any interpreting assignment is to be kept in strictest confidence.

2. Interpreting services shall always be competent, impartial and professional.

3. Messages shall be rendered faithfully, always conveying the content and spirit of the communicator and professional judgment should be exercised in assessing whether communication is being understood.

4. In accepting assignments, discretion based on skill, setting, and the consumers involved must be used.

5. Counseling or injecting personal opinion is never permitted.

6. Information on the role and appropriate use of interpreting services shall be provided to the consumers when necessary.

7. Information on available resources as appropriate should be provided.

8. Compensation for services should be pursued in a professional manner.

9. Respect of and for the deaf person's rights must always be evident.

10. Only the highest professional standards, as promulgated by the NAD, shall be pursued.

PART 1

Introduction to The Field

- **Informal Surveys Reveal . . .**
- **Definition of an Interpreter**
- **What We Do**
- **Other Terms to Be Aware Of**
- **Who We Are**
- **Registry of Interpreters for the Deaf (RID)**
- **Interpreter Profile**
- **RID Certifications**
- **Certification Maintenance Program (CMP)**
- **National Association of the Deaf (NAD)**
- **NAD Certifications**
- **National Council on Interpreting (NCI)**
- **Salary Ranges**
- **Some Things to Consider When Developing Your Fees**
- **Fee Worksheet**

PART 1

Introduction to The Field

INFORMAL SURVEYS REVEAL

WHAT WE ARE CALLED:

"signers"	"hand wavers"	"assistants"
"aides"	"translators"	"volunteers"
"servers"	"hand jive-ers"	"special little hand girls"
"helpers"	"finger girls"	"interpolators for the deef"

WHAT WE ARE ASKED TO DO:

tutor	photocopy	water plants
date	make coffee	proctor exams
baby-sit	bathroom assist	do others' errands
videotape	grade papers	take someone's temperature
chauffeur	serve coffee	divulge others' confidences
answer phones/take messages		
turn medical equipment on and off		

SOME HEARING CONSUMERS VIEW US AS:

"volunteers"	"finger people"	"good little helpers"
"a distraction"	"little finger girls"	"little angels"
"a nuisance"	"Jesus' helpers to the deaf and dumb"	

SOME D/DEAF CONSUMERS VIEW US AS:

"friends"	"ears and mouth"	"a constant necessity"
"helpful"	"too professional"	"not professional enough"
"a bridge"	"a telephone"	"not helpful enough"
"a pain"	"a nuisance"	

SOME INTERPRETERS THINK OF THEMSELVES AS:

"helpers"	"advocates"	"friends/allies of the Deaf"
"supporters"	"mind readers"	"miracle workers"
"robots"	"magicians"	"human processers"

DEFINITION OF AN INTERPRETER

"Interpreters." "Sign Language interpreters." "Interpreters Serving the Deaf Community." That is what we call ourselves.......but, what are we really? Who are we? What do we do?

DICTIONARIES DEFINE *INTERPRET* AS FOLLOWS:

- translate orally
- express in another medium
- render in another language
- change from one form, function, or state to another

SO, AN INTERPRETER IS SOMEONE WHO:

- translates orally
- expresses in another medium
- renders in another language
- changes something from one form, function, or state to another

REGISTRY OF INTERPRETERS FOR THE DEAF (RID)'S DEFINITION:

"Sign Language/spoken English interpreters are highly skilled professionals. They must be able to listen to another person's words, inflections and intent and simultaneously render them into the visual language of signs using the mode of communication preferred by the deaf consumer. The interpreter must also be able to comprehend the signs, inflections and intent of the deaf consumer and simultaneously speak them in articulate, appropriate English. They must understand the cultures in which they work and apply that knowledge to promote effective cross-cultural communications."

Reprinted with permission from RID

WHAT WE DO:

Situation:

Hearing person (**H**) wants to communicate with a Deaf person (**D**) however, (**H**) does not know sign language and (**D**) does not understand (**H**)'s oral communication/speech.

(**H**) only speaks and (**D**)'s primary language is American Sign Language (ASL).

(**H**) does not know ASL and (**H**) does not move his lips when he talks, has a full, shaggy beard, and diverts his eye gaze to the ground when he is talking. So, (**D**) cannot understand nor lip-read (**H**).

In steps the interpreter (I).

(**I**) interprets in ASL what (**H**) says to (**D**),

and

(**I**) interprets or voices what (**D**) signs in ASL to (**H**).

Voila! Communication!!! (Right?)

OTHER TERMS TO BE AWARE OF:
(because they are often confused and misused)

TRANSLITERATION/TRANSLITERATOR:

Word-for-word representation of one language form into another/a person who performs a word-for-word representation of one language form into another

TRANSLATION/TRANSLATOR:

For the purposes of this book, I will use *translation* to mean taking one form of language and changing it into another (i.e., on paper, to take one's written words and write down the corresponding meaning of those words in another written language). A *translator* is a person who takes a written representation of one language and writes down the meaning of the text in another language.

WHO ARE WE?

Well into the early 1970s, the original interpreters were most likely relatives of people who were D/deaf. They used whatever means necessary to facilitate communication between the D/deaf individual and the hearing community. Persons who were hard-of-hearing and had comprehensible oral language also functioned as early interpreters.

Children of Deaf Adults (CODAs) led the way in establishing sign language interpreting as a profession. They were among the first teachers of sign language and interpreting classes. Many continue to be quite active and instrumental in establishing present-day professional policies and practices. We owe them a debt of gratitude.

CODA International is a non-profit organization for people whose parents are D/deaf. You can find out about membership, events, conferences, publications and scholarships on the internet at this website: www.coda-international.org

REGISTRY OF INTERPRETERS FOR THE DEAF (RID)

"The Registry of Interpreters for the Deaf, Inc. (RID) is the national association dedicated to the professional development of interpreters and transliterators. Founded in 1964, RID has played a leading role in establishing a national standard of quality for interpreters and transliterators. The association encourages the growth of the profession, educates the public about the vital role of interpreters and transliterators, and works to ensure equal opportunity for all individuals."

RID's Mission:

"It is the mission of RID to provide international, national, regional, state and local forums and an organizational structure for the continued growth and development of the profession in interpretation and transliteration of American Sign Language and English."

Reprinted with permission from RID

INTERPRETER PROFILE

Note: Not all practicing interpreters are members of RID.

As of June 30, 2003, RID has 10,412 registered members, serving 5 established regions (including 58 sub-chapters).

SURVEY:

According to 3,160 respondents to a 1992 RID initiated survey, the average interpreter profile is:

Sex: Female (2,636)

Age: 26 - 39 (1,603)

Ethnic Origin: Caucasian 1,473 (out of the above 1,603)
Education: (out of 2,636 Females)
Bachelor of Arts (B.A.) or Bachelor of Science (B.S.): 802
Masters of Arts (M.A.) or Masters of Science (M.S.): 601
Doctor of Philosophy (Ph.D.) or Doctor of Education (Ed.D.): 51

Hours Interpreting (Females) 25+ hours per week: 959

Years Full-time (Females):
$\leq$ 5: 538
6 $\leq$ 10: 381
11 $\leq$ 20: 220
21+: 14
(All respondents were Female in this category; no Males responded.)

Years Part-time (Females):
$\leq$ 5: 587
6 $\leq$ 10: 326
11 $\leq$ 20: 340
21+: 44
(All respondents were Female in this category; no Males responded.)

Employment Settings (Females, time spent primarily in these categories):
Community: 707
Educational, Post -Secondary: 639
Educational, Elementary/Secondary: 446
Legal: 83
Medical/Mental Health: 182
Religious: 27
Other (not differentiated Female or Male): 419

Primary Job Function (Female):
Interpreting: 1531
Teaching/Training: 345
Administration: 234
Counseling: 96

Primary Employer (Female):
Colleges/Universities: 547
Elementary/Secondary Schools: 472
Self-Employed: 343
Rehabilitation:
      Public Funded Entities: 129
      Public Non-Profit: 171
      Private Non-Profit: 134
      Private For-Profit: 57
State: 151
      Local Government: 22
      Non-Profit: 89
      For-Profit: 6
Other (not differentiated Female or Male): 300

Primary Service Provided (Female):
Interpret:
      ("Sign"): 1406
      ("Relay"): 44
      (Tactile): 13
Transliterate:
      ("Sign"): 743
      ("Relay"): 7
      (Tactile): 3
      (Oral): 9
      (Cued Speech): 5
Other (not differentiated Female or Male): 101

Secondary Service Provided (Female):
Interpret:
      ("Sign"): 549
      ("Relay"): 162
      (Tactile): 60
Transliterate:
      ("Sign"): 1033
      ("Relay"): 59
      (Tactile): 18
      (Oral): 71
      (Cued Speech): 2
Other (not differentiated Female or Male): 23

Reprinted with permission from RID

RID CERTIFICATIONS

RID certification is recognized nationally.*
RID certification is currently available in these areas:
    Interpreting
    Transliterating
    Legal Interpreting
    Oral Transliterating

The types of certification offered are:
Certificate of Interpretation (CI)
Certificate of Transliteration (CT)
Specialist Certificate: Legal (SC: L)
Oral Transliteration Certificate (OTC)

Interpreting certification is also available to those who are D/deaf:
Certified Deaf Interpreter (CDI)

To become certified, you must complete the following requirements:
Training
Written test
Videotaped performance evaluation

Though the test for the Comprehensive Skills Certification (CSC) is no longer offered, the CSC remains a valid certification and is equal in status to achieving both the CI and CT combined.

See **RESOURCES** for Explanation of Certificates.

*Other agencies or institutions sometimes require their own system of evaluation, in spite of the fact that you may be fully certified by RID. They have their own materials, standards, and criteria. In my experience, no written test was ever presented or required. I had to fill out the agencies' application, use their videotapes, and be judged by their panel. So, regardless of the certification you obtain, expect to be re-evaluated by each and every agency or institution for which you apply to work.

DEGREE REQUIREMENTS FOR RID TEST CANDIDATES

RID test candidates must have a degree from accredited institutions by the following dates:

Associate degree minimum:
Hearing applicants must have an associate's degree by June 30, 2008.

Deaf applicants must have an associate's degree by June 30, 2012.

Bachelors degree minimum:
Hearing applicants must have a bachelor's degree by June 30, 2012.

Deaf applicants must have a bachelor's degree by June 30, 2016.

By June 30, 2006, the Certification Council will establish provisions for credit for years of professional experience, life experience, and credit hours of education that do not total a formal degree.

CERTIFICATION MAINTENANCE PROGRAM (CMP)

To maintain your certification with RID, you must take Continuing Education Units (CEUs) through the Certification Maintenance Program (CMP).

Eight CEUs must be earned every four years. Ten "contact" hours of training in an approved program is worth one CEU. Limited pre-approved Independent Study CEUs may be earned. The 8 CEUs must be divided into two Content Areas, Professional Studies and General Studies, with a minimum of 6 CEUs earned in General Studies. As of January 2002, if you have a "specialist" certification, such as Performing Arts (SC: PA) and/or Legal (SC: L), two of the Professional Studies CEUs must pertain to your area of specialty.

See **RESOURCES** for detailed information about the CMP. Also see **APPENDIX** for the following forms: Conventions/ Conferences/Workshops, Course Training Record, and Networking Information.

NATIONAL ASSOCIATION OF THE DEAF (NAD)

Established in 1880, the National Association of the Deaf (NAD) is the nation's oldest and largest nonprofit organization safeguarding the accessibility and civil rights of 28 million deaf and hard of hearing Americans across a broad range of areas including education, employment, health care, and telecommunications. The NAD is a dynamic federation of 51 state association affiliates including the District of Columbia, organizational affiliates, and national members. Primary areas of focus include grassroots advocacy and empowerment, policy development and research, legal assistance, captioned media, information and publications, and youth leadership. 301-587-1789 TTY; 301-587-1788 Voice; 301-587-1791 FAX. More information about the NAD is available at www.nad.org.

Reprinted with permission from NAD

NAD CERTIFICATIONS

Prior to 2003, NAD offered certification for levels 3-5 and rated interpreters according to levels:

Level 1: Novice I*
Level 2: Novice II*   *Levels not certified
Level 3: Generalist
Level 4: Advanced
Level 5: Master

Reprinted with permission from NAD

NAD CERTIFICATION MAINTENANCE REQUIREMENTS

If you are currently a NAD certified interpreter and wish to maintain your certification status, you must do the following:

1. Submit the NAD Certified Interpreter Special Membership Application Form along with your payment to RID by June 30, 2004.

2. Fulfill the requirements of the RID Certificate Maintenance Program (as required by the NAD) by December 31, 2006. This replaces previous NAD certification maintenance requirements.

Contact RID regarding RID and NAD certification maintenance guidelines and requirements.

See **RESOURCES** for National Association of the Deaf Certifications, NAD Certified Interpreter Special Membership Application Form, and for detailed information about the RID's Certification Maintenance Program (CMP).

NATIONAL COUNCIL ON INTERPRETING (NCI)

In June of 1996, a task force agreed to develop a new joint RID/NAD certification instrument for interpreters/transliterators. The Boards of Directors of both organizations approved this initiative. A test development committee was formed and work began in 1997 on the concept for the new test.

The NCI wants to expand its agenda to numerous other areas related to interpreting and to involve a number of other organizations in this examination of interpreting issues. Other groups have been invited and will be invited to participate in this dialogue.

NAD and RID have come a long way since the difficulties and differences of the past. Each organization, from the highest levels of leadership, fully supports the efforts of the other in many different ways. We anticipate the relationship of these two organizations to only grow stronger as time passes and more mutual efforts come to pass.

Read RID's VIEWS for further developments.

Modified and reprinted with RID's permission.

NATIONAL INTERPRETER CERTIFICATION

In June of 2004, the new National Interpreter Certification (NIC) knowledge test will be administered. Interview and Performance Tests are scheduled to be administered in 2005.

Read RID's VIEWS for further developments. See **RESOURCES** for RID Certification Updates.

SALARY RANGES

How much do interpreters get paid? Sorry to be so vague, but the answer to this question varies.

Due to the Taft-Hartley Anti-Trust Act of 1947, it is illegal for RID to establish wages or salaries that interpreters should charge/ receive or could charge/receive.

(An interesting piece of RID trivia...original guidelines titled "Suggested Fee Schedule (Revised 1973)" and included in the *REGISTRY OF INTERPRETERS FOR THE DEAF, INC., DIRECTORY*, published by Gallaudet College, Center for Continuing Education, 1976, (pages A-25 and 26), used the figures listed below:

Suggested Fee Schedule
(Revised 1973)

Interpreters Holding RID Certification
CSC: Comprehensive Skill Certificate
RSC: Reverse Skills Certificate
ETC: Expressive Translating Certificate

Interpreters Not Holding RID Certification
NCI: Non Certified Interpreter

1. OCCASIONAL Interpreting Assignments

a. CSC and RSC: Minimum three hours pay per "call"

ETC and EIC: Minimum two hours pay per "call"

b. CSC and RSCS: $11.25 to $15.00 per hour according to experience/qualifications.

ETC and/or EIC: $10.00 per hour

NCI: Minimum of $5.00 to $7.50 per hour

c. CSC and RSC: Maximum $75.00 for "full day" assignments.

ETC and/or EIC: Maximum $50.00 for "full day" assignments.

No more than six hours actual interpreting time.

2. CONFERENCES of Two or More Days Duration

a. CSC and RSC: $75.00 per day; $375.00 per 5-day week

ETC and EIC: $50.00 per day; $250.00 per 5-day week

PLUS

b. Travel expenses and per diem at prevailing agency rate.

3. CONTRACT Interpreting

a. 15 hours or less per week on regular assignment basis.

b. CSC and RSC: $11.75 to $15.00 per hour according to experience/qualifications.

ETC and/or EIC: $10.00 per hour

4. FULL TIME Interpreting

a. 4 hours daily or twenty weekly per 5-day week.

b. CSC and RSC: $260.00 per week

ETC and EIC: $200.00 per week

PLUS

c. Fringe benefits or salary commensurate to that of other professional staff within the agency.

Reprinted with permission from RID

Please keep in mind that the cost of living and inflation were a lot less in 1973 than they are today.

Bottom line: We here in America live in a capitalistic society. We are involved in "free enterprise." Independent contractors are basically "entrepreneurs" and operate their own businesses. Our "independent" fees cannot be dictated to us. We have the right to set our own fees, which include cost-of-living adjustments. Our experience and expertise should be recognized and financially compensated as in any other profession. We have a right to work hard, work ethically, and make a "good living," like every other citizen in our country.

There are no specific numbers, only "industry standards" (what interpreters in general charge) and "local standards" (what interpreters tend to charge in your geographic region). However, based on information gathered by informal surveys, here are some very general figures.

CSC/CI + CT:

$80.00 - $125.00+ Start-Up Fee (up to 2 hours)

$33.00 - $65.00+ per hour thereafter

Half-Day Rate: $150.00 - $250.00+ (up to 4 hours)

Full-Day Rate: $280.00 - $500.00+(up to 8 hours)*

Other (non-specialist) certifications:

$50.00 - $75.00 Start-Up Fee (up to 2 hours)

$15.00 - $30.00+ per hour thereafter

Half-Day Rate: $60.00 - $120.00+ (up to 4 hours)

Full-Day Rate: $120.00 - $240.00+ (up to 8 hours)*

*This includes start time to ending time with no "deduction for lunch." This is an "industry standard" (national standard), based on my informal surveys.

Note: When agencies hire you, make sure you are in agreement about the hours of the assignment and the hours that you are to bill **PRIOR** to accepting the assignment. Clear up any uncertainties before entering into an assignment. Fax a written agreement stating terms and conditions of the assignment and have it signed and faxed back if need be.

Suggestion: Contact your local sign language interpreting agencies (see **RESOURCES**), universities and other hiring entities in your local area and ask them to send you a fee schedule. Also, ask other interpreters what they tend to charge for various situations and assignments.

SOME THINGS TO CONSIDER WHEN DEVELOPING YOUR FEES

- Are you a graduate of an Interpreting Training Program (ITP)?

- Do you have a degree in interpreting?

- What is the highest level of education received?

- How long have you been interpreting?

- Are you certified?

- What level of certification have you achieved?

- How many years have you been certified?

- What are other interpreters in your area with similar education, certification, and experience charging?

- What would agencies charge?

- Is the assignment of a technical nature?

- Does the assignment involve highly specialized knowledge, training, or vocabulary (i.e., legal, medical, scientific, Ph.D. level, etc.)

- Is the assignment presented to you through a government agency? "For-Profit" company or corporation? Educational institution? "Non-Profit" agency or organization? Individual?

- Is the assignment legal in nature (i.e., deposition, attorney/client interview)?

- Is the assignment all day? All week? Half day? On-going (multiple dates involved)?

- How far do you have to travel?

- Will parking and/or mileage be included? (Find out if parking will be free, ticket validated and discounted, etc.)

First, let's consider what is called a "Start-Up Fee." This is a charge for services rendered up to (the first) two hours. A "per hour" fee can then be charged for each hour thereafter. Next, consider a half-day rate (up to four hours), full-day rate (up to eight hours). Any time worked after eight hours can either be billed per half-hour (half of your hourly fee), per hour, or per half-day rate.

This is also a good time to consider what is called a "Mutual Cancellation Policy." This is an agreement between the interpreter and the hiring source, to set up cancellation and reimbursement policies for committed times in the event that there is a "last-minute" cancellation.

EXAMPLE:

MUTUAL CANCELLATION POLICY: 72 hours or **3** full business days.

Also, make sure to specify that even if the agency does not cancel but the client does not show up, you will still be paid in full for your time reserved.

Bottom line: As the interpreter, you agree to provide interpreting services. If something comes up and you personally are not able to perform the assignment, you are agreeing to take responsibility to provide a qualified replacement for the hiring source. This means that (a) you will not leave the hiring source stranded with no interpreter once the 72-hour/3 full business day time period commences, and (b) you will take the responsibility to provide a qualified substitute in your place, if necessary. If you cancel prior to the agreed upon 72-hour/3 full business day policy, no obligation or responsibility is to be expected nor assumed by you.

Note: If you cannot fulfill either (a) or (b), you have no business making this kind of agreement.

In turn, the hiring source agrees to pay you in full if the assignment cancels at any time during either the 72 hours or 3 full business days prior to the pre-arranged starting date and time of the assignment, even if the client does not show up.

REMEMBER:

1. Include both a statement of hours and business days. This protects you if you have a cancellation on Friday afternoon for an assignment that was to take place on Monday.

2. Have everything (i.e., fees, mutual cancellation policy) in writing and signed by yourself and the hiring source representative.

3. This policy is set up to mutually benefit all parties. The hiring source does not have to scramble around looking for a qualified substitute in the event that an interpreter cancels at the last minute, the client is provided with interpreting coverage, and you are professionally compensated for time reserved. Remember, a more extensive mutual cancellation policy is beneficial to all concerned parties.

You will be asked about your rates and the conditions of your employment. Consider the above mentioned points when deciding on your fees. The following format will help you respond to such inquiries in a professional and well-thought-out manner:

FEE SCHEDULE WORKSHEET

Source of Payment	Start-Up	Per Hour	Per Half-Day	Per Full-Day	Other (Parking/ Mileage)
"For-Profit" co./corp.	$_____	$_____	$_____	$_____	$_____
General (gov't agency/school)	$_____	$_____	$_____	$_____	$_____
Non-Profit co./org.	$_____	$_____	$_____	$_____	$_____
Individual	$_____	$_____	$_____	$_____	$_____

Mutual Cancellation Policy: _____ hours or _____ full business days

PART 2

Getting Started

- **Getting Out There**
- **Federal Government Interpreting Positions**
- **Identification**
- **Business Cards**
- **Getting Organized**
- **Resumes**
- **Assignment Intake Forms**
- **Travel/Mileage Records**
- **Billing and Filing**
- **Taxes**
- **Planning for Today/Planning for Tomorrow**
- **Health Insurance**
- **Workers' Compensation Insurance**
- **Disability Insurance**
- **Professional Liability/Errors and Omissions Insurance**
- **Life Insurance**
- **Financial Planning**
- **"Tool Kit" for Interpreters**

PART 2

Getting Started

GETTING OUT THERE

If you have just graduated from an Interpreter Training Program (ITP) and/or you are relocating to another city or state, you will need to make yourself known personally and professionally within the D/deaf and interpreter communities. You should also make yourself known to agencies, organizations, and individuals who hire sign language interpreters. This section will offer suggestions on how to establish yourself.

- Get a RID directory. (If you are not a member, become one. If you do not have a current directory, order one.) Find the name, address, and telephone number of your region's representative. Call the representative and introduce yourself. Ask him or her for the name, address, and telephone number of your local area's chapter president. Call or write to that person, introduce yourself, and ask for a schedule of meetings, application forms to join the local chapter, and a copy of the most recent newsletter. Attend meetings. NETWORK!

- Attend community events, plays, captioned films, clubs, dances, parties, sporting tournaments, and so on. Introduce yourself, meet people, make new friends, run into old friends, and make business contacts. (Always be sure to have plenty of business cards with you.)

- Contact your local vocational rehabilitation office. Find out what the requirements are for the hiring of independent contractor sign language interpreters. Initiate paperwork NOW so that everything will be in place when an assignment does arise.

- Ask your interpreter trainers and mentors for references and referrals.

- Contact other organizations and agencies that tend to hire interpreters (i.e., schools for the Deaf, universities, colleges, medical centers, police stations, rehabilitation centers, and so on). Find a contact person's name, title, address, and telephone and fax numbers. Call and introduce yourself. Follow up with a short letter thanking the person for the time they spent with you and for their future consideration of hiring you. Enclose a copy of your resume and at least three business cards. I always do that in hopes that the person will keep one card for his or her files, and pass the others along to a supervisor and/or to D/deaf clients.

- Contact former ITP classmates who are in the same area. Ask them for suggestions and referrals. Remind them that you are available for substitute work ("subbing") in the event that they are not able to honor a commitment. Also ask them to think of you in the event that they are in need of a teammate.

- Contact local schools, colleges, and universities. When you speak to the location's operator, ask him or her to transfer you to the office that provides services to deaf or "disabled" students. Find out the name, title, address, and telephone and fax numbers of the person in charge of the department. Also ask if that same person "dispatches" interpreters. If it is another person, find out his or her information also. Call and introduce yourself. Set up an appointment. (Some places require you to take and pass specific forms of "evaluation" above and beyond RID certification.) I suggest that during your "introduction" call you inquire about hiring policies. Ask for details regarding the evaluation procedure (if any) and ask to take it during your introduction appointment. Bring two copies of your resume (as well as some business cards) to the meeting. After the meeting, send a follow up "thank you" letter.

- Contact sign language interpreting agencies or businesses. Use the same procedure as described above.

- Read deafness-related/interpreting-related publications, national/state/organization newsletters, magazines, etc. (i.e., *RID Views, The NAD Broadcaster*).

See **RESOURCES** for Directory of National Organizations of and for Deaf and Hard of Hearing People.

FEDERAL GOVERNMENT INTERPRETING POSITIONS

There are several ways to find out about federal government positions. First, there may be a specific job announcement that you hear about or is sent to you. Make a copy of the job announcement and use the information presented as reference while filling out the government application form (i.e., exact position title, announcement number, job series, etc.).

Another resource for government jobs is the U.S. Office of Personnel Management (OPM). This office provides an automated telephone system available 24 hours a day, 7 days a week at (478) 757-3000 or visit their website: www.usajobs.opm.gov.

Don't overlook current federal government interpreters. They are a great resource.

APPLYING FOR A FEDERAL GOVERNMENT POSITION

To be considered for a government interpreting position, you must fill out and submit a Standard Form (SF) 171 or Optional Form (OF) 612 (see **APPENDIX**).

Hint: Make several copies of the blank SF 171 and/or OF 612 application form. Keep them on file. Fill out the application and keep a copy of the completed form for your records. Periodically update your 171. Keep at least one copy of all completed 171s on file. (You will develop your new 171 based on information recorded on older forms.)

Filling out this form can be quite a lengthy process. Be patient and thorough. Always keep a copy of the completed form for your records.

IDENTIFICATION

Other than my RID membership/certification identification card, three forms of identification have also been requested of me, though not very often. Since this book is meant to thoroughly cover experiences I have encountered during my years of interpreting, I would be remiss if I did not at least mention them: (1) Birth Certificate, (2) Social Security Card (Number), and (3) Passport.

1. **BIRTH CERTIFICATE:** Procedures to obtain a copy of your birth certificate, if you do not presently have one, vary from state to state. (See **APPENDIX**)

2. **SOCIAL SECURITY CARD (NUMBER):** If you are over 18 years of age and a United States citizen and presently do not have a Social Security Number (SSN), follow the steps listed below:

   - Call (800) 772-1213 and request a Social Security card.

   - You will be asked for your zip code.

   - You will be referred to your local office.

   - You must visit the office in person with a copy of your birth certificate and one other form of picture identification (ID) (i.e., driver's license, Department of Motor Vehicles (DMV) ID card, school ID card).

   - Fill out the application.

   - A card will be issued and sent to your home address in two weeks.

If you are in need of a copy of your Social Security card, call the number listed above and request a "Duplicate Copy Application Form." You may also visit your local Social Security office to pick up and/or initiate the processing of your duplicate card. The duplicate card will be issued and sent to your home address in approximately two weeks.

Hint: It is recommended that you periodically check with Social Security regarding your work history and contributions made. Call the number listed above and request a "Detailed Information" application. You may also visit your local Social Security office to pick up and/or initiate processing of the information. The "Detailed Information" will be issued and sent to your home address in approximately two weeks.

3. **PASSPORT:** You must fill out a passport application and follow other procedural specifications (i.e., photograph) and send the completed form and $85 fee to the address listed on the application.

   (See **APPENDIX** for United States Passport Application)

Note: A driver's license or photo identification are sometimes requested. When you become certified, always carry your RID membership/certification identification card and/or NAD certification identification. Make sure you carry this identification with you at all times.

BUSINESS CARDS

This is another area that is highly individualized. My suggestion is to keep it simple:

- Name

- Certification (or training if not yet certified)

- Business telephone number (voice/TDD/fax)

- E-mail address (optional)

I strongly recommend that you DO NOT INCLUDE YOUR HOME ADDRESS. (This is for reasons of privacy and personal safety.) You can always write your address on the back of the card if you want a particular person to have it. An address label or address stamp may also be placed on the back if you so desire. Otherwise, there is no need to make your home address public knowledge.

If, however, you have a business mailing address that is separate from your home address (P.O. box, or PMB), you may include that if you feel it is important. Remember, it is a small card with limited space. Keep it simple and uncluttered.

Keep plenty of cards on hand in your briefcase, purse and/or wallet. Never leave home without them.

GET ORGANIZED!

It is essential to keep your day-to-day activities well organized and well documented. Some interpreters travel between towns, counties, and even states during a single day. In order to maximize efficiency and productivity, some sort of personalized organization system is needed.

There are many pre-produced, commercially available organizers in the marketplace today. DAY-TIMER, DAY RUNNER, FRANKLIN COVEY, and AT-A-GLANCE are a few of the companies that produce such calendars, planners, and organizers found at your local office supply store. Electronic organizers, otherwise known as Personal Digital Assistance (PDAs), are another option.

Some interpreters use highly personalized systems of their own invention with the aid of calendar/organizer type computer software programs. Bottom line: Design or incorporate a style that works best for you.

With your system in place, your goals are to:

- realistically schedule assignments
- readily eliminate conflicts
- increase productivity
- provide a place for easy access to information and documentation (i.e., directions, mileage, etc.)
- practice time management skills

Being able to glance at an entire day is extremely helpful. By organizing your day efficiently and blocking out designated assignments (bookings) and other appointments, you will be better able to judge distances and estimate travel time between commitments.

On a sheet of paper separate from the calendar page, I keep information regarding assignments - basically detailed information I can get from the "Assignment Intake Information" form (see p. 56 and **APPENDIX**). You can make a copy of the completed form and keep it in a binder to take with you. I suggest that you do not remove the sheet from the binder so that it will not get lost. Valuable and confidential information could fall into the wrong hands. In any case, make sure to keep the information in a bound form and not on separate sheets of loose paper or on sticky notes that could easily be lost or misplaced. Information pertaining to your assignment must be kept confidential!

RESUMES

It is essential for any professional in any field to have certain business tools. One of the most important tools in today's business environment is a comprehensive, yet concise, resume. While there are several excellent books devoted to the "art" of resume writing, this section will focus on how to design a resume that emphasizes those experiences that relate to the interpreting field. The purpose of your resume is to get you more interpreting-related work.

Before you begin, you must remember that resume writing is not a one-time endeavor. The goal of a well-written resume is to provide a potential employer with an accurate and current delineation of experiences related to the prospective employment. This is where you emphasize your individual experiences and skills which will make you perfect for the potential position. It is extremely important to take the time to do a well-thought-out resume. After you have completed this task, know that you will use this current effort as the "backbone" for future resumes. As we continue to have diverse experiences that contribute to the growth of our professional selves, so must our resumes reflect these experiences.

Before beginning, please know that resumes are (and should be) very individualized. There is no "right" or "wrong" resume. A lot has to do with your personal preference and style. Suggestions will be given to you regarding content, but the bottom line is that your resume is a reflection of **YOU.** I will give you suggestions to make your best interpreting-self shine through.

Some people create two resumes; each resume highlights different areas. As different employment opportunities arise, the appropriate resume can be submitted.

Let's look at resumes that emphasize sign language interpreting experiences.

SAMPLE RESUME

JANE INTERPRETER
101 Main Street
Anywhere, AB 12345
(555) 234-5678

EDUCATION

Bachelor of Science, Sociology, June 2003
Allstate University, Anywhere, AB

CREDENTIALS

Certificate of Interpretation (CI)
Certificate of Transliteration (CT)
Registry of Interpreters for the Deaf, 2003

PROFESSIONAL EXPERIENCE

INTERPRETER/INDEPENTDENT CONTRACTOR
2003 - Present
I provide sign language interpreting services in a variety
of settings to diverse clientele, in the metropolitan area
of Anywhere, AB. Experienced in post-secondary educational and technical interpreting.

REFERENCES FURNISHED UPON REQUEST

RESUME WORKSHEET WITH EXPLANATIONS

Full name: _____

Current address: _____

_____

Telephone/TDD: _____

OPTIONAL:

Professional objective: This is your opportunity to state what you are looking for in a position. This section is quite personalized and is optional. However, if you decide to incorporate this section, KEEP IT BRIEF!

Degrees: (Chronologically, starting with most recent)

    Name of academic institution

    City, state

    Type of degree, majors and minors, year awarded

Diplomas and education: If your highest level of education achieved is high school, you may state your education as follows:

    Name of high school

    City, state

    Type of diploma with any type of special emphasis (i.e., High School Diploma, General Academics or Business Emphasis, etc.)

    Year graduated

If you attended a college or university but did not complete the degree or program, try:

    Name of college or university

    City, state

    Name any special emphasis, total number of credits earned (i.e., Special Education, Total Credits: 65; or General Academics, Total Credits: 38)

    Years attended (i.e., 2002-2003)

Certifications:

    List name and abbreviation of certification

    (Certificate of Interpretation (CI))

Name of certifying organization
(Registry of Interpreters for the Deaf (RID))

Year awarded

Work experiences: (Chronologically, starting with most recent)

Title of your position, employer

City, state, and dates worked

Brief description of duties and skills used

Note: Try to emphasize areas of responsibility and qualities relevant to interpreting (i.e., office management skills, time management skills, and so on).

SUGGESTIONS FOR "BUDDING" PROFESSIONAL INTERPRETERS:

If you have not yet had any professional (in this way I mean "paid") interpreting experience but have had "intern" work experience, you may state:

Student Intern. Name of Interpreting Training Program. Name of Institution, City, State

Dates attended (starting date to ending date)

Approximate number of hours interpreting

Brief description of experiences (starting with types of interpreting performed)*

Contact person (supervisor)

Title and/or department name

Name of institution: phone number

* **Note:** Concentrate on the areas in which you have the most competence and expertise.

EXAMPLE:

Student Intern. Associate of Arts Degree Program: Interpreting for the Deaf, Allstate University, AB, September 2003 to Present.

Provided sign language interpreting and transliterating services (voice to sign/sign to voice) as a student intern. Approximate hours of supervised experience: 150 hours. Services provided in the following settings: elementary schools, universities, and hospitals.

Supervisor: Sue Astin, Director of Interpreting Interns, All-state University: (555) 546-7891

Note: Things to keep in mind while documenting work-related experiences:

- Did you help coordinate sign language interpreting services?
- Were you a mentor to other interpreters?
- Did you supervise and/or evaluate other interpreters?
- Were you responsible for maintaining a government interpreting contract?
- Were you responsible for hiring subcontractors?

References: Ask permission of at least five people to use as references. Your list should include some of the following: teachers, school administrators, program directors, professionals in related fields, professionals in unrelated fields. Make sure these people are willing to provide both written and verbal recommendations.

Things to consider: Ask for letters of recommendation. Keep letters in a file. Get updated and content specific letters as needed. The more professional experiences you have, the more likely you are to meet someone who will be able to put in a good word for you. Keep letters and reference lists current.

On the resume, simply state:

References furnished upon request.

See **APPENDIX** for Resume Worksheet and References Worksheet.

LETTERS OF INTRODUCTION

It is customary to include a brief letter of introduction with each resume. (Additionally, you will send a letter of introduction along with your resume when submitting a formal application for a specific job.)

The purpose of the letter is to introduce yourself. The secondary function is to state your interest in working for a specific agency or company and to identify which position you are applying for. Each letter should be custom written, including specific information regarding the position for which you are applying (including exact position personnel series or number). The letter should also be used to give pertinent information about the types of positions you would like to be considered for in the future. Keep copies of everything for your files.

EXPLANATION OF LETTER OF INTRODUCTION

Street Address
City, State, Zip Code
Phone (Voice/TDD)
Date

Name Of Person, Title
and/or
Department, Agency
Street Address
City, State, Zip Code

Dear _____ :

(This letter is to be highly individualized according to the type of position and how you would like to introduce yourself. If you are applying for a specific position and have a job description in hand, state all pertinent identifying information such as the job series number, position name and number, and so on.)

(State that you are enclosing a resume that gives details regarding your qualifications and experiences.)

(Inform the person that you will be contacting him or her in a week's time regarding the status of the application.)

(Closing: Thank the person for his or her consideration. State that you are available to provide further information or clarification, and that he or she should feel free to contact you.)

Sincerely,
Signature
Type Name

Enclosures

Hints:

Always keep at least one copy of all resumes ever used. They are good for future reference to keep track of past work experiences.

To save money, have your resume saved on a computer disk. This will make life easier when it comes to making further revisions. Have several copies of the resume printed from a computer laser printer. Go to an office supply store or copy center and select bond paper with matching envelopes. Have the resume photocopied onto the bond paper you chose. Make several copies at this time. Purchase additional sheets of paper to use for letters of introduction and future photocopying.

(By getting high quality laser printouts and having them photocopied, you will save a great deal in printing costs.)

Resumes should be one page long, using only one side, or two pages at the very most (using two pieces of paper printing on only one side).

OTHER TOOLS:

Contact your past colleges and universities and get a copy of your academic transcripts. Keep copies of all records on file. Also, have transcript request forms from the various institutions on hand. While applying for some positions, the initial application may require you to send copies of your transcripts along with the application and letters of reference. It may also require "official" copies of your transcripts to be forwarded to the application-receiving office. This is where the transcript request forms come in handy. It will expedite the process if you have the forms available and know whether or not a fee is required in the processing and submission of your transcripts. Do your homework.

Another way of handling the "official" transcript is as follows: You may request that formal "official" copies of your transcript be sent to you. This way you will have copies at your disposal when you need them. When you do receive the "official" copies, it is important that you file them as is, and not open the sealed envelope. What makes them "official" is the college or university seal used on the outside of the envelope. The seal is most likely from the registrar's office of the institution and indicates that the contents of the envelope have not been tampered with.

Keep a copy of your certification on file as well. You may also want to make copies of your RID membership and certification identification card (especially if you do not have a handy copy of your certificate). The cards are updated and renewed with your current status every year. You may use a copy of your card when asked to furnish proof of certification.

ASSIGNMENT INTAKE FORMS

The purpose of devising an intake form is to help you gather assignment-related information in a quick and precise manner.

When someone calls to request your interpreting services and the initial information presented seems agreeable to both parties (i.e., date, time, location, topic, and so on), additional detailed information is then needed.

The Assignment Intake Information form provided illustrates pertinent information that is both necessary and beneficial for a sucessful interpreting assignment.

ASSIGNMENT INTAKE INFORMATION

Today's date & time: _____

Caller: _____ Position: _____

Company/Agency Representing: _____

Telephone: _____ Fax: _____ E-mail: _____

ASSIGNMENT INFORMATION

Date(s): _____ Time(s): _____

Address: _____

Directions: _____

_____

Parking Provided: _____Yes _____ No   Where to Park: _____

Site Contact Person: _____ Telephone: _____

Person(s) Interpreting for : _____

Sign Language Preferences: _____

Description of Assignment: _____

_____

Partner: _____

BILLING

Price quoted: _____ Per: _____

Cancellation
Policy: _____

PAYMENT EXPECTED IN 30 CALENDAR DAYS UNLESS OTHERWISE STATED
LATE FEE POLICY: $_____ PER 30 DAYS DELINQUENT

_____ Send Invoice to: _____

_____

Contact: _____ Telephone: _____

_____ Payment: On-Site Pickup   Location: _____

_____

Contact: _____ Telephone: _____

ASSIGNMENT COMPLETION DATE: _____

_____ ON-SITE PAYMENT RECEIVED   INVOICE MAILED: _____

PAYMENT RECEIVED:

Date: _____ Check#: _____

Amount: _____

TRAVEL/MILEAGE RECORDS

It is always a good idea to keep a record of your mileage and travel expenses for tax purposes. Ask your accountant or tax preparer what information and receipts you must keep or record. You may request a travel log from your accountant, purchase one from an office supply or stationery store, or create your own.

See **APPENDIX** for Travel/Mileage Record Form.

BILLING AND FILING

If an invoice (bill) is to be submitted at the appointment site after completion of the assignment, make a copy of your invoice, attach the copy to the intake sheet, and file them in your office. File the papers in an organized manner, either by company, client name, month, fiscal quarter, year, or another system that makes sense to you. (You may need to obtain quick access to the materials, so make your system efficient and uncomplicated.)

Set up a "Payment Pending" file. Place a copy of the invoice and attached intake sheet in this file. When a payment arrives from the completed assignment and if the information and numbers are accurate, make a copy of the check before you cash it and attach it to the intake form and invoice. Place the three attached copies (intake, invoice, and check) in a file for "Payment Received."

If you have a computer and a scanner, you can simply scan in the Assignment Intake Information form, invoice, and check received. You can place this information in a special file on a special disk. You can also set up a "tickler" file to remind you of "Payment Pending" accounts.

REMEMBER: MAKE BACKUP COPIES OF ALL COMPUTER DISKS AND FILES.

LATE OR DELINQUENT ACCOUNTS:

Periodically check through your "Payment Pending" file for late or delinquent accounts. Accounts not paid in 30 days after the date of billing should be followed up with a phone call or letter. Remember to charge a late fee for delinquent accounts.

INVOICE

This is the bill you submit for services rendered. Information to be included on the invoice should be obtained from the Assignment Intake Information form. Your invoice should include the following information in whatever format you choose:

Purpose of invoice:
(Sign Language Interpreting Services)

Bill to:
Address:
Contact Person:
Telephone:

Mail check to:
Your name
Mailing address:
Telephone (V/TDD):
Social Security Number:

Brief description of assignment:
(including date and location)

Total amount due:

Due date:

Late fees:

This is another area where you will have to devise a form that suits your individual needs.

Note: Always make a copy of the invoice for your files before you mail it. You can make your invoices into "carbon-less" copies. See your local printing center and inquire about this. You can always invoice from your computer and print out a copy. Always backup your files.

SAMPLE INVOICE

INVOICE:

SIGN LANGUAGE INTERPRETING SERVICES

May 31, 2004

BILLED TO:
ABC COMPANY
2232 American Way
Heartland, AB 12345

Contact Person:
Dave Richardson
(111) 555-0111

SEND CHECK TO:
JANE INTERPRETER
101 Main Street
Anywhere, AB 12345
(111) 555-4567
SSN: 000-00-0000

For Sign Language Interpreting Services Rendered

May 31, 2004
9:00am - 5:00pm
"Communications in the Next Century"
Hyatt Regency
Heartland

AMOUNT NOW DUE:
$350.00

A LATE FEE OF $25 WILL BE ASSESSED IF THE AMOUNT
IS NOT PAID IN FULL BY:
June 30, 2004

(PER AGREEMENT: $25 PER 30 DAYS DELINQUENT)

TAXES

Bottom line:
Find Yourself A Good Accountant!

Because the area of taxes is too broad, too in-depth, too far outside of my expertise, and ever changing, I suggest that you find an accountant or tax preparer that you like and trust. I love my accountant and would not think of doing my tax returns on my own. If you have done your own tax returns or if you are planning to do your own, I am in awe of you.

How can you find a "good" accountant or tax preparer? Simply ask family, friends, or other interpreters for a referral. If, however, you end up not being satisfied with the recommendation, shop around. Do, however, make sure that the person you choose to prepare your tax return has a thorough knowledge of recent tax rules and regulations. Ask about his or her certification or qualifications. Remember, no matter who you hire to prepare your tax returns, **YOU** are ultimately responsible for the accuracy of the information provided.

This section is a limited source of information and references regarding taxes. In the **APPENDIX** you will find information regarding Internal Revenue Service (IRS) and state tax resources, as well as other information that has helped me to document, gather, and provide thorough information to the persons or agencies involved.

Remember: These are only guidelines. You must consult a qualified tax preparer and the IRS for specific and appropriate advice and information.

The information presented is designed to assist those freelance interpreters who are independent contractors (ICs). I am assuming that you have minimal or no Federal, State and Social Security taxes deducted from the checks you receive for services performed.

Suggestions:

Make "quarterly" payments. This spreads out the tax payments you owe into four smaller payments rather than one lump sum with financial penalties. Remember, if insufficient funds are paid and if payments are not made on time, financial penalties will be charged. Any discrepancy or penalty must be paid by April 15 of the present year to reconcile the entire previous calendar year's records. (In some cases, extensions may be filed and granted. Ask your tax preparer for the details.)

For a fiscal year of January 1 - December 31, the quarterly payment dates are as follows:

April 15, June 15, September 15, January 15

Steps:
1. Contact the IRS and request form 1040 ES and begin making quarterly payments.

2. Contact your state taxation department and request quarterly forms and begin making quarterly payments.

ESTIMATED QUARTERLY TAXES:

Since the amount of the quarterly payments is formulated on an estimate of your total earnings for the present year and exact figures cannot be verified until the present fiscal year has ended, I use a formula to calculate my Estimated Quarterly Taxes. Before examining the specific quarterly approximation formula, it would be helpful to understand a general concept behind the taxes.

SAMPLE ESTIMATED QUARTERLY TAXES WORKSHEET

Estimate the amount of money you will earn (gross) this year:
Gross = (A) **$30,000**

APPROXIMATE PERCENTAGES

Federal Taxes = **30%** of gross (approximate)

Social Security Taxes = **4%** of gross (approximate)
(to be added to Federal Tax payments)

State Taxes = **6%** of gross
(percent varies from state to state)

Approximation Formula for Estimated Quarterly Taxes Example:

"QUARTERLIES":

Federal Taxes: **30%** of (A) **$30,000** = **$9,000** / 4 = **$2,250** *

SS Taxes: **4%** of (A) **$30,000** = **$1,200** / 4 = **$300** *

*Add Federal and SS "Quarterlies" to make the total Estimated Federal Tax Quarterly payment.

Total Estimated Federal Tax Quarterly Payment = $2,550

PLUS

State Taxes: **6%** of (A) **$30,000** = **$1,800** / 4 = **$450**

TOTAL AMOUNT DUE EACH QUARTER: $3,000

See **APPENDIX** for Estimated Quarterly Taxes Worksheet.

PLANNING FOR TODAY / PLANNING FOR TOMORROW

While there are certain things we wish never to happen to us (i.e., a disabling incident, problems with health, and so on), we should still have plans in place should the unfortunate happen. You should consider several essential areas in which to insure yourself against adverse events and situations: (1) health insurance, (2) workers' compensation insurance, (3) disability insurance, (4) professional liability insurance, and (5) life insurance.

HEALTH INSURANCE

Rationale: To cover expenses accrued during a medical emergency or for medical treatment.

Suggestion: There are several ways to go about getting health insurance. I have two very simple suggestions:

1. Assuming you are a member, call RID (703) 838-0030 (V). Ask them to send you information re: group health insurance.

   AND/OR

   Contact: Group Insurance Plans
   Albert H. Wohlers & Co., Administrator
   1440 N. Northwest Highway
   Park Ridge, Illinois 60068-1400

Explain that you are a member of RID and would like information sent to you.

2. You may also want to talk to an insurance broker/ financial planner. Ask your family, friends, and other professionals (particularly other independent contractors) for a referral to a broker with whom they have had a positive relationship and whom they trust. Contact the broker and explain your needs. Set up an introductory meeting to spell out your requirements and preferences. If you feel comfortable with this broker, ask for a presentation of your options and the insurance company's requirements and stipulations.

Things to think about prior to your meeting:

- How much of a deductible are you willing/able to pay (out of your own pocket) in the event of an accident or injury? (Ordinarily the higher the deductible, the lower the cost of insurance.)

- What type of coverage is important to you? Medical? Dental? Eye care?

- How much can you afford to comfortably spend on insurance per month?

- What type of insurance coverage will that amount entitle you to? (Hospitalization? If so, how many days? Prescriptions? General medical? Co-payments? If so, how much?)

Note: I had my insurance broker look over my current plan to check out coverage "loopholes." She reviewed my existing coverage and made recommendations for additional coverage. (I chose to stick with my current health insurance. I did, however, branch out and get a life insurance policy.)

WORKERS' COMPENSATION INSURANCE

I AM NOT A LAWYER. THIS INFORMATION IS NOT MEANT TO BE CONSTRUED AS LEGAL ADVICE OR THE SOLE SOURCE OF INFORMATION REGARDING THIS TOPIC. FOR FURTHER INFORMATION AND ANSWERS TO ANY CONCERN AND QUESTIONS, SEE RESOURCES: WORKERS' COMPENSATION: DIRECTORY OF ADMINISTRATORS. YOU MAY ALSO WANT TO CONSIDER OBTAINING THE SERVICES OF AN ATTORNEY.

Rationale: If you are self-employed - even part time - you should take out a workers' compensation insurance policy. The reasons for doing this are obvious. If you are hurt, money will be paid to you for your lost income, medical treatment, and so on. In addition, there are times when an employment contract will require you to produce a "certificate of insurance" (issued by your insurance agent) to show that you have workers' compensation coverage. You may be asked to provide this even before you will be considered for employment and/or prior to the commencement of work.

If you work for interpreting agencies as an independent contractor or freelance interpreter and are not an employee of the agency or company (meaning taxes are not taken out of your pay), you probably are not covered by workers' compensation.

Do not assume, "Oh, well. So-and-so agency will take care of me. I was hired through them. They will file for me." If you do contact them after an accident to report it, they will most likely say, "Gee. What a shame. Hope you feel better."

DO NOT BE FOOLED INTO THINKING THAT THIS WILL MAGICALLY AND MYSTICALLY BE TAKEN CARE OF FOR YOU.

Suggestion: You must take the responsibility of looking into this and getting coverage on your own. Make certain that any workers' compensation policy covers you and anyone you might hire to work for you. Follow "Health Insurance" Steps 1 and 2 and inquire specifically about workers' compensation insurance.

DO NOT DELAY! DO THIS AS SOON AS POSSIBLE !

FRIENDLY REMINDER:

ALWAYS REMEMBER:

SAFETY FIRST!

DISABILITY INSURANCE

Rationale: If you become incapacitated due to an injury or illness that is not covered by workers' compensation insurance and you are unable to earn income, this insurance provides interim financial support for a specified period of time and for a specified amount.

Note: Here it is important to have the broker explain to you about the waiting period involved (when no benefits are paid), whether you must be disabled from interpreting only or from any type of work, partial versus total disability, and how benefits are calculated. (The calculations are usually based on a percentage of your prior earnings.) Remember to make certain that you are covered by your own workers' compensation policy. Then check with your broker regarding how the workers' compensation and the disability policies dovetail or complement each other, if at all.

PROFESSIONAL LIABILITY INSURANCE

Rationale: This will provide limited monetary compensation to pay damages in the event that you are sued by someone and you are proven to be professionally liable for a harmful or negative outcome due to "professional error." This insurance covers damages up to a specific amount during a specific period of time.

Note: Ask your insurance agent or broker for the exact conditions, circumstances, and amounts that are covered.

> REMEMBER, I AM NOT A LAWYER AND THE INFORMATION PROVIDED IS NOT MEANT TO BE THE SOLE SOURCE OF INFORMATION REGARDING PROFESSIONAL LIABILITY INSURANCE COVERAGE. THIS SECTION IS TO BE USED AS A RESOURCE ONLY. TALK TO A LAWYER. TALK TO A BROKER. EDUCATE YOURSELF.

Suggestion: Follow "Health Insurance" Steps 1 and 2 and inquire specifically about professional liability insurance.

Note: Some RID members are insured by:

Marsh Affinity Group Services
Seabury & Smith
1440 Rennaissance Drive
Park Ridge, IL 60068-1400
(800) 503-9230

LIFE INSURANCE

Rationale: This insurance is really to provide financial compensation for others in the event of your death.

Suggestion: Follow "Health Insurance" Steps 1 and 2 and inquire specifically about disability insurance and life insurance.

FINANCIAL PLANNING

The most important thing I can tell you regarding this area is to DO IT! DO IT NOW! The sooner you do it, the better. This actually should have been done yesterday, so do not delay!

Many interpreters walk around totally clueless in this area

and have such a laissez-faire attitude about it! Take responsibility for yourself here and now! If you know nothing about financial planning, do not let it intimidate you. Do not allow your discomfort to hinder your research. Dive in! Educate yourself! Ask questions! Read materials! Hire the services of a professional financial planner! EMPOWER YOURSELF! It will totally behoove you to be informed in this area. Strive to be financially secure and independent. There is no shame in this. It is a smart business practice. IT IS A SMART, COMMON SENSE THING FOR EVERYONE ON THE FACE OF THIS PLANET TO DO!

SOME TOPICS YOU MAY WANT TO INVESTIGATE:

- Independent Retirement Accounts (IRAs): For anyone with income

- Self-Employed Pensions (SEPs): For those who are small business employees or for those who are self-employed

- 403 (B): For non-profit organizations' employees

- 401 (K): For employees who work for a "for-profit" business

Another Tip: Write a last will and testament. Regardless of your age, health condition, or economic status, you should write a last will and testament. You may not "have much" in the way of material things but, if you make a will, you determine the disposition of your estate. Otherwise, the government will become your beneficiary by default. If you do not have a beneficiary, consider stipulating that your possessions go to a specific charitable organization or that they be sold and the proceeds go to that organization. Consider this, please.

"TOOL KIT"*
FOR INTERPRETERS

Even before you go to your first assignment, take some time to put together your personal "Tool Kit." Listed below are things that I have found beneficial to have close at hand, in your briefcase or in your car. Place the items you will keep in your car in an easily accessible container that is solely devoted to these items. Lists will vary from individual to individual. The list below reflects what I consider essential after years of trial and error in the field. I hope this list will save you time, energy, and potential embarrassment. (Time may be saved by having a complete, experience-proven list. Energy may be saved by having what you need all in one place. Embarrassment may be saved by ...well, you'll see ....)

Things You Might Want To Consider Having In Your Personal "Tool Kit":

briefcase

appointment book; PDA

business cards

extra blank invoices

envelopes

stamps

pens with erasers

correction fluid

stapler (with ample supply of staples)

paper clips

tape

blank pieces of paper

flashlight with functioning batteries

glasses (if necessary)

eye drops (if necessary)

sunglasses

umbrella

adhesive bandages

aspirin (or other medication)

hand lotion

towel, towelettes, tissues

hair supplies (hair spray, pins, comb)

bottled water

snacks

spare blouse, slip, jacket or sweater, nylons

spare shirt, tie, pants, jacket

shoes (heels, flats, sneakers)

hygiene products, make-up

books, magazines

coins (for parking meters, vending machines, pay telephones)

telephone calling card

safety pins (different sizes)

compact sewing kit

scissors

watch or compact timing device

cellular telephone, spare charged battery, battery recharger

identification

proof of certification

emergency telephone numbers

emergency survival kit (see **APPENDIX**)

What else can you think of to add to your "Tool Kit"??? Not everyone's will be the same. What would yours include?

*Original "Tool Kit" and contents assembled in 1981 as part of a classroom exercise at Gallaudet University, Washington, D.C. Additions made throughout the years as technologies were invented and implemented.

PART 3

Interpreting Situations and Circumstances

- **AIDS-Related Interpreting**
- **Agency or "Staff" Interpreting**
- **Business/Corporate Interpreting**
- **Community Services Interpreting**
- **Deaf-Blind Interpreting**
- **Educational/Academic Interpreting**
- **Emergency Interpreting**
    - **Public Emergency Situations**
    - **"911" Interpreting**
- **Government Interpreting**
- **Legal Interpreting**
- **Medical Interpreting**
- **Mental Health Interpreting**
- **Platform/Performing Arts Interpreting**
- **Religious Interpreting**
- **Spiritual/Metaphysical/"Alternative" Interpreting**
- **Social Interpreting**
- **Support Groups Interpreting**
- **Technical Interpreting**
- **Video Relay Service (VRS) Interpreting**

PART 3

Interpreting Situations and Circumstances

Note:

In the following section, some "Positive" and "Possible Challenge" aspects of interpreting situations are mentioned for your consideration. Some of the "Positives" may be viewed as "Possible Challenges" by some people, while other people may view the "Possible Challenges" as "Positives." I am simply trying to give you some food for thought. You will have to make your own decisions regarding the pros and cons for each situation. These aspects are mentioned merely to help you so you can think and prepare in advance for anything that may happen.

AIDS-RELATED INTERPRETING

WHAT?

This refers to interpreting for those who are HIV-Positive and/or have AIDS.

WHERE?

- doctors' offices
- clinics
- hospitals
- hospices
- support groups
- lectures
- workshops

POSITIVES TO CONSIDER:

You work with a group of great individuals. You may already know some of the individuals involved. Sometimes, just by you being there, being the one interpreting can be a great comfort and relief to those involved. (I have been told by some people that just seeing the warm, smiling face of a familiar interpreter can make a world of positive difference to those involved.)

POSSIBLE CHALLENGES TO CONSIDER:

This kind of work can tear your heart apart. You love some of these people. You see people you love in pain. You see people you love die. This is, emotionally, tough work to do.

INTERPRETER ATTRIBUTES:

- kindness
- warmth
- compassion
- love of people
- non-judgmental attitude towards others

PREPARATION ADVICE:

Familiarize yourself with medical terminology: vocabulary and signs used by HIV/AIDS community, human sexuality terms and signs (both "technical" and "everyday" terms used), current research topics regarding testing, treatments, prevention, and so on. Set up (if you do not already have) a strong emotional support system for yourself in which you can vent, in confidence, for your own personal emotional release and support. This could translate into having one really good friend in whom you can trust and confide, and on whose shoulder you can cry.

Remember: There are such things as "advocates," persons who are paid or who volunteer to advocate for services and treatments. Do not overstep your interpreting boundaries. You may be asked to, you may want to. Remember who you are and the function you were hired to perform. Suggest to parties involved that an advocate be called in when you are being pressed upon to do non-interpreting related duties and functions. Everyone always expects the interpreter to take care of things. "After all, they are there." Be careful. Do yourself a favor. Do our profession a favor. Do the client a favor. Do the other parties involved a favor. Remain in the interpreter's role and suggest that an advocate be contacted.

AGENCY OR "STAFF" INTERPRETING

WHAT?

Working for an agency/organization that is or has an interpreting service. These interpreters are "dispatched" to do community service interpreting (i.e., emergency, social, legal, and so on), and to interpret for other staff members who are D/deaf.

WHERE?

- within organizations serving the D/deaf community

- within organizations that solely provide sign language interpreting services

Positives to Consider:

You have regular hours with stable income and benefits. Staff interpreters may be offered their choice of freelance work (non-staff hours sometimes at freelance pay) before "outside" freelance interpreters are offered work. You are part of a team. Opportunities to be mentored or to mentor may be available.

Possible Challenges to Consider:

You may not make as much money per hour (in spite of a benefits package) compared to a freelance interpreter. You are given assignments. Sometimes you may be able to switch your schedule or assignments; other times you may not be able to switch (unlike freelance interpreters who have full freedom to "pick and choose" their assignments). After completion of an assignment, you may be required to report back to the office where you may have "other duties as assigned."

Interpreter Attributes:

- flexibility

- willingness to be a team player

- ability to cooperate and compromise

Preparation Advice:

Gain life experiences and general knowledge to prepare for a variety of assignments. Get a dependable car that gets good mileage because a lot of driving may be involved.

BUSINESS/CORPORATE INTERPRETING

What?

This includes interpreting for conferences, conventions, training, staff meetings, business appointments, and so on.

Where?

- corporate offices

- hotel ballrooms

- convention centers

- board rooms

- training facilities

- retreat centers

- outdoor facilities

POSITIVES TO CONSIDER:

You become exposed to a variety of fields, businesses, and topics. You may be hired per hour, per half-day, per day, per week, per month, per quarter.

POSSIBLE CHALLENGES TO CONSIDER:

Each business or corporation has its own structure and "corporate-ese," which may include many acronyms. Sometimes acronyms are spoken as a word instead of individual letters. It may take a while to understand and get used to the corporate "lingo."

INTERPRETER ATTRIBUTES:

- flexibility

- good people skills

- basic neutrality

- ability to blend in with "corporate America" (attire-wise; behavior-wise)

PREPARATION ADVICE:

Arrive extra early. Introduce yourself to the meeting coordinator. Get a copy of the agenda/program. Ask about special acronyms or acronym-words that may be used and may not be familiar to the general public. Know how to spell the names of the presenters or people to be introduced. Survey the seating and lighting arrangements. (Will videos be shown? Are they captioned? Will all the lights be dimmed? Can some be left on? Will the interpreter be "spotlighted"?) Check out the acoustics. (Are you directly in front of or behind a loud speaker?) Ask to do a sound/lighting check, if necessary. (Better to do these things beforehand. Do not wait until it is too late to make adjustments - meaning after the meeting or presentation has already begun.) If the coordinator seems to be "put-off" by your requests, explain that you want the meeting to run smoothly and without interruptions. Explain that you want to make sure that the interpreting end of things goes smoothly, so that you can comfortably and proficiently perform the task for which you have been hired. Dress in business attire, a business suit/dress/pants suit for women or business suit with tie for men.

COMMUNITY SERVICES INTERPRETING

WHAT?

This includes interpreting for Social Security appointments, IRS audits, job interviews, home loan/re-financing application appointments, and so on. Basically, it means anything and everything not included in other categories.

WHERE?

- government office buildings
- banks
- warehouses
- docks
- stores
- company/manufacturer's offices
- parks
- recreation centers
- auditoriums
- community centers

POSITIVES TO CONSIDER:

You get to do everyday "slice of life" interpreting, where familiar topics in any person's everyday life are discussed. No intense "homework" is involved. These assignments are usually short in duration (interpreting-wise).

POSSIBLE CHALLENGES TO CONSIDER:

You may experience a lot of down time, sitting around, waiting to interpret. Sometimes you leave the assignment feeling discouraged by "the system" (i.e., government bureaucracy).

INTERPRETER ATTRIBUTES:

- patience

- flexibility

- some knowledge about "everything"

PREPARATION ADVICE:

Have exposure to general life experiences.

DEAF-BLIND INTERPRETING

WHAT?

This type of work can involve and include any of the other interpreting situations, however services are rendered to persons who are D/deaf with a visual impairment or blindness.

WHERE?

- anywhere

- everywhere

POSITIVES TO CONSIDER:

If you develop the necessary skills for working with deaf-blind individuals, you open your world to a wonderful and unique group of people.

POSSIBLE CHALLENGES TO CONSIDER:

This kind of interpreting work can be quite fatiguing if the client is "heavy handed." Consider switching with your teammate every 15-20 minutes (depending on the client and pace of speakers).

INTERPRETER ATTRIBUTES:

- flexibility

- kindness

- calmness

- stamina

PREPARATION ADVICE:

Learn various methods of guiding blind and visually-impaired individuals. Practice clear fingerspelling. Learn to sit up straight at all times. Arrive early to meet with the client to discuss his or her communication preferences such as room arrangement, acoustics, lighting, and so on. Before you make decisions or start re-arranging anything, discuss details with the client. The client is his or her own best advocate and certainly the most knowledgeable about his or her own needs and preferences. Find yourself a comfortable chair.

Note: Interpreting for deaf-blind individuals is as varied as interpreting for individuals within the general D/deaf community. Some preferences of the individuals I have worked with include (but are not limited to) the following:

- Signing/fingerspelling within a specific range of space (the person's field of vision)

- "Tactile" interpreting: refers to a literal "hands-on" method of interpreting. The client places his or her hand(s) on your wrist or hand and tactilely receives the signs/fingerspelling. Some individuals also use their limited vision. The client may also prefer to use this mode depending on the lighting situation. Some persons may prefer "regular" interpreting during the day, but "tactile" interpreting during the evening. This is sometimes due to eye strain and fatigue, other times due to "night blindness" (an aspect of Usher's Syndrome).

- One-handed manual alphabet (fingerspelling) only: manually spelling out individual letters of each word while client's hands rest "on top" of your fingerspelling hand. The client may also hold your wrist into his or her field of vision or specify to you the field of vision in which to fingerspell.

- Drawing outlines of letters into the individual's palm.

- Doing what we Americans tend to call the "two-handed European" method of fingerspelling, into the palm of the individual.

AGAIN, PLEASE NOTE THAT EACH INDIVIDUAL IS DIFFERENT AND HAS DIFFERENT COMMUNICATION/INTERPRETING NEEDS AND PREFERENCES.

Also, interpreting for some individuals may require a few "extras":

- **Guiding:** client to chair, to refreshments, to restroom, to bus, cab, and so on.

- **Describing:** the room set up, guests, food at refreshment table, voice or tone of person speaking, directions (i.e., instead of pointing as if to say "over there", be precise as in "10 feet to your left"), and so on.

You may need to request changes in the set up to aid you in providing the service you were hired to perform.

THINGS TO CONSIDER OR REQUEST:

- Make sure that you, the interpreter, can hear things clearly and distinctly. If microphones and speakers will be used, make sure that you will be in a position to hear well. If not, and if the client prefers to stay in a particular location, locate the contact person or the facilitator of the room. Request that a speaker be turned in your direction or that an additional speaker be added and placed closer to where you will be seated.

- If at all possible, especially if it is a small group meeting and discussion, have people identify themselves before they speak. Most likely, your back may be turned towards the speakers and this will help you. You do not want to get "whiplash" from straining to see and identify who is talking.

- You may have to ask people to slow down. (FYI: They may slow down for 30 seconds, then due to nervousness or forgetfulness fall back into the same old pattern. It is highly unlikely that people will slow down for the duration of the meeting.) You may have to remind people repeatedly.

- Ask for a comfortable chair if you are not able to find one.

EDUCATIONAL/ACADEMIC INTERPRETING

WHAT?

This includes interpreting for students, faculty, staff, administrators, guest lecturers, and parent/teacher/counselor sessions in an academic environment.

WHERE?

- pre-kindergarten and kindergarten programs

- elementary schools

- junior high schools

- middle schools

- high schools

- colleges/universities

- trade/vocational/technology schools and programs

POSITIVES TO CONSIDER:

You may be offered a salaried position with benefits and guaranteed hours. The known variables include having the same clients and the same coworkers every day. Sometimes you may work as a "team" with a "teammate." You can expect exposure to new information and theories.

POSSIBLE CHALLENGES TO CONSIDER:

You may be offered a low salary or hourly pay with no or minimal benefits. Other duties beside interpreting may be assigned. Your skills may plateau due to constant interpreting of very basic information and repetitious subject matter. Consider the topic matter or grade level. Will the subject matter and interpreting of it provide the chance to grow interpreting-wise? Will you be challenged? Depending on the age and signing skill of a child in a primary level, you may feel more like a "glorified baby-sitter" than an interpreter. You may also be asked to do teacher or teacher-like duties while not being compensated with a teacher-like salary.

INTERPRETER ATTRIBUTES:

- broad general knowledge of a variety of different subjects

- a strong foundation of basic academic principles (i.e., math, English grammar, and so on)

- a love of children (if that is the population you will be serving)

- good people skills

- a love of learning in an academic environment

- a love of academia

- patience

PREPARATION ADVICE:

Expose yourself to any and all inf[...]
a "Jacqueline/Jack" of all trades [...]
matter. Read newspapers, magazi[...]
sics. Become a sponge of general i[...]
Become familiar with technical sig[...]
the manual alphabet and brush up [...]

Note for the freelance interprete[...]
tend to pay less per hour than [...]
sources. If you do get offered wo[...]
will be provided at no charge to [...]
hires you should provide free pa[...]
small way, for the lower hourly pay[...]
a team partner if the assignment la[...]
If the subject to be interpreted is cle[...]
ized knowledge and vocabulary, ask[...]
(paid time to study information to [...]
interpreting assignment).

Description of Post-Secondary setting

Qualifications JM

Role Delineation JM
— responsibilities
pg. 13.6 - 137

Interpreter Attributes

Working Conditions SL
— not < B-8

Positives / Negatives SL

Pay for Services pg 13-9+10+11
contracts SL
Benefits

Placement —M

Supervision + Evaluation SL
Professional Development SM
Ethical Considerations SM
Prepping for an Assignment —M

EMERGENCY INTERPRETING:
PUBLIC EMERGENCY SITUATIONS

WHAT?

This means interpreting during a public emergency or crisis.

WHERE?

- scenes of natural or man-made disasters or accidents (i.e., Oklahoma City bombing site, Northridge, CA earthquake sites, World Trade Center)

- Red Cross stations

- food and shelter relief sites

POSITIVES TO CONSIDER:

Here, more than with any other kind of interpreting, you really do make a difference. Here, you roll up your sleeves and start interpreting. You are there "where the action is," providing communication to those truly in need. This can be extremely rewarding.

POSSIBLE CHALLENGES TO CONSIDER:

Emergency situations can be stressful and anxiety producing. It can be emotionally traumatizing to witness victims and their families in the midst of a crisis.

Note: Do this work within reason. First, take care of yourself and your own family's personal health, safety, and welfare. The reason for this is that when you are not personally stressed, worried, or preoccupied about your own family, you can be more calm, more "there" for the people who need you. Do what you can. Do not overdo it. No one wants you to die a martyr. (Besides, if you die, you cannot interpret and that does not do anybody any good.) Afterwards, you may want to seek emotional/stress relief support for yourself.

BOTTOM LINE:

Do what you can. Know your limits and boundaries. Be good to yourself while you are being good to others. Know and remember that you did the best you could do. Know you contributed and did make a difference. As we saw with the rescue workers at the Oklahoma City bomb site and at the World Trade Center, you may need to get emotional/psychological/ Post Traumatic Stress Disorder (PTSD) support after, or even during the event. Doing so is not a negative; nor is it a sign of weakness. Doing so is positive - a sign of being human.

INTERPRETER ATTRIBUTES:

- ability to be calm, level-headed and centered in the midst of chaos and tragedy

- ability to work without severely depleting your physical/emotional reserves

- physical, mental and emotional stamina

PREPARATION ADVICE:

Always remember: **SAFETY FIRST!** Do not stand in harm's way. Have personal safety and survival supplies in your car (i.e., safety supplies/survival kit). (See **APPENDIX**.) Other than that, how can one ever really prepare for such unforeseen events?

EMERGENCY: "911" INTERPRETING

WHAT?

This means interpreting for someone's personal emergency (i.e., medical, law enforcement, or safety related).

WHERE?

- scene of accident

- hospital emergency room (see **MEDICAL INTER-PRETING** pages 91-93)

- scene of an arrest (see **LEGAL INTERPRETING** pages 89-90)

POSITIVES TO CONSIDER:

Providing an important service at a time when someone is really in need of your assistance can be rewarding work. Wisely use the time between your intake conference and the actual assignment to mentally prepare yourself. This mental preparation is extremely important for creating a calm place inside from which you can deliver clear communication despite any potentially chaotic or stressful situation in which you may find yourself.

POSSIBLE CHALLENGES TO CONSIDER:

Emergency interpreting involves chaotic situations, unusual circumstances, and stressed people. Your work environment may be frenzied.

INTERPRETER ATTRIBUTES:

- calmness in the face of chaos

- flexibility

- ability to quickly survey a situation and the environment

- ability to stay out of harm's way while interpreting

PREPARATION ADVICE:

Use your general life experiences. Become familiar with medical terms and conditions, law enforcement terms and procedures, and general health and safety rules. Get legal interpreting training prior to accepting any assignment involving the police or any kind of law enforcement entity. Remember: "SAFETY FIRST!" here, too!

GOVERNMENT INTERPRETING POSITION

WHAT?

This is a position interpreting for the government as a government employee.

WHERE?

- department/agency/office headquarters

- field offices

- laboratories

- testing sites

- conferences/workshops/trainings

- hotel ballrooms

- auditoriums

- office/team/branch/division meetings

- one-on-one meetings

- small group meetings

- agency-wide presentations

POSITIVES TO CONSIDER:

Enjoy stable work in a salaried position with benefits, pay increments (steps, grades, cost of living adjustments), and the potential for professional growth, advancement, and training, which may lead to other career paths.

POSSIBLE CHALLENGES TO CONSIDER:

Often the job description includes an "other duties as assigned by the supervisor" clause. These "slash" positions (i.e., "Interpreter/Assistant Program Manager") may be quite inclusive. While you may like the interpreting portion, you may not care for the other duties that are included in your job title.

Employees, both D/deaf and hearing, will see you day in and day out at the office; a camaraderie may develop. This camaraderie may lead to a more relaxed work environment, which in turn, might cause your co-workers to forget the professional Code of Ethics. For example, your supervisor or staff members might question you about information presented or the behavior of other employees during your assignment. It is extremely important to set firm boundaries regarding the Code of Ethics and perhaps issue gentle reminders to others that confidentiality is a must during interpreting assignments.

Your supervisor or the person doing your employee performance evaluation may not be familiar with the training, skills, and ethics required for the position. Often the person doing the evaluation (which can affect grade, step, or merit increases or awards) is not an interpreter and does not know the intricacies involved. Further, he or she may not be able to tell whether the level of interpreting services rendered were "good" or "bad," "appropriate" or "inappropriate," and whether they "exceeded standards" or "failed to meet standards."*

*SUGGESTIONS:

Regarding "OTHER DUTIES": Get detailed information about that part of the position. Get information from the job description, job announcement, government personnel classification, interviewing supervisor, other employees in the department with similar positions, and perhaps even the vacating interpreter (if one is leaving the position you are interviewing for). Ask questions. Do some homework prior to the interview to know what kind of questions to ask regarding possible duties and responsibilities that may be involved.

Regarding EMPLOYEE EVALUATIONS: This is an area where you might consider doing some "public relations" (PR) for yourself. You should consider doing some interpreter education in a kind and gentle manner, without attitude or condemnation. Supervisors do not tend to appreciate others' negative attitudes or contempt towards them. Supervisors may also not want to admit their lack of familiarity or understanding of the work you do. After all, evaluating you (which requires knowledge and understanding of exactly what you do and how well you do it) is part of their job description! They get evaluated on how well they perform their evaluations on employees like you.

INTERPRETER ATTRIBUTES:

- patience

- preference for stability

- flexibility

- willingness to do "other duties as assigned"

- willingness to be part of a team

PREPARATION ADVICE:

Become familiar with government acronyms including agency, department, and division acronyms as well as general "government-ese" or "government-speak." Become familiar with the general mission of the specific agency and with the agency's structure. Ask for brochures or publications sponsored/ endorsed/ published by the agency. Ask questions.

AND

Do your homework. Investigate the agency you are considering. Research the mission statement of the agency. Who do they serve? What kind of public services do they perform? What is the structure of the organization? Information of this kind helps you to see how you may fit into the grand scheme of the government workplace and how you can contribute to the agency's mission.

Note: You may also need a government security clearance to do certain kinds of government interpreting. Make a list of addresses you have had over the past ten years. Be prepared to furnish names of people whom government agents can interview, either by telephone or in person, about your character and background. Your neighbors (past and current) may be interviewed as well.

LEGAL INTERPRETING

WHAT?

This involves court proceedings, legal meetings, depositions, arbitrations, mediations, hearings, arrests, and court ordered counseling and evaluation sessions.

WHERE?

- court houses

- police departments

- lawyer's offices

- jails/prisons

- juvenile detention centers

- court sanctioned counseling facilities

- mental health facilities and programs

POSITIVES TO CONSIDER:

You are exposed to interesting cases. The work is challenging both intellectually and technically, especially in the conversion of legal terminology into ASL or even Signed English. You will usually earn more money per hour, per half-day, per day than for other types of interpreting.

POSSIBLE CHALLENGES TO CONSIDER:

This type of assignment can be stressful and often involves high pressure work. Participants communicate at a rapid fire pace. At times it is difficult to bridge D/deaf culture with that of the courtroom. Professional liability issues abound. Occasionally, you are exposed to very disturbing cases and to the darker side of human behavior.

INTERPRETER ATTRIBUTES:

- a great vocabulary

- "nerves of steel"

- ability to remain calm in highly stressful situations

- patience

- in-depth knowledge of the legal system, the court system, and legal procedures

PREPARATION ADVICE:

GET TRAINING! Know what you are doing. Know what people are saying ("legal-ese"). Sign-to-voice well. Know aspects of the D/deaf culture thoroughly. Become familiar with "street" language, slang and signs regarding drugs, drug culture, and "street life." Know about courtroom etiquette and protocol. Study the judicial system and know about the various proceedings. Purchase professional liability insurance. Build your vocabulary . Know Latin roots of words. **GET TRAINING! FIND A MENTOR!** Work towards getting legal interpreting certification. Visit courthouses and spend time in courtrooms. Expose yourself to legal proceedings. Study the Miranda Warning. Study jury instructions.

MEDICAL INTERPRETING

WHAT?

This is interpreting for medically related appointments, hospital staff meetings, hospital emergencies and medical training programs including conferences, seminars, and pre- and post-operation meetings with doctors, midwives, nurse practitioners, and other health care providers, and their patients.

WHERE?

- doctors' offices

- hospitals

- clinics

- medical training centers

- hospices

- rehabilitation facilities

POSITIVES TO CONSIDER:

This work is professionally challenging (interpreting medical terminology into ASL or even Signed English, while it comes to you at machine gun pace), provides varied experiences (i.e., medical conditions, clients), gives you a sense of really contributing, and provides the opportunity to learn about anatomy, physiology, medicine, and pathologies. Sometimes, if you are lucky enough to interpret for a couple's labor and delivery, you may become a surrogate "aunt" or "uncle."

POSSIBLE CHALLENGES TO CONSIDER:

Here, highly complex material and information is "shot" at you at a rapid pace. This can be quite frustrating and very stressful. You witness some disturbing conditions (i.e., sights, sounds, smells). Other challenges include professional liability issues and exposure to illnesses (some of which are contagious). You may see people suffer and perhaps even die. Sometimes these people are individuals you have gotten to know and love.

INTERPRETER ATTRIBUTES:

- a strong stomach

- must not faint easily
  (Some medical interpreting is not for those who are "faint of heart" nor for those who are "weak of stomach.")

- compassion

PREPARATION ADVICE:

Know basic biology, anatomy, physiology, chemistry, and pharmacology concepts. Many medical terms are Latin based. Know these roots. Know technical words/signs. Expose yourself to medical information (i.e., journals, articles, research).

SUGGESTIONS:

PROTECT YOURSELF! TAKE PRECAUTIONS! AVOID EXPOSING YOURSELF TO CONDITIONS THAT MAY BE HAZARDOUS TO YOUR HEALTH! If the person you are interpreting for is entering a room marked "CAUTION!" (of any kind), TAKE PRECAUTIONARY MEASURES! If the doctor and/or the client is suiting up in "scrubs" (protective clothing of any kind) or is wearing a robe, face mask, or eye protection, then ask where you can get your scrubs, mask, robe, and eye protection. If you are told, "Well, we will only be there for a moment," then ask the client whether or not he or she needs you in the room. If the answer is "No," then fine, just wait outside the room. However, if the client does want you in the "CONTAMINATION RISK: TAKE APPROPRIATE PRECAUTIONS" room, you should take precautions! Everyone else is!!! Simply inform your client that to enter the room, you require the appropriate gear. End of discussion.

Also, if your client is getting X-rays, get out of the way! You do not have to stay with your client during the actual photography process. The technicians don't!

NOTE: WHAT IS WRITTEN BELOW IS NOT TO BE PERCEIVED OR CONSTRUED AS MEDICAL ADVICE. I AM NOT A PHYSICIAN. I AM NOT QUALIFIED TO GIVE MEDICAL ADVICE, ORDERS, OR CONSULTATIONS. THE PURPOSE OF THIS SECTION IS TO PROVIDE YOU WITH SOME THINGS TO CONSIDER AND TO LOOK INTO WITH YOUR OWN PHYSICIAN FOR YOUR OWN PERSONAL SAFETY AND WELFARE.

I suggest you look into getting the hepatitis inoculation series (shots given over a period of time). After these shots, you may consider getting a blood titer (blood test) that detects the presence of hepatitis antibodies. If a positive detection has been found, the series is over. However, if no antibodies are found, you may have to get another hepatitis inoculation (or two) and then retake the blood titer to determine the presence of hepatitis antibodies.

MAKE SURE THAT YOU HAVE HAD ALL OTHER VITAL VACCINATIONS AND INOCULATIONS! (Did you get a polio vaccination? If so, in what year? If you had a polio shot or if you had serum drops on sugar cubes, what year was it? If it was prior to a certain year, you might have to have it redone to be protected.)

Check into your past history of measles, mumps, rubella (MMR), and chicken pox. Make a list of all previous inoculations and inoculation dates. Have you been exposed? Tell your private physician about your history of exposure. If you have not been exposed, ask your doctor what, if any, inoculations you may need or ask about other precautions you should take.

LOOK INTO GETTING A TUBERCULOSIS (TB) TEST. If your skin reaction is positive to the skin test, it may be an indication of either exposure to TB or of having TB. IF YOU DO TEST POSITIVE, RETURN TO YOUR DOCTOR FOR ADDITIONAL TREATMENTS/THERAPIES IMMEDIATELY!

Consider getting a tetanus shot. (Hey ... you never know. Lock jaw is a terrible thing to get, especially if you are an oral interpreter.) It is a good idea to get a tetanus shot every five years. If you cannot remember when your last shot was, you probably need one.

Listed above are just a few of the things that you should check into. There are also certain things that you must be mindful of if you are pregnant, have a pacemaker, or have certain other conditions.

AGAIN NOTE: I AM NOT A PHYSICIAN. I AM NOT QUALIFIED TO GIVE MEDICAL ADVICE OR CONSULTATION. THIS IS TO PROVIDE YOU WITH SOME COMMON SENSE MEASURES THAT YOU SHOULD LOOK INTO WITH YOUR OWN PHYSICIAN FOR YOUR OWN PERSONAL SAFETY AND WELFARE.

IF YOU HAVE ANY CONCERNS OR QUESTIONS, ASK YOUR PHYSICIAN!

MENTAL HEALTH INTERPRETING

WHAT?

This includes interpreting for counseling/therapy appointments, "in-patient" treatment, "out-patient" treatment, evaluations for intake, group therapy, mental health providers' staff meetings, and mental health trainings and seminars.

WHERE?

- mental health facilities

- mental health programs

- therapist's or psychiatrist's office

- hospital emergency rooms

- offices

- training sites

POSITIVES TO CONSIDER:

You have the opportunity to learn about/be exposed to different and interesting aspects of human behavior/psychosis/emotions. This work gives you the chance to see "textbook cases" in real life.

POSSIBLE CHALLENGES TO CONSIDER:

Topics/issues/situations may be personally uncomfortable/frustrating/ depressing for the interpreter who may have experienced similar circumstances. Even for those who have not had similar experiences, it can be very sad. At times, voicing may be difficult due to the general incoherent state of the client. Your personal safety may be threatened. (Always stay next to the therapist or staff person and near the door for prompt exit in case of a violent outbreak.) Interpreting in this situation may be frustrating because linguistically and culturally, it can be a difficult gap to bridge. You can sometimes leave the assignment feeling uncertain. "Did I get through? Did the client understand, not only my signs, but the concepts being communicated?"

INTERPRETER ATTRIBUTES:

- a strong, grounded sense of self

- not only knowledge of, but full integration into practice of the Code of Ethics (a given for all situations)

- not easily affected by other people's energy

PREPARATION ADVICE:

Have some knowledge of "abnormal" psychology and pharmacology (both "chemical" and generic medication names). Wear flat shoes or something to walk fast or run easily. Do not wear dangling earrings, necklaces, or scarves which can be pulled on or used to choke you. If in a treatment center, find out who the staff members are and never let them leave you alone with a patient or unescorted. If they leave the room, you leave with them. If they must leave to tend to someone else, have them escort you to the "nurses' station." Remain there, after introducing yourself to the staff, until an interpreting need arises.

If the client/patient tries to engage you in personal conversation, ask them, "Who? Which staff?" until they indicate which of the staff people they wish to talk to. If they are belligerent and keep pointing to you, as if to say, "I want to talk to you!", get the attention of the head nurse or another staff member and let him or her know that the patient wishes to communicate.

- **Do not engage in one-to-one personal conversation with the client/patient.**

- **Never be left alone with a client/patient.**

- **Never sit next to the client/patient.**

- **Always sit next to the counselor and close to a door.**

PLATFORM/PERFORMING ARTS INTERPRETING

WHAT?

This means interpreting for theater productions, awards ceremonies, poetry readings, concerts, speeches, rallies, and the like.

WHERE?

- auditoriums

- concert halls

- convention centers

- amphitheaters

- stadiums

- pavilions

- small stages

- festivals

- fairs, and other outdoor venues

POSITIVES TO CONSIDER:

These jobs can be lots of fun! This kind of interpreting may allow for a bit more animation due to signing "large" (in an effort to make signs more visible to audience members).

POSSIBLE CHALLENGES TO CONSIDER:

This work may be nerve-wracking if you are "weak-kneed." Performers may go off the rehearsed script, become quite nervous, and improvise in a difficult-to-follow (interpret) manner. Unscripted, metaphoric, esoteric poems and songs may be sprung on you at the last moment. These can be culturally and linguistically difficult to "bridge."

INTERPRETER ATTRIBUTES:

- flexibility

- sense of humor

- some "stage presence" (comfort and ease at being on stage)

- strong sense of professional purpose*

PREPARATION ADVICE:

Arrive extra early. Introduce yourself to the meeting coordinator. Get a copy of the agenda/program. Ask about special acronyms or acronym-words that may be used and may not be familiar to the general public. Know how to spell the names of the presenters or people to be introduced. Survey the seating and lighting arrangements. (Will videos be shown? Are they captioned? Will all the lights be dimmed? Can some be left on? Where on stage will the interpreter be positioned? Will the interpreter be spotlighted?) Check out the acoustics. (Are you directly in front of or behind a loud speaker?) Ask to do a sound/lighting check, if necessary. Better to do these things beforehand. If the coordinator seems to be "put-off" by your request, explain that you want the event to run smoothly and without interruptions on your part. Explain that you want to make sure that the interpreting end of things runs smoothly, so that you can comfortably and proficiently perform the task for which you have been hired.

Get a script of the show, words to the songs/poems, copies of the speeches (if possible), show programs, and so on. Many theaters pay for preparation/script translation time. Check it out. Consult a "Sign Master" for sign choices. Listen to taped songs of what you will be interpreting. Attend rehearsals. Wear comfortable shoes!

Directors, theatres, and performing arts companies may have a preference for the positioning of sign language interpreters during performances. Interpreters may sit or stand to one side of the stage in front of a designated section for D/deaf patrons. In some instances interpreters "shadow" the performers, moving around the stage during the performance. Be flexible.

Note: A strong sense of professional purpose means you are conscious, at every moment, that this is not YOUR show. You are there for the sole purpose of interpreting someone else's show and performance. Many actor "wannabes" get carried away and truly "act" as if it were THEIR show. For instance, do not make up your own rendition of instrumental music when asked to interpret. You are not hired as a "performing artist"; this is something entirely different. My point here is that if you were hired to interpret, simply do that.

RELIGIOUS INTERPRETING

WHAT?

This is interpreting for observances, worship services, holidays, weddings, baptisms, dedications, circumcisions, confirmations, funerals, bar mitzvahs, bat mitzvahs, Sunday school, Saturday school, ordinations, and so on.

WHERE?

- churches

- chapels

- temples

- mosques

- shrines

- auditoriums

- hotel ballrooms

- classrooms

- "store front" gathering rooms

POSITIVES TO CONSIDER:

The material you are interpreting can be inspirational at times. You are exposed to a strong sense of community. You also get the opportunity to be exposed to and learn about a group or belief system that may be different than your own.

POSSIBLE CHALLENGES TO CONSIDER:

Sometimes people in this setting will try to convert you. Some people may be upset by the fact that you charge money for professional services rendered in this setting. Some people expect you to donate your money, your time, and your resources, even though you are not a "believer" nor a member of their church, nor do you subscribe to their belief system. Some beliefs and practices may be offensive to you and directly opposed to your own belief system.

INTERPRETER ATTRIBUTES:

- comfortable and at peace with yourself (know who you are, what you believe, and stay true to that)

- ability to act with love and acceptance of others

- respect for and appreciation of the diversity among people

- non–judgmental/non-critical attitude towards others

- ability to say, "No" (able to turn down an assignment if you feel that you cannot convey the content of the message clearly, accurately, and in a neutral manner)*

PREPARATION ADVICE:

Get to know special terms, signs, chants, refrains and symbolism of the event to be interpreted or of the religion. Do some homework prior to the assignment. Ask other interpreters or members of the D/deaf community for specific signs if you do not already know them. Ask for a program or bulletin in advance. Know the order or flow of events, people's names, and terminology to be used. Find out which books are referenced. Glance at them beforehand. Ask the contact person if any special attire is required or appreciated. (Do you have to wear a veil/head covering? Will one be provided? If not, what kind/what color?) If a female is interpreting, should she wear a dress only and not dress pants?

*Note: If you feel that exposure to a specific community or belief system will be too personally upsetting to you, do not take the assignment.

SPIRITUAL/METAPHYSICAL/"ALTERNATIVE" INTERPRETING

WHAT?

This entails interpreting non-traditional, metaphysical, spiritual and philosophical concepts. Some people refer to this as "New Age" interpreting. (The concepts are actually very ancient. They are just being "re-visited.") This includes observances, worship services, guided meditations, healing/clearing/balancing "circles"/sessions/rituals, private practitioner sessions, workshops, conferences, holidays, marriages, baptisms, dedications, "transition ceremonies", Sunday school, ordinations, and so on.

WHERE?

- churches

- chapels

- temples

- mosques

- shrines

- auditoriums

- hotel ballrooms

- classrooms

- "store front" gathering rooms

- offices

- outdoor venues

POSITIVES TO CONSIDER:

The material you are interpreting can be inspirational at times. You are exposed to a strong sense of community. You also get the opportunity to be exposed to and learn about a group or belief system that may be different from your own.

POSSIBLE CHALLENGES TO CONSIDER:

Sometimes people in this setting will try to convert you. Some people may be upset by the fact that you charge money for professional services rendered in this setting. Some people expect you to donate your money, your time, and your resources, even though you are not a "believer" nor a member of their church, nor do you subscribe to their belief system. Some beliefs and practices may be offensive to you and directly opposed to your own belief system.

INTERPRETER ATTRIBUTES:

- comfort and peace within yourself (know who you are, what you believe, and stay true to that)

- ability to act with love and acceptance of others

- respect for and appreciation of the diversity of people

- non–judgmental/non-critical attitude towards others

- ability to say, "No," (able to turn down an assignment if you feel that you cannot convey the content of the message clearly, accurately, and in a neutral manner)*

PREPARATION ADVICE:

Get to know special terms, signs, chants and refrains and symbolism of the event to be interpreted or of the religion. Do some homework prior to the assignment. Ask other interpreters or members of the D/deaf community for specific signs if you do not already know them. Ask for a program or bulletin in advance. Know the order or flow of events, people's names, and terminology to be used. Find out which books are referenced. Glance at them beforehand. Ask the contact person if any special attire is required or appreciated. (Do you have to wear a veil/head covering? Will one be provided? If not, what kind/what color?) If a female is interpreting, should she wear a dress only and not dress pants?

*Note: If you feel that exposure to a specific community or belief system will be too personally upsetting to you, do not take the assignment.

SOCIAL INTERPRETING

This differs from **PLATFORM/PERFORMING ARTS INTERPRETING** (see pages 96-97) because you do more "table talk" or "chitchat." This tends to be more small-group and one-on-one interactions. It can be formal, informal, or more of a networking/information gathering kind of interaction.

WHAT?

Dinners, banquets, receptions, ceremonies, awards programs, benefits, and so on.

WHERE?

- hotel ballrooms

- convention centers

- restaurants

- private homes

- outdoor venues

POSITIVES TO CONSIDER:

These events can be a lot of fun! You get exposure to new and interesting people and attend events in beautiful surroundings with great food! "Time flies when you are having fun!"

POSSIBLE CHALLENGES TO CONSIDER:

Of course, these events can turn out to be completely the opposite! Some events are in awful surroundings and seem to drag on forever with lousy food!

INTERPRETER ATTRIBUTES:

- ability to "blend in"

- polite

- knowledge of manners and social etiquette

PREPARATION ADVICE:

This may not be the most important thing nor the first thing to do, but this is important: Find out what to wear! Is it a formal event? (Evening gown? Nice dress? Tux? Nice suit?) Dress to "blend in" not to "stand out" or to "knock out." Will you be with one client throughout the entire evening, or will you be rotating tables/clients with other interpreters throughout the evening? Wear comfortable shoes!

Get a copy of the program/agenda ahead of time. Familiarize yourself with the spelling of the speakers' names and titles. What are the scheduled events? (Here I am assuming that someone else will be hired to do the platform interpreting/ceremonial responsibilities or to interpret for a guest speaker. You will simply focus on the individuals to whom you are assigned.)

Guests at your table will want to talk to you because you are a "warm body"; you are there, and it is after all, a social event. Practice polite ways of declining conversation, stating who you are and what your function is for the evening.

If you are teaming with someone, work out eating arrangements. If meals are provided for the interpreters, you may want to consider having the "off" interpreter leave and eat, while you remain at the table interpreting. When your partner is finished eating, alternate. If it seems uncomfortable to sit there while others are eating, perhaps nibble some salad, sip water, or eat a little bread until you are replaced. Diners can become quite uncomfortable and self-conscious if someone is just sitting there. Be aware that we must blend in and not cause undo attention to ourselves in this particular situation.

You may also consider eating before the assignment so that you are not sitting at the table hungry with a growling stomach.

Use your best judgment. Use general, common sense rules of etiquette and exhibit polite behavior.

SUPPORT GROUP INTERPRETING

WHAT?
This includes interpreting for participants in support groups such as Alcoholics Anonymous (AA), Narcotics Anonymous (NA), ALANON (for family of AA members), as well as of groups for people who are divorced or widowed, single parents, grieving a loss, and so on.

WHERE?

- general meeting halls

- lodges

- office conference rooms

- library conference rooms

- church halls and basements

- hospitals

- treatment facilities

POSITIVES TO CONSIDER:

You participate in a supportive environment where positive living and coping skills are taught and reinforced. These are gatherings of people who share interesting life stories.

POSSIBLE CHALLENGES TO CONSIDER:

Topics/issues/situations may be personally uncomfortable/ frustrating/ depressing for the interpreter who may have experienced similar circumstances. Even for those who have not had similar experiences, it can be very sad.

INTERPRETER ATTRIBUTES:

- good people skills

- an understanding of and empathy for human nature

- ability not be easily shocked nor surprised by honest personal stories

- non-judgmental/non-critical attitude toward others

PREPARATION ADVICE:

General and varied life experiences are helpful here; understanding of human nature and psychology are valuable. Become familiar with "street" language, slang, and signs regarding drugs, drug culture, and "street life." Familiarize yourself with THE TWELVE STEPS, THE TWELVE TRADITIONS,

PREAMBLE, SERENITY PRAYER, (see **APPENDIX**), and slogans used. The following are some common slogans:

- "Keep coming back!"

- "It works if you work it! It won't if you don't! You will die if you don't try! SO DO IT!"

- "Let go and let God" (sometimes said and signed, "L-G, L-G")

- "One day at a time!"

- "Fake it 'til you make it!"

- "K.I.S.S." (Keep It Simple, Silly!)

TECHNICAL INTERPRETING

WHAT?
Topics for technical interpreting include: computers, programming, chemistry, physics, engineering, and any of the maths or sciences.

WHERE?
- government agencies

- technology corporations

- pharmaceutical companies

- laboratories

- staff meetings

- conferences

- classrooms

POSITIVES TO CONSIDER:
You gain exposure to "state-of-the-art" information within the various fields. Comprehending and interpreting technical information can provide an intellectual challenge for the interpreter.

POSSIBLE CHALLENGES TO CONSIDER:

If you are not interested in the topic, information can be quite tedious when discussed in minutia. Sometimes there are no standardized signs for some of the highly specialized vocabulary. Some speakers have quite heavy or "thick" accents and they present highly technical and unfamiliar (to the average person) material at a rapid fire pace. This can contribute not only to hand fatigue (if you have to fingerspell a lot), but to mental fatigue as well. Discuss with your partner the possibility of switching off every 20-25 minutes if need be. (Also, if it is an international conference, discuss the foreign accents with your partner. You may need to switch off back and forth based on your familiarity with and understanding of the accent of the speaker.)

INTERPRETER ATTRIBUTES:

- flexibility

- interest in/appreciation for/knowledge of topics involved

- broad knowledge base of math and sciences

PREPARATION ADVICE:

Study; read; ask questions; expose yourself to any and all types of technical information. If you can meet with the client prior to the start of the assignment, do it. Ask for any acronyms, specialized signs, and topics to be discussed. Ask for a related article you can glance over prior to interpreting. If you are new to the topic, tell your client. Also welcome sign input from him or her.

VIDEO RELAY SERVICE (VRS) INTERPRETING

WHAT?

Video relay service interpreting is performed via the computer using a video web camera, internet protocol, and a telephone. The D/deaf person connects to a Video Relay Service (VRS) provider and makes an interpreting request to the video interpreter (VI) on the receiving end. The VI receives the request and makes the connection with the other party via telephone.

The VI interprets in sign language to the D/deaf person via web camera and voices into the telephone what the D/deaf person is signing.

WHERE?

- Video Relay Service centers

POSITIVES TO CONSIDER:

Interpreting takes place through live interaction with only a slight time lag between responses. Communication flows in a more natural manner using signs, facial expressions, and body language. VRS centers offer interpreting support, allowing frequent breaks to prevent eye and hand fatigue.

POSSIBLE CHALLENGES TO CONSIDER:

Sluggish internet connections or delays caused by large volumes of "traffic" on your ISP (Internet Service Provider) may cause slow transmission/reception of signs. Additionally, the quality of the equipment itself affects the clarity of the interpreting. Even if state-of-the-art equipment is used, picture quality may still be poor because the person signing may not be aligned within the frame, possibly being too far from the camera, improperly lit, or situated at a poor angle for delivering/receiving the signed message. If clear images are not received, the quality of the interpreting may be affected. Additionally, keep in mind that VRS centers are independently owned and operated. Be sure to read the employment contract carefully. Limited breaks and little or no support can lead to both mental and physical fatigue, possibly leading to eye and/or hand strain.

INTERPRETER ATTRIBUTES:

- flexibility

- good people skills

- excellent voicing skills and, specifically, excellent voicing skills in a two-dimensional environment

- calm demeanor

- patience

- great stamina (not prone to eye fatigue/mental/

general body fatigue while being in front of a computer screen for hours)

PREPARATION ADVICE :

Practice voicing in a two-dimensional environment by voicing signed video tapes. While performing VRS interpreting you will find that some clothing colors enhance the face and hands while others wash them out and make it challenging to impossible for the receiver to decipher the signs on their screen. Ask the VRS personnel what colors they prefer you to wear. Request a visit to the VRS center and ask to observe the process, or ask for a demonstration and mock practice session if possible. Ask about breaks and interpreter support.

PART 4

Professional Challenges

- **Your Role? Follow the Code of Ethics**

- **Preparation**

- **Taking Precautions Prior to the Assignment**

- **Workers' Compensation**

- **Carpal Tunnel Syndrome/Repetitive Motion Disorder**

- **Stress**

- **Sometimes, You May Have to Just Say "No"**

- **Personal Safety Considerations**

PART 4

Professional Challenges

YOUR ROLE? FOLLOW THE CODE OF ETHICS

Sometimes interpreters are asked to perform duties, relay information, or are invited or "given permission" to participate in situations that are not in line with their professional role.

BOTTOM LINE:

DON'T. AVOID STEPPING OUT OF YOUR ROLE. YOU ARE A PROFESSIONAL INTERPRETER!

Remember that the Code of Ethics was written by interpreters and D/deaf people to protect the D/deaf community's rights and to maintain the integrity and neutrality of interpreters. Anything performed outside of these guidelines compromises the integrity of the communication, our neutrality, and the rights of the communicators involved. Period.

I do not accept anyone's "permission" to step out of my role. I do not need anyone's permission. I won't make that misstep. Ethics are not something that should be turned on and off at a whim.

If there are any questions about the Code of Ethics, or if you are being pressured to breach the Code, I suggest that you hand out copies to the persons involved, right then and there. Explain that you cannot continue to function as a "neutral facilitator of communication" until all parties are familiar with these guidelines and adhere to them.

If you are a bit "shaky" about the Ethics and what they mean or how they apply to you, reread them before each assignment. Have them forefront in your mind. If you still feel unsure, discuss your concerns with other interpreters who have reputations for being neutral and ethical.* Role play, explore hypothetical situations, ask questions, pick their brains. Do whatever you can, whatever is necessary, to have the Ethics ingrained in your mind so you will instinctively be true to the Code. Have an ethical response on speed-dial at all times.

I suggest that you keep several copies of the Code of Ethics in your briefcase, ready to distribute if necessary.

* One way to decide if another interpreter is neutral and ethical is to evaluate how he or she speaks of others. When an interpreter is known to speak ill of other interpreters or clients, this should be a huge red flag to you. This is NOT a neutral or ethical person if he or she is idly gossiping about other interpreters to clients or co-workers. A neutral and ethical interpreter is one who tries to make a *positive* difference, knows his or her boundaries, and respects others.

PREPARATION

THE ENVIRONMENT

Interpreting assignments occur in a variety of locations and each place offers a unique environment for communication. Some are conducive to interpreting, others are not. You may be faced with conditions that hinder your ability to sign such as poor lighting, inadequate climate control, glaring sunshine, smokers, hecklers or worse.

Always be prepared. Bring a jacket or sweater appropriate for interpreting should you become cold. Dress in tasteful layers of clothing so that you may shed the outer layer if you become too warm. Remember to bring sunglasses to outdoor assignments and position yourself in the most advantageous light. If it is a windy day at an outdoor assignment, position yourself bedside a windbreak and be sure to secure your hair, hat, and loose clothing so they will not be a distraction. If the environmental conditions are interfering with your ability to interpret, speak to the location contact person or if indoors, speak to the person responsible for the room setup. Talk with your partner about your discomfort. If necessary, leave the area during your non-interpreting times and refresh yourself. Remember, do not be a martyr.

KNOW YOURSELF. KNOW YOUR LIMITS. SET BOUNDARIES.

OFF DAY? BE GENTLE ON YOURSELF

Everyone experiences an "off" day occasionally. While these days strain confidence in our own proficiency, they don't happen often and we should not beat-up on ourselves. Off days are usually the ones we remember most vividly, reliving the embarrassment of inefficiency. Keep in mind that part of our human experience involves making mistakes and learning from them. Don't waste energy on the past, hone your skills and perform well in the future.

BOTTOM LINE:

Be gentle on yourself. Lighten up. Get over it. We are all human. Do the best you can. After all, that is all anyone can ask of you and all you can ask of and expect from yourself.

NEGATIVE SELF-TALK: TURN IT OFF!

Who needs it? You certainly do not, especially while you are trying to interpret!

BOTTOM LINE:

Turn it off! Shut it out! Lighten up!

Instead of tuning into the negative, cultivate and perpetuate the positive. Make positive inner feedback your new mantra. You must replace the negative with positive images, words and energy. Replace the inner voice of the harsh critic with that of your own personal cheerleader!

TOTALLY STRESSED OUT? GET A LIFE!

Nothing, I repeat, nothing is worth totally stressing over!

Get a clue! Don't become unglued!

Have a life separate from your interpreting work. Start a new hobby. Exercise. Relax. Visit with non-interpreting friends. Do volunteer work.

Strive For Mastery, Not Perfection!

We can be misguided by seeking a false sense of perfection and be woefully disappointed when we do not attain that illusion. Try your best; that is all anyone can ask of you. Simply find satisfaction in being the best person, best interpreter you can be.

KNOW YOURSELF. KNOW YOUR LIMITS. SET BOUNDARIES.

Believe me, the better care you take of yourself, both physically and mentally, the more you can contribute to the communities you serve and to your profession. No one wants to be around someone who is burned-out, injured or stressed! Everyone will benefit if you take good care of yourself so that you can continue to have a long and healthy career full of positive contributions. You will be able to stay in this profession and acquire skills, knowledge, and experiences that you can pass on to interpreting students and young professionals.

Care for yourself. Choose to be a bright light instead of a frazzled interpreter.

Bottom line:

KNOW YOURSELF!

KNOW YOUR LIMITS!

SET BOUNDARIES!

TAKE PRECAUTIONS PRIOR TO THE ASSIGNMENT

Contact your partner prior to the assignment. If it is someone you have never met before, introduce yourself and tell him or her that you are looking forward to meeting. Ask if he or she has received the agenda or program. If not, you might want to run through the information you have received. Confirm the address, date, and times you were given. By doing this, you are verifying the assignment details and you are getting confirmation that your teammate was given the same information. If you make the call several days prior to the assignment and find out that your teammate was given different and conflicting information, you will have enough time to reach the contact person to clear up any misunderstandings or miscommunications.

During your conversation with the other interpreter, suggest arriving a little early to check out the interpreting setup (chairs, acoustics, and lighting), to chat and to find out each other's interpreting preferences (replacement times, support, and so on).

If your partner does not show and you have not called ahead to confirm (as I suggested above), you will wonder why. Perhaps he or she was given incorrect or different information and thought that the assignment was to take place tomorrow instead of today. Perhaps the other interpreter got sick or was in a car accident. Perhaps he or she is a "flake" and just "flaked out." Again, I want to emphasize the importance of eliminating variables and assumptions. Make contact, communicate, clarify!

If you are stuck alone with no partner, what can you do? First, call the contact person to find out if your partner has called to explain his or her absence. You will want to know if his or her excuse is valid. Do not harbor a needless grudge against another interpreter; discover the facts before making harsh judgments.

If your partner has *not called,* ask the contact person to find out what happened and when or if to expect the interpreter. Explain to the contact person and to the clients involved that you were expecting to work as a member of a team for this assignment and that efforts should be made to find a replacement for your absent partner.

You can then present the contact person and the client(s) several options. First, you may continue interpreting but insist that the interpreted sessions be arranged to provide you ample break time. Explain that interpreting is demanding both mentally and physically; adequate break time is essential to quality service.

Second, you may suggest rescheduling the meeting for a time when two interpreters can be present.

I asked interpreters what they would do if stranded at a teamed assignment without a teammate. Here are their responses:

1. "If I felt up to doing the work by myself, but with frequent breaks, I would negotiate with the contact person to double bill (full day x 2) for having to do double the work. If an agency hired me, I would negotiate it with them. If not, then a) I would take off every half hour for a half hour, or take off for 45 minutes after 45 minutes of interpreting, or take off for one hour after an hour of interpreting; b) if

none of the above were an option, I would suggest rescheduling."

2. "I would not even think of doing the entire assignment alone, and I do not want to be pressured into trying!"

3. "I would not attempt to do the entire assignment alone if:

(a) I did not feel up to it. After all, it would be a disservice to all the parties involved and

(b) I would definitely not do it if I was not doubly compensated for doing double the amount of work."

What I would do:

I would tell the agency (if the agency was the hiring party) that continuing in this manner (no team/no additional breaks/no adjustment in pay) is not an option. I would say: "Let's negotiate a 'win-win' scenario that serves the client's communications needs, that I am physically comfortable with, and that I feel that I am being adequately compensated for as a professional."

BOTTOM LINE:

Do not endanger yourself physically. You hurting yourself will not do anyone any good. It will only cause damage to you, diminish service to your present client, and perhaps compromise the service you render to your next client. No one wins! Being self-sacrificing does no one any good. Set up the best possible "win/win" situation. Take care of your needs without hurting yourself or causing damage, while providing the best service you can.

KNOW YOURSELF. KNOW YOUR LIMITS. SET BOUNDARIES.

If the other interpreter did have an emergency, try to be understanding and supportive. You never know when your own emergency may arise and you may need the understanding and support of other interpreters. If the other interpreter just "flaked" with no good reason, I would call him or her after the assignment. (Remember, calling prior to the assignment can help avoid this situation altogether.) Explain that you were expecting to be part of a team, and by not showing up, he or she put you in an uncomfortable bind. We should all assume responsibility in trying to establish good professional relationships with our fellow interpreters, and to clear the air if there are any misunderstandings or hurt feelings. Do your best to resolve your concerns. Remember, as independent contractors, we are sometimes in the position of choosing our partners or suggesting other interpreters if not able to do an assignment ourselves. If you feel that you did your best to resolve your concerns and the other person repeatedly "flaked" or if you find that interpreter not to be the kind of professional with whom you want to be associated, do not call to partner with him or her again. Do not recommend that person to others. If the person did "flake" on you, the contact person will know because of your request that he or she follow up. The contact person might reward your professionalism by requesting or contacting you for future assignments. The other interpreter might never be called again.

WORKERS' COMPENSATION

I AM NOT A LAWYER. THIS INFORMATION IS NOT TO BE CONSTRUED AS LEGAL ADVICE OR THE SOLE SOURCE OF INFORMATION REGARDING THE TOPIC. FOR FURTHER INFORMATION AND ANSWERS TO ANY CONCERNS OR QUESTIONS, SEE APPENDIX: WORKERS' COMPENSATION: DIRECTORY OF ADMINISTRATORS. YOU MAY ALSO WANT TO CONSIDER OBTAINING THE SERVICES OF AN ATTORNEY.

In the event you are hurt or injured while performing your job, there are several things you may want to consider doing (not in order):

- Report injury/accident/event to the "contact person" and with the location's administrator's office (which is perhaps called the "Human Resources Department").

- Report injury/accident/event to your state's workers' compensation entity and ask for their policies and procedures.

- If you were hired through an interpreting agency, report the injury or accident to them immediately.

- Get names and telephone numbers of any witnesses (if applicable).

- Get medical attention, treatment, and documentation of such.

- You may want to consider getting legal advice at this time.

- Contact your health insurance provider regarding policies and treatment options.

- Contact your workers' compensation insurance policy provider and initiate a claim.

- Keep detailed records and notes. Document everything in one easy-to-access place. Keep copies of reports, test results, and so on.

ALWAYS REMEMBER:

SAFETY FIRST !

CARPAL TUNNEL SYNDROME/ REPETITIVE MOTION DISORDER

An entire book could be written about this topic. In this section you will find a general definition of Carpal Tunnel Syndrome (CTS)/ Repetitive Motion Disorder (RMD), signs and symptoms, and suggestions of possible avenues for relief.

WHAT IS PRESENTED HERE IS GENERIC INFORMATION WHICH IS INTENDED TO PROVIDE GENERAL AWARENESS. IT IS NOT INTENDED TO BE TAKEN EITHER AS MEDICAL ADVICE OR AS A PRESCRIPTION FOR RELIEF. IF YOU SUSPECT THAT YOU ARE SUFFERING FROM ANY CONDITION, SEEK THE ADVICE AND ASSISTANCE OF A TRAINED MEDICAL PROFESSIONAL. MEDICAL PROFESSIONALS WILL BE THE BEST RESOURCE TO PROPERLY DIAGNOSE YOUR CONDITION AND PRESCRIBE INDIVIDUALIZED AND SPECIFIC REMEDIES AND TREATMENTS.

There is a narrowing of bones at the region of the wrist. There is a space in this area called the carpal tunnel. Different tendons and the median nerve run through this space. CTS (sometimes referred to as RMD) results from chronic overuse, repetitive movements and actions that pinch, compress or irritate the median nerve. Severe pain to the hand region, elbow, shoulder and neck region may result. Numbness may result in an impaired and weakened grasp. Some people experience a buildup of tissue fluid at the wrist. (Stedt) (See **APPENDIX** for Carpal Tunnel Syndrome/Repetitive Motion Disorder References.)

A woman with CTS described what she experiences as "pins and needles," sometimes a burning sensation, and at other times a total numbness. She must often shake her hand to retrieve a semblance of normal sensation, to "wake it up and feel something."

As I mentioned earlier, if you notice persistent pain, numbness, or swelling, seek medical attention.

SUGGESTIONS:

- **Rest:** Stop all intense wrist movements or flexing.

- **Physical Therapy:** Perhaps some specific exercises could be recommended to warm up the region before use.

- **Chiropractic Adjustments:** Ask friends, relatives, and fellow interpreters about their experiences with chiropractors. Perhaps they can recommend a reliable practitioner. Call the doctor and ask questions prior to your appointment, questions about your condition or treatment options. Ask the chiropractor if he or she has any experience with other CTS patients. Ask how those patients benefited from the treatment.

For more information about finding a qualified (board certified) chiropractor, try these two sources of chiropractic information:

National Board of Chiropractic Examiners
901 54th Avenue
Greeley, Colorado 80634
(970) 356-9100

International Chiropractic Association
1110 N. Glebe Road
Arlington, Virginia 22201
(800) 423-4690
FAX: (703) 528-5023

CONSIDERATIONS:

- Wrist brace? Ask your doctor or physical therapist about the benefits of wearing a wrist brace during your non-working hours, perhaps even while you sleep.

- Anti-inflammatory medication? Aspirin?

- Steroid and cortisone injections? Temporary relief? Ask your doctor or physical therapist about this.

- Acupuncture? Check it out. Currently 26 states and Washington, D.C. license acupuncturists. Call your state's acupuncturist licensing board to find an acupuncturist in your area.

- Surgery? Last resort. Success rate? Ask surgeon.

My personal strategy is to soak my hands every morning in hot water. When I arrive at the assignment, I soak my hands again or run warm water over my hands for several minutes in the restroom. I then apply a non-oily hand lotion and massage my hands and fingers. My hands feel "revved up" and raring to go. In the evening, I again soak my hands in hot water and apply lotion.

See **APPENDIX** for "Signer-cises" and Carpal Tunnel Syndrome/ Repetitive Motion Disorder References.

STRESS

I am sure you have heard people say that a little stress can be good for you because it keeps you sharp, focused, "on your toes." What I address here is negative stress and constructive ways to deal with it.

YES...INTERPRETING CAN BE STRESSFUL.

- The pressure and stress of interpreting assignments is real. Dealing with traffic, parking, finding the correct building or room, and so on, can be frustrating. Even before you lift your hands to interpret, you may already be "stressed out." (See page 55-56.)

- You may find yourself interpreting an unfamiliar topic or a topic for which you were unprepared. An unexpected change in venue often causes stress. (See pages 55-56.)

- Your partner may show up late - or not at all! How will you deal with your negative feelings toward the other interpreter and yet not strain your professional relationship? How will you explain to both the hearing and D/deaf clients why you cannot interpret alone for the next eight hours? What is the best way to serve your client's needs while still protecting yourself both physically and mentally? (See pages 114-117.)

- Clients, both hearing and D/deaf, might make in-appropriate requests of you. They might ask you to perform tasks outside the boundaries of your role as an interpreter and in violation of the Code of Ethics! (See pages 111-112.)

- The room may be hot and stuffy and you feel as if you are going to melt. The building is freezing and you are so cold that you can see your breath! The speaker or participants begin to smoke and you are allergic to cigarette smoke. (See page 112.)

- You may be having an "off" day (as we all some-times do) when you are required to execute platform interpreting. You are already a little "off kilter" when platform jitters kick in. This is perfor-mance stress. (See pages 113-114.)

- Negative self-talk can get the better of you while you are interpreting. Interpreters can be their own worst enemy and harshest critic. This negative thinking often kicks in while experiencing an "off" day, perhaps the same day that you are doing that platform interpreting. It is difficult to turn off the negative self-talk in your head. (See page 113.)

- You arrive home from work totally stressed...and start stressing-out about the day to come.

I am sure that you have your own list of situations that causes you stress. I hope your list will not be too long or too complex. In the next section I will offer coping strategies to help you manage your stress.

SUGGESTED REMEDIES:

BUDGET YOUR TIME:

To avoid hassles related to any aspect of travel or location, I strongly suggest four things:

- First, during the intake process, record specific address, cross streets, building number, room number, and parking information. (See pages 55-56.) If the parking is not on site, write down the names of the cross streets where the parking lot is located. If the job is to take place on a campus or military base, be sure to inquire about specifics such as where to obtain a parking pass, where to park, in which building the assignment will take place, and the telephone number of the contact person who may need to escort you to the interpreting location. Prior to the assignment, have the contact person mail/fax you the facility's map indicating buildings, parking lots, and the exact entrance you are required to use.

- Second, on the night before the assignment, map out your route and record it clearly. Consider alternate routes in case primary roads are impassable due to weather conditions, accidents or heavy traffic.

- Third, always leave early, especially if you are going to an unfamiliar location. Learn to budget your time. Estimate the time it will take you to arrive at the exact location (room, office, or auditorium). Remember that it may only take you 45 minutes to arrive at the site, but it may take an additional 20 minutes to find the specific room. Tack on another 15-30 minutes as a cushion in case of an unforeseen event (storm or traffic accident). Will you need extra time to stop at your local ATM or gas station? Be sure to allot enough time!

- Fourth, carry enough cash with you to pay for parking, meals, and gas. Check your wallet the night before to make sure that you can easily cover these three expenses.

SOMETIMES, YOU MAY HAVE TO JUST SAY "NO"

It is imperative to get thorough and accurate information regarding an assignment prior to accepting it. If possible, have the contact person send you a copy of the program or agenda. Ask questions. Never assume anything. You will never feel as though you are "thrown" into a situation if you screen your assignments carefully. There will be times when you will have to decline when asked to do an assignment. Accept the fact that there will be times when you:

> a) may not be qualified to accept the assignment
>
> **and/or**
>
> b) may be qualified but there is a conflict of interest or role conflict

Although you may have the appropriate certifications and credentials, it still may not be appropriate for you to accept certain assignments. We all have "buttons" and inevitably, there will be a type of work that will push your particular button. Although we cannot always foresee our reactions, politely and graciously decline any job offer which you know will adversely affect you.

Examine your thoughts and feelings to identify specific situations and content areas you should avoid. If you feel that you are "button-less," I encourage you right here and now to sit yourself down, take the time and opportunity to get to know yourself better, and be brutally honest. Identify situations which might make you upset, uptight, distraught, judgmental, disgusted, or contemptuous. Likewise, in what situation might you lose sight of the Code of Ethics? Is there any content that you wouldn't interpret under any circumstances? In which situations would you feel a need to "tell it like it really is," preach/sermonize, omit information, offer "the interpreter's perspective" or "the real deal" to the client? In which situations would you go home upset and lose sleep? Feel personally oppressed? Give some thought to these questions; save yourself and your clients a lot of grief, heartache, and lost sleep. In order to decide which situations might adversely affect you, ask yourself these questions regarding:

ETHNICITY

Can you relay thorough and accurate information without prejudice when interpreting for persons of a different national, cultural or ethnic group?

RELIGION

Can you remain neutral while interpreting religious services? Will you be upset when interpreting services or lectures espousing the beliefs of religions other than your own? Religious organizations that are vehemently opposed to yours? Yours to theirs?

VALUES

If you support the Right to Life movement, could you impartially interpret a meeting for a pregnant woman discussing procedures for an abortion? Could you interpret for her during the procedure? If you are Pro-Choice, could you interpret during a Right to Life seminar? Counseling session?

SEX

If you are opposed to certain sexual preferences, practices, or lifestyles, could you interpret sexual information impartially? If a client has a high-risk, sexually transmitted disease, could you be neutral/non-judgmental and interpret for this person?

POLITICS

If you are a member of a political party and if that is an important part of your personal identity, could you be neutral and interpret for the opposing parties?

The more you reflect on these and other charged topics, the more your personal "buttons" list will grow. **SELF-AWARENESS** is your vantage point when deciding whether you will take an assignment. Remember, you can always **just say "no."**

KNOW YOURSELF!

KNOW YOUR LIMITS!

SET BOUNDARIES!

In large metropolitan areas, there is usually a substantial pool of interpreters and an abundance of work from which to pick and choose your assignments. What about areas that have few qualified professional interpreters and the work is not as plentiful? You may worry that if you do not accept a certain job, other work may not come your way. You may be anxious that the D/deaf person may be stranded and "interpreter-less."

Please think about the following when considering a "button-pushing" assignment. While it's true that you may not immediately get other offers of work and your calendar may remain blank while the bills keep coming in, you must decide for yourself if the upset is worth it. Is it fair for you to do that to yourself? Is it fair to the client or others involved? Can you truly stay neutral and not impact the message and intent of the persons involved?

Also consider that sometimes, having no interpreter is better than having an interpreter who cannot remain objective. Having no interpreter present may then create the opportunity for the parties to reschedule with a more appropriate interpreter. Just think about it.

PERSONAL SAFETY PRECAUTIONS

A friend taught me her definition of harassment. She states that harassment is any behavior exhibited by another that is unsolicited, inappropriate, unwarranted, unwanted, and unwelcome.

Unfortunately, I have heard horror stories from other interpreters involving these behaviors, have witnessed such conduct toward fellow interpreters, and have personally been on the receiving end.

This is not a "comfortable" issue to bring up, but it is even more uncomfortable being on the receiving end of this conduct. Listed below are a few suggestions about precautions you can take:

- If inappropriate comments are made to you by the hearing person, you may want to interpret the comments, then sign and voice that the comments are inappropriate. Indicate the behavior must stop. Tell the person that you view the comments as inappropriate and as harassment. Also, remind the person that everything said is being interpreted by you for all to see.

- If inappropriate words are being signed to you by the D/deaf person while you are interpreting, you might do a similar thing. Remind the client that everything signed will be voiced and then continue to voice what is being signed to you. (After all, that is your job.) Tell the D/deaf person that you view the comments as inappropriate and as harassment, and that he or she must stop immediately.

- If the inappropriate behavior ceases during the actual interpreting but continues during breaks, simply remind the person involved of your role as a neutral facilitator. Tell him or her that you view such behavior as inappropriate and as harassment. Explain that if the behavior persists, you will no longer be able to comfortably perform your job and will depart. Add that you will be forced to inform the hiring party of the reasons for your departure. You might choose to say, "Due to a hostile environment involving harassment, I am not able to comfortably continue providing services." Additionally, inform the hiring party that the meeting will have to be rescheduled with another interpreter.

- Report the harassment to the Human Resources/ Equal Employment Opportunity Departments of the sponsoring event and hiring entity.

- Never have your home address printed on your business cards.

- Never give out your home address. The only reason for anyone to have your address is for payment of interpreting services and it would be more prudent for you to have an alternate billing address. You should have a post office (P.O.) box and list that address for billing. There really is no reason for clients to have your home address. If a client needs to contact you professionally, have him or her call your business telephone number, the contact person who hired you, or the agency that hired you. If you have a computer and are connected to the internet, you may have the option of setting up several e-mail addresses and mailboxes through your internet service provider. Designate one e-mail address and mailbox for your interpreting business. Keep your personal e-mail address separate from that of your business; the client should only use your business e-mail address.

TYPICAL SAFETY PRECAUTIONS:

- Park in well lit areas.

- Never walk to your car alone. Have someone you trust escort you to your car.

- Have your keys ready to unlock the door as soon as you get to your car. Do not fumble or scrounge for your keys in the parking lot.

- Be aware of your surroundings.

- Look out for each other. Make sure that your fellow interpreter makes it safely to his or her car (walk together), and that both of your cars start. Then leave at the same time.

- If you suspect that someone is trying to follow you home, simply drive to a police station. This will send the message that you are aware that you are being followed and this may be enough so that the person leaves you alone. If this does not work, get the license plate number, make, model, and color of the car and go into the police station and report your concern. You may even want to call the police on your cellular telephone while you are being followed.

- If in the future you are asked to interpret for the "harassing" client, remember, you can simply say, "No thank you" to that assignment.

- Do not stress yourself out and put yourself in uncomfortable situations. You do not need to be the martyr, the victim, or just plain stupid. Harassment, of any kind, is simply inappropriate and unacceptable.

- Use common sense. Remember,
  SAFETY FIRST!!!

PART 5

Working With Others

- **Professional Presentation**
- **Professional Courtesy**
- **Giving Back to the Community**

PART 5

Working With Others

PROFESSIONAL PRESENTATION

There is a correct way to comport oneself at a professional interpreting assignment. Appropriate attire and proper grooming are a must. I am continuously shocked and dismayed at the "professionals" showing up for assignments wearing inappropriate attire and accessories.

Listed are grooming faux pas actually committed by "professional" interpreters on assignment. These outfits and accoutrements run contretemps to a professional interpreting experience:

- Sandals and soiled socks with holes in the toes

- A referee's striped shirt

- A spaghetti-stained gray sweatshirt, wrinkled white jacket, jeans, and tennis shoes at a formal platform assignment

- A sheer, white, skimpy tank top with no bra and no jacket at a formal auditorium setting

- Short shorts, tank top, sandals, and colored nail and toe polish at an assignment in a very conservative setting (male interpreter)

- A stained and wrinkled smock at a formal "black-tie" event for platform interpreting

If **you** were in need of interpreting services, would you want the interpreter to show up exhibiting any of the above?

Personally, if it ever happened to me, I would be embarrassed. I would rather go interpreter-less than have the interpreter draw undo negative attention. **THINK ABOUT IT!!!**

I am **NOT** going to address fashions, trends, styles, or "*GLAMOUR* Do's/*GLAMOUR* Don'ts." I encourage you to cultivate and use common sense and thoughtfulness towards your client when presenting your "professional" self.

Additionally, wearing political, social, or religious statement pins and buttons on coats, backpacks, jackets, and so on has no place in our work environment. These should never be worn to an assignment. As a "neutral facilitator of communication," wearing these things contradicts the very essence of who and what we are and what we do as interpreters. We are hired to be NEUTRAL. Professionally speaking, we should not be human billboards for any "cause." Express yourself **OUTSIDE** the work environment during non-working hours. Leave your opinions at home.

I will never forget the time I saw a client's eyes "bug out of his head" when my teammate walked through the door. She had so many pins and buttons, she clinked and clanked when she walked! For every button she wore, a "button" was being pushed in the audience. Several buttons showed a red circle with a slash and the word "NOT!" along with the respective cause for which she was opposed, "POPE/NOT!", "ABORTION (coat hanger)/NOT!" She also sported a marijuana leaf pin, an Alcoholics Anonymous button, a "Gays and Lesbians United" button, and an anti-male button, to name just a few. This is a far cry from neutral behavior. To top things off, the event was a fundamentalist/separatist religious group meeting and prayer session. I do not remember who "squirmed" the most, the client, the interpreter, or the speaker. The tone and focus of the meeting shifted to the interpreter as the speaker hovered over her, preaching to and trying to convert the back of her head.

Later that same interpreter told me that she felt discriminated against on several levels during the assignment. She stated she needed to attend a support group meeting to deal with the prejudice she felt at this meeting. I kept wondering how she could have been so surprised? Hadn't she been responsible for bringing the negative attention on herself? Hadn't she presented herself as a "walking billboard/poster child" for her biases and beliefs? She then turned around and felt victimized by other peoples' opposing biases and beliefs.

During my 20+ years of experience, 95% of the interpreting situations have been conservative. Many environments within that framework have been run and dominated by conservatives. Good or bad, right or wrong, this is the environment and hierarchy in which you may also find yourself doing the vast majority of your work during your professional lifetime as an interpreter. Business/corporate, political, judicial, medical, religious, and academic environments happen to be "power structured" in this manner. The point is that we must remain neutral in these environments

PROFESSIONAL COURTESY

SHOW UP ON TIME!

Arriving early is better, but being on time is a must. I was always taught that to be truly on time, I had to be at least 10 minutes early. If I arrived at the appointed time, I was considered late.

DO NOT ARRIVE LATE AND THEN EXPECT TO LEAVE EARLY!

Discuss replacement timing with your partner. At some assignments we replace each other every 20 minutes; at others, up to 45 minutes (or whenever is the most appropriate break period).

DO NOT ARRIVE LATE TO REPLACE THE OTHER INTERPRETER!

Once you agree to a 30/30 split hour, switching after 45 minutes is not acceptable. Switching after 35 minutes is not appreciated. Occasional oversights do happen but habitual lateness is not acceptable.

ALWAYS HAVE A WATCH WITH YOU!

It is your responsibility to be your own timekeeper. When you go on break, be conscious of the time so you will not be late returning. Punctuality is a must in all interpreting situations.

DON'T MAKE ASSUMPTIONS! DISCUSS PREFERENCES!

Each interpreter is a unique individual. No two interpreters have the same background, training, skills, and work ethic. The best way to set the stage for a pleasant working relationship is to open channels of communication between you and your partner. Dialogue. Share. Do not impose your expectations. Discuss preferences.

Discuss the issue of professional feedback with your partner. Some interpreters expect to be "fed" information, praise, and constructive criticism during interpreting and non-interpreting seat time. They want or need someone to observe and critique their skills. Other interpreters resent receiving this unsolicited information. They also consider the need to provide such feedback to the other interpreter as "babysitting." Arrive early to your assignment and determine your partner's preference before the assignment and also be sure to make *your* conditions for feedback known.

DO NOT IMPOSE UNSOLICITED PROFESSIONAL CRITICISM ON ANOTHER INTERPRETER. DO NOT ASSUME THAT OTHERS WILL OR SHOULD PRAISE OR ANALYZE YOUR PERFORMANCE. DO NOT ASSUME THAT OTHERS HAVE THE SAME STYLES AND PREFERENCES AS YOU. BE FLEXIBLE. DON'T BE INTRUSIVE.

If you have a special circumstance arise, for example the need to leave early or arrive late, call your partner ahead of time to discuss the details. Keep in mind that your special request may not be acceptable to your partner and he or she has every right to express his or her preference and to decline any changes to the prior arrangement.

If you are teaming with an interpreter with whom you have not previously worked, remember to call and introduce yourself prior to the assignment. Establishing a friendly rapport with your fellow interpreter is always a good idea.

Remember that you are a member of a team; act accordingly. Be a team player.

Small considerations can make a big difference. Be kind to your fellow interpreters. Perhaps they are having a bad day and they need some understanding and encouragement. Let's work on creating a supportive interpreting community.

BOTTOM LINE:

Be supportive of each other. We have a very demanding job. Sometimes we serve difficult clients, both hearing and D/deaf, in complicated situations. The last thing we need is to be stuck with a troublesome partner or for us to be perceived as troublesome by other interpreters. Be encouraging. Be flexible. Be respectful. Try to provide what your fellow interpreter needs when he or she needs it.

Discuss Expectations:

Communicate your needs and expectations to your partner and ask the same in return. No one is a mind reader; it is best to communicate issues prior to the start of the assignment so that you both have a clear understanding of what to expect from each other.

Final Note:

You and your partner may have style or personality differences which may lead to disagreements. Put these aside during your current assignment. However, if things are so bad between you that your work performance is suffering, do not accept any future assignments with this interpreter.

Do not try to impose your ideals on another interpreter and then speak badly about him or her to others because he or she would not conform to your standards. During a teamed assignment, each partner's preferences should be respected. Your partner may make professional choices that differ from yours; this does not make the individual a "bad" interpreter. The interpreter's style is not "wrong," it is simply different. Remember that things cannot always be done your way.

Respect Each Other

Try to reach a comfortable compromise. Please consider either attempting to work out differences or just agreeing to disagree. Then, just move on.

Reminder: Not everyone, including the clients (hearing or D/deaf) and the other interpreter, has to be your "friend." You should, however, be as pleasant and supportive as you can be to one another.

GIVING BACK TO THE COMMUNITY: PRO BONO

Explore your heart, conscience, values, and spirit. This section of the book examines charity and provides you the opportunity to personally investigate this important matter. This subject should be given serious thought and consideration.

Every interpreter, every individual, has a different concept of what it means to give back to the community. Some interpreters do volunteer work. Some interpreters choose to support organizations or causes that they care deeply about by contributing in "non-interpreting" ways. I respect that. I know interpreters who send donations to organizations, write letters to members of Congress, participate in walk-a-thons, make baked goods for fund-raisers and sell raffle tickets for schools, churches, or other community organizations. The list of ways to contribute is expansive. I have found my fellow interpreters to be generous, big-hearted people.

I suggest that you explore your own conscience to discover how you can best give back to your community. Within a one-year time frame, how much time, energy, money, or materials can you contribute? Make a commitment to yourself to give something that will help others.

AS I EXPLAINED BEFORE, I AM NOT AN ACCOUNTANT AND WHAT IS WRITTEN BELOW IS NOT TO BE CONSTRUED AS TAX ADVICE. CONSULT WITH YOUR ACCOUNTANT.

Consult with your accountant to explore a legal and advantageous way to donate your services while reaping tax benefits. To me, this is a perfect example of a "win/win" venture.

If your contribution takes the form of donating interpreting services, ask your accountant if the value of donated interpreting services can be used as a deduction. If so, ask the receiving organization to send you a letter confirming the assignment with all details including location, date, times, hourly pay, and so on. Be sure the letter states that the organization acknowledges the services you are donating are worth "X" dollars and that these services are your contribution. Ask your accountant to advise you about any other details the letter should contain.

OR

Discuss with your accountant if your tax records are better served by receiving payment for your services and then writing a check for that amount to the charitable organization. This may help you because your cancelled check will document your contribution. There is a possibility that this method may not prove advantageous if your earnings project you into a higher tax bracket. Consult your accountant.

There are some drawbacks. Consider these statements from professional interpreters who have had negative experiences while doing pro bono work.

> • "I volunteered once before. Now, when I am called and quote my interpreting rates, the same client is irate and rude because he doesn't want to pay the standard fee."

- "I was asked to provide pro bono services by a very rude, pressuring person of the D/deaf community."

- "I worry that if I volunteer more often, no one will want to pay me in the future. I feel a lack of respect and a lack of professional worth for my services."

- "I feel that it [pro bono work] sends out a 'mixed message' regarding value or worth of services and maintaining a professional (paying) career."

Additionally, consider the following disadvantages to pro bono work:

- Some interpreters feel that clients already view them as volunteers, friends, or relatives instead of trained professionals. These clients balk when they are charged for services. Volunteering sometimes reinforces the image of interpreters as "helpers" and not certified experts working to earn a living.

- Some interpreters have experienced negative attitudes from members of the D/deaf community who expect or demand volunteer interpreting services. Interpreters have reported that some people act as if giving back to the community means giving back only to the D/deaf community.

- While most interpreters feel they are providing a valuable service to the D/deaf community, they are sometimes undervalued by this same community. Reportedly, some members of the D/deaf community view interpreters as "takers" and feel that they "abuse deafness" and profit from the D/deaf individual's disability. Interpreters are expected to "give, give, give" with no thought of compensation for their services.

I was asked to volunteer interpret for a week-long training program offered by a for-profit, Fortune 500 corporation. This corporation was written up in an article featuring the 100 fastest growing, most-profitable corporations in America. Needless to say, I did not "volunteer" for that corporation.

Despite the problems inherent in pro bono work, many interpreters continue to serve the D/deaf community by volunteering their services. Here is a sampling of the reasons why interpreters donate their time:

- They enjoy it.

- It makes them feel good.

- They feel appreciated.

- It is a good public relations (PR) tool to enhance the bridge of "good will" between interpreters and the D/deaf community.

- Volunteer services may be tax deductible.

- They feel it is fun, less pressure, more relaxing.

- Some feel a stronger sense of community by being connected in this way.

- They like the exposure and want others (meaning other interpreters and members of the D/deaf community) to know that they "are doing something good."

- It furnishes great opportunities to participate in business, education, and service functions with their friends/peers.

- It provides a way to express gratitude to the D/deaf community for being able to make their living as an interpreter, a profession they enjoy and love.

BOTTOM LINE:

No one has the right to impose his or her values or expectations on another. Volunteerism/contributing to society is a private and personal thing. I suggest you explore your thoughts and feelings about your preferences, limits, and boundaries and come up with a cogent response and a practical guideline *before* you are asked to offer your services pro bono.

My personal plea is that you contribute something back to your community in whatever form you feel most comfortable.

See **APPENDIX** for Donations Sample Worksheet.

APPENDIX

- **Conventions/Conferences/Workshops**
- **Course Training Record**
- **Networking Information**
- **Applying for a Federal Job**
- **Application for Federal Employment – SF 171**
- **General Information**
- **Optional Application for Federal Employment –OF 612**
- **Birth Certification Location Information**
- **Social Security Application**
- **Request for Earnings and Benefit Estimate Statement**
- **United States Passport Application**
- **United States Passport Application by Mail (Renewals Only)**
- **Resume Worksheets**
- **Reference Worksheet**
- **Assignment Intake Information**
- **Travel/Mileage Record Form**
- **Estimated Quarterly Taxes Worksheet**
- **Internal Revenue Service Centers**
- **State Tax Information**
- **"Tool Kit" for Interpreters Worksheet**
- **Emergency Essentials**
- **Alcoholics Anonymous Preamble/Serenity Prayer**
- **Twelve Steps/Twelve Traditions**
- **"SIGNER-CISES"**
- **Carpal Tunnel Syndrome/Repetitive Motion Disorder References**
- **Donations Sample Worksheet**

CONVENTIONS/CONFERENCES/WORKSHOPS

Name of Event: _____ Dates: _____

Location: _____ CEU's: _____

Sponsoring Organization: _____

Address: _____

Contact Person: _____ Telephone: _____

E-mail Address: _____

WORKSHOPS

Topic: **Presenter:**
                                              Contact:

Notes:

WORKSHOPS

Topic: **Presenter:**
                                              Contact:

Notes:

COURSE TRAINING RECORD

Date(s) Completed: _____ CEU's: _____

Name of Course: _____

Location: _____

Sponsoring Organization: _____

Contact Person: _____ Telephone: _____

Address: _____

E-mail: _____

Instructor's Name: _____ Telephone: _____

Address: _____

E-mail: _____

Topics Included:

_____

Notes:

NETWORKING INFORMATION

Name: **E-mail:**

Address:

Telephone:

Reference:

Name: **E-mail:**

Address:

Telephone:

Reference:

Name: **E-mail:**

Address:

Telephone:

Reference:

Name: **E-mail:**

Address:

Telephone:

Reference:

Name: **E-mail:**

Address:

Telephone:

Reference:

Name: **E-mail:**

Address:

Telephone:

Reference:

Applying for a Federal Job

United States
Office of
Personnel
Management

OF 510
(September 1994)

VETERANS' PREFERENCE IN HIRING

I If you served on active duty in the United States Military and were separated under honorable conditions, you may be eligible for veterans' preference. To receive preference if your service began after October 15, 1976, you must have a Campaign Badge, Expeditionary Medal, or a service- connected disability. For further details, call OPM at **912-757-3000**. Select "Federal Employment Topics" and then "Veterans." Or, dial our electronic bulletin board at **912-757-3100.**

☐ Veterans' preference is not a factor for Senior Executive Service jobs or when competition is limited to status candidates (current or former Federal career or career-conditional employees).

☐ To claim 5-point veterans' preference, attach a copy of your DD-214, *Certificate of Release or Discharge from Active Duty,* or other proof of eligibility.

☐ To claim 10-point veterans' preference, attach an SF 15, *Application for 10-Point Veterans' Preference,* plus the proof required by that form.

OTHER IMPORTANT INFORMATION

☐ Before hiring, an agency will ask you to complete a *Declaration for Federal Employment* to determine your suitability for Federal employment and to authorize a background investigation. The agency will also ask you to sign and certify the accuracy of all information in your application. **If you make a false statement in any part of your application, you may not be hired; you may be fired after you begin work; or you may be fined or jailed.**

☐ If you are a male over age 18 who was born after December 31, 1959, you must have registered with the Selective Service System (or have an exemption) to be eligible for a Federal job.

☐ The law prohibits public officials from appointing, promoting, or recommending their relatives.

☐ Federal annuitants (military and civilian) may have their salaries or annuities reduced. All employees must pay any valid delinquent debts or the agency may garnish their salary.

PRIVACY AND PUBLIC BURDEN STATEMENTS

The Office of Personnel Management and other Federal agencies rate applicants for Federal jobs under the authority of sections 1104, 1302, 3301, 3304, 3320, 3361, 3393, and 3394 of title 5 of the United States Code. We need the information requested in this brochure and in the associated vacancy announcements to evaluate your qualifications. Other laws require us to ask about citizenship, military service, etc.

☐ We request your Social Security Number (SSN) under the authority of Executive Order 9397 in order to keep your records straight; other people may have the same name. As allowed by law or Presidential directive, we use your SSN to seek information about you from employers, schools, banks, and others who know you. Your SSN may also be used in studies and computer matching with other Government files, for example, files on unpaid student loans.

☐ If you do not give us your SSN or any other information requested, we cannot process your application, which is the first step in getting a job. Also, incomplete addresses and ZIP Codes will slow processing.

☐ We may give information from your records to: training facilities; organizations deciding claims for retirement, insurance, unemployment or health benefits; officials in litigation or administrative proceedings where the Government is a party; law enforcement agencies concerning violations of law or regulation; Federal agencies for statistical reports and studies; officials of labor organizations recognized by law in connection with representing employees; Federal agencies or other sources requesting information for Federal agencies in connection with hiring or retaining, security clearances, security or suitability investigations, classifying jobs, contracting, or issuing licenses, grants, or other benefits; public or private organizations includng news media that grant or publicize employee recognition and awards; and the Merit Systems Protection Board, the Office of Special Counsel, the Equal Employment Opportunity Commission, the Federal Labor Relations Authority, the National Archives, the Federal Acquisition Institute, and congressional offices in connection with their official functions.

☐ We may also give information from your records to: prospective nonfederal employers concerning tenure of employment, civil service status, length of service, and date and nature of action for separation as shown on personnel action forms of specifically identified individuals; requesting organizations or individuals concerning the home address and other relevant information on those who might have contracted an illness or been exposed to a health hazard; authorized Federal and nonfederal agencies for use in computer matching; spouses or dependent children asking whether an employee has changed from self-and-family to self-only health benefits enrollment; individuals working on a contract, service, grant, cooperative agreement or job for the Federal Government; non-agency members of an agency's performance or other panel; and agency-appointed representatives of employees concerning information issued to an employee about fitness-for-duty or agency-filed disability retirement procedures.

☐ We estimate the public burden for reporting the employment information will vary from 20 to 240 minutes with an average of 40 minutes per response, including time for reviewing instructions, searching existing data sources, gathering data, and completing and reviewing the information. You may send comments regarding the burden estimate or any other aspect of the collection of information, including suggestions for reducing this burden, to the U.S. Office of Personnel Management, Reports and Forms Management Officer, Washington, DC 20415-0001.

Send your application to the agency announcing the vacancy.

Form Approved: OMB 3206-0219

Here's what your resume or application must contain

(in addition to specific information requested in the job vacancy announcement)

JOB OPENINGS

For job information 24 hours a day, 7 days a week, call **912-757-3000**, the U.S. Office of Personnel Management (OPM) automated telephone system. Or, with a computer modem dial **912-757-3100** for job information from an OPM electronic bulletin board. You can also reach the board through the Internet (Telnet only) at FJOB.MAIL.OPM.GOV.

APPLICANTS WITH DISABILITIES

You can find out about alternative formats by calling OPM or dialing the electronic bulletin board at the numbers above. Select "Federal Employment Topics" and then "People with Disabilities." If you have a hearing disability, call **TDD 912-744-2299**.

HOW TO APPLY

Review the list of openings, decide which jobs you are interested in, and follow the instructions given. **You may apply for most jobs with a resume, the *Optional Application for Federal Employment*, or any other written format you choose.** For jobs that are unique or filled through automated procedures, you will be given special forms to complete. (You can get an *Optional Application* by calling OPM or dialing our electronic bulletin board at the numbers above.)

WHAT TO INCLUDE

Although the Federal Government does not require a standard application form for most jobs, we do need certain information to evaluate your qualifications and determine if you meet legal requirements for Federal employment. If your resume or application does not provide all the information requested in the job vacancy announcement and in this brochure, you may lose consideration for a job. Help speed the selection process by keeping your resume or application brief and by sending only the requested material. Type or print clearly in dark ink.

JOB INFORMATION

☐ Announcement number, and title and grade(s) of the job you are applying for.

PERSONAL INFORMATION

☐ Full name, mailing address *(with ZIP Code)* and day and evening phone numbers *(with area code)*
☐ Social Security Number
☐ Country of Citizenship *(Most Federal jobs require United States citizenship.)*
☐ Veterans' preference *(See reverse.)*
☐ Reinstatement eligibility *(If requested, attach SF 50 proof of your career or career-conditional status.)*
☐ Highest Federal civilian grade held *(Also give job series and dates held.)*

EDUCATION

☐ High School
   Name, city, and State *(ZIP Code if known)*
   Date of diploma or GED
☐ Colleges or universities
   Name, city, and State *(ZIP Code if known)*
   Majors
   Type and year of any degrees received *(If no degree, show total credits earned and indicate whether semester or quarter hours.)*
☐ Send a copy of your college transcript only if the job vacancy announcement requests it.

WORK EXPERIENCE

☐ Give the following information for your paid and nonpaid work experience related to the job you are applying for. *(Do not send job descriptions.)*
   Job title *(include series and grade if Federal job)*
   Duties and accomplishments
   Employer's name and address
   Supervisor's name and phone number
   Starting and ending dates *(month and year)*
   Hours per week
   Salary
☐ Indicate if we may contact your current supervisor.

OTHER QUALIFICATIONS

☐ **Job-related** training courses *(title and year)*
☐ **Job-related** skills, for example, other languages, computer software/hardware, tools, machinery, typing speed
☐ **Job-related** certificates and licenses *(current only)*
☐ **Job-related** honors, awards and special accomplishments, for example, publica-tions, memberships in professional or honor societies, leadership activities, public speaking, and performance awards *(Give dates but do not send documents unless requested.)*

THE FEDERAL GOVERNMENT IS
AN EQUAL OPPORTUNITY EMPLOYER

Application for Federal Employment - SF 171

Read the instructions before you complete this application. *Type or print clearly in dark ink.*

Form Approved
OMB No. 3206-0012

GENERAL INFORMATION

1 What kind of job are you applying for? *Give title and announcement no. (if any)*

2 Social Security Number

3 Sex   ☐ Male   ☐ Female

4 Birth date (*Month, Day, Year*)

5 Birthplace *(City and State or Country)*

6 Name (*Last, First, Middle*)

Mailing address (*include apartment number, if any*)

City   State   ZIP Code

7 Other names ever used (*e.g., maiden name, nickname, etc.*)

8 Home Phone   Area Code   Number

9 Work Phone   Area Code   Number   Extension

10 Were you ever employed as a civilian by the Federal Government? If **"NO"** go to Item 11. If **"YES"**, mark each type of job you held with an **"X"** .

☐ Temporary   ☐ Career-Conditional   ☐ Career   ☐ Excepted

What is your **highest** grade, classification series and job title?

Dates at **highest** grade: FROM   TO

AVAILABILITY

11 When can you start work? (*Month and Year*)

12 What is the **lowest** pay you will accept? *(You will not be considered for jobs which pay less than you indicate.)*

Pay $ per   **OR** Grade

13 In what geographic area(s) are you willing to work?

14 Are you willing to work:

	YES	NO
A. 40 hours per week *(full-time)*?		
B. 25-32 hours per week *(part-time)*?		
C. 17-24 hours per week *(part-time)*?		
D. 16 or fewer hours per week *(part-time)*?		
E. An intermittent job *(on-call/seasonal)*?		
F. Weekends, shifts, or rotating shifts?		

15 Are you willing to take a temporary job lasting:

A. 5 to 12 months *(sometimes longer)*?		
B. 1 to 4 months?		
C. Less than 1month?		

16 Are you willing to travel away from home for:

A. 1 to 5 nights each month?		
B. 6 to 10 nights each month?		
C. 11 or more nights each month?		

MILITARY SERVICE AND VETERAN PREFERENCE

17 Have you served in the United States Military Service? *If your only active duty was training in the Reserves or National Guard, answer "NO". If "NO", go to item 22* ......   YES   NO

18 Did you or will you retire at or above the rank of major or lieutenant commander? ......

PREVIOUS EDITION USABLE UNTIL 12-31-90

Page 1

FOR USE OF EXAMINING OFFICE ONLY

DO NOT WRITE IN THIS AREA

Date entered register

Form reviewed:

Form approved:

Option	Grade	Earned Rating	Veteran Preference	Augmented Rating
			☐ No Preference Claimed	
			☐ 5 Points *(Tentative)*	
			☐ 10 Pts.*(30% Or More Comp. Dis.)*	
			☐ 10 Pts.*(Less Than 30% Comp. Dis.)*	
			☐ Other 10 Points	

Initials and Date

☐ Disallowed   ☐ Being Investigated

FOR USE OF APPOINTING OFFICE ONLY

Preference has been verified through proof that the separation was under honorable conditions, and other proof as required.

☐ 5-Point   ☐ 10-Pt.-- 30% or more Compensable Disability   ☐ 10-Pt.-- Less Than 30% Compensable Disability   ☐ 10-Point-- Other

Signature and Title

Agency   Date

MILITARY SERVICE AND VETERAN PREFERENCE *(Cont.)*

19 Were you discharged from the military service under honorable conditions? *(If your discharge was changed to "honorable" or"general" by a Discharge Review Board, answer "YES". If you received a clemency discharge, answer "NO".)* If **"NO"**, provide below the date and type of discharge you received.   YES   NO

Discharge Date (*Month, Day, Year*)	Type of Discharge

20 List the dates (Month, Day, Year), and branch for all **active duty** military service.

From	To	Branch of Service

21 If all your active military duty was after October 14, 1976, list the full names and dates of all campaign badges or expeditionary medals you received or were entitled to receive.

22 **Read the instructions that came with this form before completing this item.** When you have determined your eligibility for veteran preference from the instructions, place an **"X"** in the box next to your veteran preference claim.

☐ NO PREFERENCE

☐ 5-POINT PREFERENCE -- You must show proof when you are hired.

10-POINT PREFERENCE -- If you claim 10-point preference, place an "X" in the box below next to the basis for your claim. **To receive 10-point preference you must also complete a Standard Form 15, Application for 10-Point Veteran Preference, which is available from any Federal Job Information Center. ATTACH THE COMPLETED SF 15 AND REQUESTED PROOF TO THIS APPLICATION.**

☐ Non-compensably disabled or Purple Heart recipient.

☐ Compensably disabled, less than 30 percent.

☐ Spouse, widow(er), or mother of a deceased or disabled veteran.

☐ Compensably disabled, 30 percent or more.

NSN 7540-00-935-7150   171-109   Standard Form 171 (Rev. 6-88)
U.S. Office of Personnel Management
FPM Chapter 295

23 May we ask your present employer about your character, qualifications, and work record? A "NO" will not affect our review of your qualifications. If you answer "NO" and we need to contact your present employer before we can offer you a job, we will contact you first.....

YES	NO

24 READ **WORK EXPERIENCE** IN THE INSTRUCTIONS BEFORE YOU BEGIN.

- Describe your current or most recent job in Block **A** and work backwards, describing each job you held **during the past 10 years.** If you were **unemployed** for longer than 3 months within the past 10 years, list the dates and your address(es) in an experience block.

- You may sum up in one block work that you did **more than 10 years ago.** But if that work **is related** to the type of job you are applying for, describe each related job in a separate block

- INCLUDE VOLUNTEER WORK (non-paid work) – **if the work** (or a part of the work) **is like the job you are applying for,** complete **all** parts of the experience block just as you would for a paying job. You may receive credit for work experience with religious, community, welfare, service, and other organizations.

- INCLUDE MILITARY SERVICE-- You should complete **all** parts of the experience block just as you would for a non-military job, including all supervisory experience. Describe each major change of duties or responsibilities in a separate experience block.

- IF YOU NEED MORE SPACE TO DESCRIBE A JOB--Use sheets of paper the same size as this page (be sure to include all information we ask for in **A** and **B** below). On each sheet show your name, Social Security Number, and the announcement number or job title.

- IF YOU NEED MORE EXPERIENCE BLOCKS, use the SF 171-A or a sheet of paper.

- IF YOU NEED TO UPDATE (ADD MORE RECENT JOBS), use the SF 172 or a sheet of paper as described above.

A Name and address of employer's organization (include ZIP Code, if known)

Dates employed *(give month, day and year)*	Average number of hours per week	Number of employees you supervised
From: To:		

Salary or earnings	Your reason for wanting to leave
Starting $ per	
Ending $ per	

Your immediate supervisor Name	Area Code	Telephone No.	Exact title of your job	If Federal employment *(civilian or military)* list series, grade or rank, and, if promoted in this job, the date of your last promotion

Description of work: Describe your specific duties, responsibilities and accomplishments in this job, **including the job title(s) of any employees you supervised.** *If you describe more than one type of work (for example, carpentry and painting, or personnel and budget), write the approximate percentage of time you spent doing each.*

For Agency Use. (skill codes, etc.)

B Name and address of employer's organization (include ZIP Code, if known)

Dates employed *(give month, day and year)*	Average number of hours per week	Number of employees you supervised
From: To:		

Salary or earnings	Your reason for leaving
Starting $ per	
Ending $ per	

Your immediate supervisor Name	Area Code	Telephone No.	Exact title of your job	If Federal employment *(civilian or military)* list series, grade or rank, and, if promoted in this job, the date of your last promotion

Description of work: Describe your specific duties, responsibilities and accomplishments in this job, **including the job title(s) of any employees you supervised.** *If you describe more than one type of work (for example, carpentry and painting, or personnel and budget), write the approximate percentage of time you spent doing each.*

For Agency Use (skill codes, etc.)

EDUCATION

25 Did you graduate from high school? *If you have a GED high school equivalency or will graduate within the next nine months, answer "YES".*

| YES | | ► If "YES", give month and year graduated or received GED equivalency:........................ |
| NO | | ► If "NO", give the highest grade you completed: |

26 Write the name and location *(city and state)* of the last high school you attended or where you obtained your GED high school equivalency.

27 Have you ever attended college or graduate school?

| YES | ► If "YES", continue with 28. |
| NO | ► If "NO", go to 31. |

28 NAME AND LOCATION *(city, state and ZIP Code)* OF COLLEGE OR UNIVERSITY. *If you expect to graduate within nine months, give the **month** and **year** you expect to receive your degree:*

Name	City	State	ZIP Code	MONTH AND YEAR ATTENDED From	To	NUMBER OF CREDIT HOURS COMPLETED Semester	Quarter	TYPE OF DEGREE *(e.g.B.A., M,A,)*	MONTH AND YEAR OF DEGREE
1)									
2)									
3)									

29

CHIEF UNDERGRADUATE SUBJECTS *Show major on the first line*	NUMBER OF CREDIT HOURS COMPLETED Semester	Quarter
1)		
2)		
3)		

30

CHIEF GRADUATE SUBJECTS *Show major on the first line*	NUMBER OF CREDIT HOURS COMPLETED Semester	Quarter
1)		
2)		
3)		

31 If you have completed any **other courses or training related to the kind of jobs you are applying for** *(trade, vocational, Armed Forces, business)* give information below.

NAME AND LOCATION *(city, state, and ZIP Code)* OF SCHOOL	MONTH AND YEAR ATTENDED From	To	CLASS-ROOM HOURS	SUBJECT(S)	TRAINING COMPLETED YES	NO
1) School Name						
City — State — ZIP Code						
2) School Name						
City — State — ZIP Code						

SPECIAL SKILLS, ACCOMPLISHMENTS AND AWARDS

32 Give the title and year of any honors, awards or fellowships you have received. List your special qualifications, skills or accomplishments that may help you get a job. *Some examples are: skills with computers or other machines; most important publications (do not submit copies); public speaking and writing experience; membership in professional or scientific societies; patents or inventions; etc.*

33 How many words per minute can you:
TYPE?   TAKE DICTATION?

Agencies may test your skills before hiring you.

34 List **job-related** licenses or certificates that you have, such as: *registered nurse; lawyer; radio operator; driver's; pilot's; etc.*

LICENSE OR CERTIFICATE	DATE OF LATEST LICENSE OR CERTIFICATE	STATE OR OTHER LICENSING AGENCY
1)		
2)		

35 Do you speak or read a language other than English *(include sign language)*? *Applicants for jobs that require a language other than English may be given an interview conducted solely in that language.*

| YES | ► If "YES", list each language and place an "X" in each column that applies to you. |
| NO | ► If "NO", go to 36. |

LANGUAGE(S)	CAN PREPARE AND GIVE LECTURES Fluently	With Difficulty	CAN SPEAK AND UNDERSTAND Fluently	Passably	CAN TRANSLATE ARTICLES Into English	From English	CAN READ ARTICLES FOR OWN USE Easily	With Difficulty
1)								
2)								

REFERENCES

36 List three people who are not related to you and are not supervisors you listed under 24 who know your qualifications and fitness for the kind of job for which you are applying. At least one should know you well on a personal basis.

FULL NAME OF REFERENCE	TELEPHONE NUMBER(S) *(Include Area Code)*	PRESENT BUSINESS OR HOME ADDRESS *(Number, street and city)*	STATE	ZIP CODE
1)				
2)				
3)				

	YES	NO
37 Are you a citizen of the United States? *(In most cases you must be a U.S. citizen to be hired. You will be required to submit proof of* identity and citizenship at the time you are hired.) If **"NO"**, give the country or countries you are a citizen of:		

> **NOTE:** It is important that you give complete and truthful answers to questions **38 through 44.** If you answer **"YES"** to any of them, provide your explanation(s) in **Item 45. Include** convictions resulting from a plea of nolo contendere (no contest). **Omit:** 1) traffic fines of $ 100.00 or less; 2) any violation of law committed before your 16th birthday; 3) any violation of law committed before your 18th birthday, if finally decided in juvenile court or under a Youth Offender law; 4) any conviction set aside under the Federal Youth Corrections Act or similar State law; 5) any conviction whose record was expunged under Federal or State law. We will consider the date, facts and circumstances of each event you list. In most cases you can still be considered for Federal jobs. However, **if you fail to tell the truth or fail to list all relevant** events or circumstances, this may be grounds for not hiring you, for firing you after you begin work, or for criminal prosecution (18 USC 1001).

	YES	NO
38 During the last **10 years**, were you **fired from any job** for any reason, did you **quit after being told that you would be fired**, or did you leave by mutual agreement because of specific problems?		
39 Have you **ever been convicted of, or forfeited collateral for any felony violation?** *(Generally, a felony is defined as any violation of law punishable by imprisonment of longer than one year, except for violations called misdemeanours under State law which are punishable by imprisonment of two years or less.)*		
40 Have you **ever been convicted of, or forfeited collateral for any firearms or explosives violation?**		
41 Are you **now** under charges for **any** violation of law?		
42 During the **last 10 years** have you forfeited collateral, been convicted, been imprisoned, been on probation, or been on parole? Do **not include** violations reported in 39, 40, or 41, above.		
43 Have you **ever** been convicted by a military **court-martial?** If no military service, answer **"NO"**		
44 Are you **delinquent** on any Federal debt? *(Include delinquencies arising from Federal taxes, loans, overpayment of benefits, and other debts to the U.S. Government **plus** defaults on Federally guaranteed or insured loans such as student and home mortgage loans.)*		

45 If **"YES"** in: **38** - Explain for each job the problems(s) and your reason(s) for leaving. Give the employer's name and address.
        39 through 43 - Explain each violation. Give place of occurrence and name/address of police or court involved.
        44- Explain the type, length and amount of the delinquency or default, and steps you are taking to correct errors or repay the debt. Give any identification number associated with the debt and the address of the Federal agency involved.
    NOTE: If you need more space, use a sheet of paper, and include the item number.

Item No.	Date (Mo./Yr.)	Explanation	Mailing Address
			Name of Employer, Police, Court, or Federal Agency
			City State ZIP Code
			Name of Employer, Police, Court, or Federal Agency
			City State ZIP Code

	YES	NO
46 Do you receive, or have you ever applied for retirement pay, pension, or other pay based on military, Federal civilian, or District of Columbia Government service?		
47 Do any of your relatives work for the United States Government or the United States Armed Forces? Include: *father; mother; husband; wife; son; daughter; brother; sister; uncle; aunt; first cousin; nephew; niece; father-in-law; mother-in-law; son-in-law; daughter-in-law; brother-in-law; sister-in-law; stepfather; stepmother; stepson; stepdaughter; stepbrother; stepsister; half brother; and half sister*		

If **"YES"**, provide details below. If you need more space, use a sheet of paper.

Name	Relationship	Department, Agency or Branch of Armed Forces

SIGNATURE, CERTIFICATION, AND RELEASE OF INFORMATION

YOU MUST SIGN THIS APPLICATION. Read the following carefully before you sign.

- A false statement on any part of your application may be grounds for not hiring you, or for firing you after you begin work. Also, you may be punished by fine or imprisonment (U.S. Code, title 18, section 1001).
- If you are a male born after December 31, 1959 you must be registered with the Selective Service System or have a valid exemption in order to be eligible for Federal employment. You will be required to certify as to your status at the time of appointment.
- I **understand** that any information I give may be investigated as allowed by law or Presidential order.
- I **consent** to the release of information about my ability and fitness for Federal employment by *employers, schools, law enforcement agencies and other individuals and organizations, to investigators, personnel staffing specialists, and other authorized employees of the Federal Government.*
- I **certify** that, to the best of my knowledge and belief, **all** of my statements are true, correct, complete, and made in good faith.

48 Signature *(Sign each application in dark ink)*	**49** DATE SIGNED *(Month, day, year)*

Page 4

GENERAL INFORMATION

You may apply for most Federal jobs with a resume, the attached *Optional Application for Federal Employment* or other written format. If your resume or application does not provide all the information requested on this form and in the job vacancy announcement, you may lose consideration for a job. Type or print clearly in dark ink. Help speed the selection process by keeping your application brief and sending only the requested information. If essential to attach additional pages, include your name and Social Security Number on each page.

- For information on Federal employment, including job lists, alternative formats for persons with disabilities, and veterans' preference, call the U.S. Office of Personnel Management at **912-757-3000, TDD 912-744-2299,** by computer modem **912-757-3100,** or via the Internet (Telnet only) at FJOB.MAIL.OPM.GOV.

- If you served on active duty in the United States Military and were separated under honorable conditions, you may be eligible for veterans' preference. To receive preference if your service began after October 15, 1976, you must have a Campaign Badge, Expeditionary Medal, or a service-connected disability. Veterans' preference is not a factor for Senior Executive Service jobs or when competition is limited to status candidates (current or former career or career-conditional Federal employees).

- Most Federal jobs require United States citizenship and also that males over age 18 born after December 31, 1959, have registered with the Selective Service System or have an exemption.

- The law prohibits public officials from appointing, promoting, or recommending their relatives.

- Federal annuitants (military and civilian) may have their salaries or annuities reduced. All employees must pay any valid delinquent debts or the agency may garnish their salary.

- Send your application to the office announcing the vacancy. If you have questions, contact that office.

THE FEDERAL GOVERNMENT IS AN EQUAL OPPORTUNITY EMPLOYER

OPTIONAL APPLICATION FOR FEDERAL EMPLOYMENT - OF 612

FORM APPROVED
OMB No. 3206-0219
Electronic Form Approved by CGIR
03/23/95

You may apply for most jobs with a resume, this form, or other written format. If your resume or application **does not provide** all the information requested on this form and in the job vacancy announcement, you may lose consideration for a job.

1. Job title in announcement	2. Grade(s) applying for	3. Announcement number
4. Last name First and middle names		**5. Social Security** Number
6. Mailing address		**7. Phone numbers** (include area code) **Daytime**
City State ZIP Code		**Evening**

WORK EXPERIENCE

8. Describe your paid and nonpaid work experience related to the job for which you are applying. Do **not** attach job **descriptions.**

A) Job title (if Federal, include series and grade)

From (MM/YY)	To (MM/YY)	Salary $	per	Hours per week
Employer's name and address				Supervisor's name and phone number

Describe your duties and accomplishments   Unprotected Form Field. Only eleven lines of data will print in this area. You may continue on another sheet of paper.

B) Job title (if Federal, include series and grade)

From (MM/YY)	To (MM/YY)	Salary $	per	Hours per week
Employer's name and address				Supervisor's name and phone number

Describe your duties and accomplishments   Unprotected Form Field

50612-101   NSN 7540-01-351-9178   Optional Form 612 (September 1994)
U.S. Office of Personnel Management

9. May we contact your current supervisor?

YES (☐)   NO (☐)▶   If we need to contact your current supervisor before making an offer, we will contact you first.

EDUCATION

10. Mark highest level completed. Some HS (☐)   HS/GED (☐)   Associate (☐)   Bachelor (☐)   Master (☐)   Doctoral (☐)

11. Last high school (HS) or GED school. Give the school's name, city, State, ZIP Code (if known), and year diploma or GED received.

12. Colleges and universities attended. Do **not** attach a copy of your transcript unless requested.

A) Name			Total Credits Earned		Major(s)	Degree	Year Received
			Semester	Quarter		(if any)	
City	State	ZIP Code					
B) Name							
City	State	ZIP Code					
C) Name							
City	State	ZIP Code					

OTHER QUALIFICATIONS

13. Job-related training courses (give title and year). **Job-related** skills (other languages, computer software/hardware, tools, machinery, typing speed, etc.). **Job-related** certificates and licenses (current only). **Job-related** honors, awards, and special accomplishments (publications, memberships in professional/honor societies, leadership activities, public speaking, and performance awards). Give dates, but do **not** send documents unless requested.

        Unprotected Form Field

GENERAL

14. Are you a U.S. citizen?   **YES** (☐)   **NO** (☐) ▶   Give the country of your citizenship.

15. Do you claim veterans' preference?   **NO** (☐)   **YES** (☐) ▶   Mark your claim of 5 or 10 points below.

5 points   (☐) ▶ Attach your DD 214 or other proof.   10 points   (☐) ▶ Attach an Application for 10-Point Veterans' Preference (SF15) and proof required.

16. Were you ever a Federal civilian employee?

				Series	Grade	From (MM/YY)	To (MM/YY)

     NO (☐)   **YES** (☐) ▶ For highest civilian grade give:

17. Are you eligible for reinstatement based on career or career-conditional Federal status?

     NO (☐)   **YES** (☐) ▶ If requested, attach SF 50 proof.

APPLICANT CERTIFICATION

18. I certify that, to the best of my knowledge and belief, all of the information on and attached to this application is true, correct, complete and made in good faith. **I understand** that false or fraudulent information on or attached to this application may be grounds for not hiring me or for firing me after I begin work, and may be punishable by fine or imprisonment. **I understand** that any information I give may be investigated.

SIGNATURE	DATE SIGNED

BIRTH CERTIFICATION LOCATION INFORMATION

ALABAMA $12.00

Center for Health Statistics
State Department of Public Health
P.O. Box 5625
Montgomery, AL 36103-5625

State office has had records since January 1908. Additional copies at same time are $4.00 each. Fee for special searches is $10.00 per hour. Personal check or money order should be made payable to Alabama Vital Records. To verify current fees, call (334) 206-5418 (recorded message). Information on how to obtain certified copies is also available via the Internet at http://www.adph.org.

ALASKA $15.00

Department of Health and Social Services
Bureau of Vital Statistics
5441 Commercial Boulevard
Juneau, AK 99801

State office has had records since January 1913. Personal check or money order should be made payable to Bureau of Vital Statistics. To verify current fees, the telephone number is (907) 465-3391 (recorded message). Information on how to obtain certified copies is also available via the internet at http://www.hss.state.ak.us.

ALL REQUESTS MUST INCLUDE A COPY OF A PICTURE ID OF THE APPLICANT. Enlarge the copy and lighten it as much as possible to be sure that it is clear and readable when sent to the Bureau. A signature under the copied ID is also required.

ARIZONA long form: $15.00/ short form: $10.00

Vital Records Section
Arizona Department of Health Services
P.O. Box 3887
Phoenix, AZ 85030-3887

State office has had records since July 1909 and abstracts of records filed in counties before then. Birth certificates prior to 1990 cost $15.00 and 1990 to the present cost $10.00 (certified computer copies). Check or money order should be made payable to Office of Vital Records. Personal checks are accepted. To verify current fees, the telephone number is (602) 364-1300 (recorded message). Information on how to obtain certified copies is also available via the internet at http://www.hs.state.az.us. Applicants must submit a copy of picture identification or have their request notarized.

ARKANSAS $ 8.00

Division of Vital Records
Arkansas Department of Health
4815 West Markham Street
Little Rock, AR 72205-3867

State office has had records since February 1914 and some original Little Rock and Fort Smith records from 1881. Additional copies of the same birth record, when requested at the same time are $5.00 each. Check or money order should be made payable to Arkansas Department of Health. Personal checks are accepted. To verify current fees, the telephone number is (501) 661-2174 (recorded message). Information on how to obtain certified copies is also available via the internet at http://www.healthyarkansas.com.

CALIFORNIA $15.00
Department of Health Services
Office of Vital Records
M.S. 5103
P.O. Box 997410
Sacramento, CA 95899-7410
State office has had records since July 1905. For earlier records, write to County Recorder in county where event occurred. Personal check or money order should be made payable to Office of Vital Records. To verify current fees, the telephone number is (916) 445-2684 (recorded message). Information on how to obtain certified copies is also available via the internet at
http://www.dhs.cahwnet.gov/hisp/chs/OVR/Ordercert.htm#birth.

COLORADO $15.00
Vital Records
Colorado Department of Public Health and Environment
4300 Cherry Creek Drive South
HSVRD-VS-A1
Denver, CO 80246-1530
State office has had death records since 1900 and birth records since 1910. State office also has birth records for some counties for years before1910. Additional copies of the same record ordered at the same time are $6.00. Pocket size birth cards are available for birth years 1960 to present and contain name, sex, date, place of birth, state file number, date filed, and date issued. Personal check or money order should be made payable to Vital Records. To verify current fees, call (303) 756-4464 (recorded message). Information on how to obtain certified copies is also available via the Internet at
http://www.cdphe.state.co.us/hs/cshom.html

CONNECTICUT $ 5.00
Certified copies are not available from State Office. Request must be submitted to town where event occurred. PLEASE NOTE: A photocopy of picture identification must be submitted with any request for a birth certificate. Personal check or money order should be made payable to town where the event occurred.

DELAWARE $ 10.00
Office of Vital Statistics
Division of Public Health
P.O. Box 637
Dover, DE 19903
State office has death records since 1963 and birth records since 1931. Additional copies of the same record requested at the same time are $4.00 each. For previous years, write to Archives Hall of Records, Dover, DE (302) 744-5000. A photo identification is REQUIRED for all transactions. If submitting by mail, a copy of ID IS REQUIRED. Personal check or money order should be made payable to Office of Vital Statistics. To verify current fees, the telephone number is (302) 744-4549.

DISTRICT OF COLUMBIA   short form $18.00/long form $23.00

Vital Records Office
825 North Capitol Street NE
Washington, DC 20002

Office has birth records since 1874. Personal check or money order should be made payable to DC Treasurer. To verify current fees, the telephone number is (202) 442-9009 (recorded message). Information on how to obtain certified copies is also available via the internet at http://www.dchealth.dc.gov.

FLORIDA $ 9.00

Office of Vital Statistics
P.O. Box 210
1217 Pearl Street
Jacksonville, FL 32231

The majority of records date from January 1917. If the exact date is unknown, the fee is $9.00 (births) or $5.00 (deaths) for the first year searched and $2.00 for each additional year up to a maximum of $50.00. Fee includes one certification of record if found or certified statement stating record not on file. Additional copies are $4.00 each when requested at the same time. Personal check or money order should be made payable to Office of Vital Statistics. To verify current fees, call (904) 359-6900 (recorded message). Information on how to obtain certified copies is also available via the Internet at http://www.doh.state.fl.us.

GEORGIA $10.00

Georgia Department of Human Resources
Vital Records Service
2600 Skyland Drive, NE
Atlanta, GA 30319-3640

State office has had records since January 1919. Additional copies of same record ordered at same time are $5.00 each except birth cards, which are $10.00 each. Certified check or money order should be made payable to Vital Records Service. Personal checks are not accepted. To verify current fees, call (404) 679-4701 (recorded message). Information on how to obtain certified copies is also available via the Internet at http://state.ga.us/programs/vitalrecords

HAWAII $10.00

State Department of Health
Office of Health Status Monitoring
Vital Records Section
P.O. Box 3378
Honolulu, HI 96801-9984

State office has had records since 1853. Additional copies ordered at the same time are $4.00 each. Cashier's check or money order should be made payable to State Department of Health. Personal checks are not accepted. To verify current fees, call (808) 586-4533 (recorded message). Information on how to obtain certified copies is also available via the Internet at http://www.hawaii.gov/health/records/index.html

IDAHO $13.00

Vital Statistics Unit
Center for Vital Statistics and Health Policy
450 West State Street, 1st Floor
P.O. Box 83720
Boise, ID 83720-0036

State office has had records since July 1911. For records from 1907 to 1911, write to County Recorder in county where event occurred. Check or money order should be made payable to Idaho Vital Statistics. Personal checks are accepted. To verify current fees, the telephone number is (208) 334-5988 (recorded message). Information on how to obtain certified copies is also available via the internet at http://www.state.id.us/dhw. Applicants must provide a copy of their drivers license or other State picture identification. If this is not available, the applicant must provide a copy of two other forms of identification with a signature.

ILLINOIS $15.00 certified copy/$10.00 certification

Division of Vital Records
Illinois Department of Public Health
605 West Jefferson Street
Springfield, IL 62702-5097

State office has had records since January 1916. For earlier records and for copies of State records since January 1916, write to County Clerk in county where event occurred (county fees vary). The fee for a search of the State files is $10.00. If the record is found, one certification is issued at no additional charge. Additional certifications of the same record ordered at the same time are $2.00 each. The fee for a full certified copy is $15.00. Additional certified copies of the same record ordered at the same time are $2.00 each. Money orders, certified checks, or personal checks should be made payable to Illinois Department of Public Health. To verify current fees, the telephone number is (217) 782-6553 (recorded message). Information on how to obtain certified copies is also available via the internet at http://www.idph.state.il.us.

INDIANA $ 10.00

Vital Records Section
State Department of Health
2 North Meridian Street
Indianapolis, IN 46204

State office has had birth and death records since October 1907. Additional copies of the same record ordered at the same time are $4.00 each. For earlier records, write to Health Officer in city or county where event occurred. Check or money order should be made payable to Indiana State Department of Health. Personal checks are accepted. To verify current fees, the telephone number is (317) 233-2700. Information on how to obtain certified copies is also available via the internet at http://www.in.gov/isdh/index.htm.

IOWA $10.00
Iowa Department of Public Health
Bureau of Vital Records
Lucas Office Building
321 East 12th Street
Des Moines, IA 50319-0075
State office has had records since July 1880. Personal check or money order should be made payable to Iowa Department of Public Health. To verify current fees, call (515) 281-4944 (recorded message). Information on how to obtain certified copies is also available via the Internet at http://www.idph.state.ia.us/pa/vr.htm

KANSAS $12.00
Office of Vital Statistics
Kansas State Department of Health and Environment
Landon State Office Building
1000 SW Jackson Street, Suite 120
Topeka, Kansas 66612-2221
State office has had records since July 1911. For earlier records, write to County Clerk in county where event occurred. Additional copies of same record ordered at same time are $7.00 each. Personal check or money order should be made payable to Vital Statistics. Personal checks are accepted. To verify current fees, the telephone number is (785) 296-1400. This will be a recorded message with the option to speak with a Customer Service Representative. Information on how to obtain certified copies is also available via the internet at http://www.kdhe.state.ks.us/vital/.

KENTUCKY $10.00
Office of Vital Records
Department for Health Services
275 East Main Street
Frankfort, KY 40621-0001
State office has had records since January 1911. Personal check or money order should be made payable to Kentucky State Treasurer. To verify current fees, the telephone number is (502) 564-4212. Information on how to obtain certified copies is also available via the internet at http://publichealth.state.ky.us/vital.htm.

LOUISIANA $15.00 long form/$9.00 short form
Vital Records Registry
Office of Public Health
325 Loyola Avenue
New Orleans, LA 70112
State office has had records since July 1914. Check or money order should be made payable to Vital Records. Personal checks are accepted. To verify current fees, call (504) 568-5152 (recorded message). Information on how to obtain certified copies is also available via the Internet at http://www.dhh.state.la.us

MAINE $10.00 certified/$6.00 uncertified
Office of Vital Records
Maine Department of Human Services
State House Station 11
Augusta, ME 04333
State office has had records since 1892. Records for 1892-1922 are available at the Maine State Archives. For earlier records, write to the municipality where the event occurred. Additional copies of same record ordered at same time are $4.00 each. Check or money order should be made payable to Treasurer, State of Maine. Personal checks are accepted. To verify current fees, the telephone number is (207) 287-3181. This will be a recorded message. Information on how to obtain certified copies is also available via the internet at http://www.state.me.us

MARYLAND $ 12.00
Division of Vital Records
Department of Health and Mental Hygiene
6550 Reisterstown Road
P.O. Box 68760
Baltimore, MD 21215-0020
State office has had records since August 1898. Records for city of Baltimore are available from January 1875. Fee for Commemorative Birth Certificates is $25.00. Will not do research for genealogical studies. Must apply to State of Maryland Archives, 350 Rowe Blvd., Annapolis, MD 21401, (410) 974-3914. Check or money order should be made payable to Division of Vital Records. Personal checks are accepted. To verify current fees, the telephone number is (410) 764-3038 (recorded message). Information on how to obtain certified copies is also available via the internet at http://mdpublichealth.org/vsa.

MASSACHUSETTS $12.00 (In person)/$22.00 (Mail request)/$6.00 (State Archives)
Registry of Vital Records and Statistics
150 Mount Vernon Street
1st Floor
Dorchester, MA 02125-3105
State office has records since 1906. For earlier records, write to The Massachusetts Archives at Columbia Point, 220 Morrissey Boulevard, Boston, MA 02125 (617) 727-2816. Check or money order should be made payable to Commonwealth of Massachusetts. Personal checks are accepted. To verify current fees, the telephone number is (617) 740-2600 (recorded message). Information on how to obtain certified copies is also available via the internet at http://www.state.ma.us/dph/bhsre/rvr/vrcopies.htm.

MICHIGAN $15.00
Vital Records
3423 North Martin Luther King Blvd.
P.O. Box 30195
Lansing, MI 48909
State office has records of births and deaths that occurred and were filed with the state since 1867. Check or money order should be made payable to State of Michigan. Personal checks are accepted. Additional copies of the same record, ordered at the same time are $5.00

each. To verify current fees, the telephone number is (517) 335-8656 (recorded message). Information on how to obtain certified copies is also available via the internet at http://www.mdch.state.mi.us/pha/osr/index.asp

MINNESOTA $13.00
Minnesota Department of Health
Section of Vital Statistics
717 Delaware Street, SE
P.O. Box 9441
Minneapolis, MN 55440
State office has had birth records since January 1900. Additional copies of the birth record when ordered at the same time are $7.00 each. Personal check or money order should be made payable to Minnesota Department of Health. To verify current fees, call (612) 676-5120 (recorded message). Information on how to obtain certified copies is also available via the Internet at http://www.health.state.mn.us.

MISSISSIPPI $12.00 long form/ $7.00 short form
Vital Records
State Department of Health
P.O. Box 1700
Jackson, MS   39215-1700
State office has had records since 1912. Full copies of birth certificates obtained within 1 year after the event are $7.00. Additional copies of same record ordered at same time are $3.00 each. For out-of-state requests only bank or postal money orders are accepted and should be made payable to Mississippi Vital Records. Personal checks are accepted only for in-state requests. To verify current fees, call (601) 576-7981. A recorded message may be reached on (601) 576-7450.

MISSOURI $10.00
Missouri Department of Health
Bureau of Vital Records
930 Wildwood
P.O. Box 570
Jefferson City, MO   65102-0570
State office has had records since January 1910. Certified copies of most Missouri birth also available from local county health department or the St. Louis City or Kansas City Health Departments. For details, please contact these offices directly. If event occurred in St. Louis (City), St. Louis County, or Kansas City before 1910, write to the city or county Health Department. Copies of these records are $10.00 each in St. Louis City and St. Louis County. In Kansas City, the fee is $6.00 for the first copy and $3.00 for each additional copy ordered at same time. Computer issued copies containing the state certification are $10.00 each. Check or money order should be made payable to Missouri Department of Health. Personal checks are accepted. To verify current fees on birth records, the telephone number is (573) 751-6400. Information on how to obtain certified copies is also available via the internet at http://www.health.state.mo.us.

MONTANA $12.00
MT Dept of Public Health and Human Services
Vital Statistics Bureau
P.O. Box 4210
Helena, MT 59604
State office has had records since late 1907. Additional copies of the same record requested at the same time are $5.00. Photocopy of picture ID and signature required. Check or money order should be made payable to Montana Department of Public Health and Human Services. Personal checks are accepted. To verify current fees, the telephone number is (406) 444-4228. Information on how to obtain certified copies is also available via the internet at http://www.dphhs.state.mt.us.

NEBRASKA $ 8.00
Bureau of Vital Statistics
Department of Health and Human Services
301 Centennial Mall South
P.O. Box 95065
Lincoln, NE 68509-5065
State office has had records since late 1904. If birth occurred before then, writethe State office for information. Check or money order should be made payable to Bureau of Vital Statistics. Personal checks are accepted. To verify current fees, the telephone number is (402) 471-2871 (recorded message). Information on how to obtain certified copies isalso available via the internet at http://www.hhs.state.ne.us/ced/nevrinfo.htm.

NEVADA $13.00
Office of Vital Records and Statistics
Capitol Complex
505 East King Street #102
Carson City, NV 89710
State office has records since July 1911. Personal check or money order should be made payable to Office of Vital Records and Statistics. To verify current fees, the telephone number is (775) 684-4280 (recorded message). Information on how to obtain certified copies is also available via the internet at http://health2k.state.nv.us.

NEW HAMPSHIRE $12.00
Bureau of Vital Records
Health and Welfare Building
6 Hazen Drive
Concord, NH 03301
State office has had records since 1883. Copies of records may be obtained from State office or from City or Town Clerk in place where event occurred. Additional copies ordered at the same time are $6.00 each. Check or money order should be made payable to Treasurer, State of New Hampshire. Personal checks are accepted. To verify current fees, the telephone number is (603) 271-4654 (recorded message). Information on how to obtain certified copies is also available via the internet at http://www.dhhs.state.nh.us.

NEW JERSEY $4.00
New Jersey State Department of Health and Senior Services
Vital Statistics Registration
P.O. Box 370
Trenton, NJ 08625-0370
State office has had records since June 1878. Additional copies of same record ordered at same time are $2.00 each. If the exact date is unknown, the fee is an additional $1.00 per year searched. Check or money order should be made payable to State Registrar. Personal checks are accepted. To verify current fees, the telephone number is (609) 292-4087 (recorded message). Information on how to obtain certified copies is also available via the internet at http://www.state.nj.us.health/vital/vital.htm.

NEW MEXICO $10.00
New Mexico Vital Records
P.O. Box 26110
Santa Fe, NM 87502
State office has had records since 1920 and delayed records since 1880. Personal check or money order should be made payable to NM Vital Records. To verify current fees, the telephone number is (505) 827-2338 (recorded message).

NEW YORK $30.00
(except New York City)
Certification Unit
Vital Records Section
P.O. Box 2602
Albany, NY 12220-2602
State office has had records since 1880. Personal check or money order should be made payable to New York State Department of Health. To verify current fees, the telephone number is (518) 474-3075 (recorded message).

NEW YORK CITY $15.00
Division of Vital Records
NYC Department of Health and Mental Hygiene
125 Worth Street, CN4, Rm. 133
New York, NY 10013
Office has birth records since 1910 for those occurring in the Boroughs of Manhattan, Brooklyn, Bronx, Queens, and Staten Island. There are strict identification requirements. A 24-hour automated telephone system is available that provides detailed information. The number is (212) 788-4520. Information on how to obtain certified copies and applications are available via the internet at http://www.nyc.gov/health.

NORTH CAROLINA $15.00
NC Vital Records
1903 Mail Service Center
Raleigh, NC 27699-1903
State office has had birth records since October 1913. Additional copies of the same record ordered at the same time are $5.00 each. Check or money order should be made payable to NC Vital Records. Personal checks are accepted. To verify current fees, the telephone

number is (919) 733-3526. Information on how to obtain certified copies is also available via the internet at http://www.schs.state.nc.us/SCHS.

NORTH DAKOTA $7.00
Division of Vital Records
State Capitol
600 East Boulevard Avenue
Dept. 301
Bismarck, ND 58505-0200
State office has had some records since July 1893. Years from 1894 to 1920 are incomplete. Additional copies of birth records are $4.00 each. Copies are generally processed within 5-7 working days after request is received. Personal check or money order should be made payable to ND Department of Health. To verify current fees, the telephone number is (701) 328-2360 (automated attendant with a recorded message). Information on how to obtain certified copies is also available via the internet at http://www.vitalnd.com.

OHIO $15.00
Bureau of Vital Statistics
Ohio Department of Health
246 North High Street, 1st Floor
Columbus, OH 43216
State office has had birth records since December 20, 1908. Personal check or money order should be made payable to Treasury, State of Ohio. To verify current fees, the telephone number is (614) 466-2531 (recorded message). Information on how to obtain certified copies is also available via the internet at http://www.vitalrec.com/oh.html.

OKLAHOMA $10.00
Vital Records Section
State Department of Health
1000 Northeast 10th Street
P.O. Box 53551
Oklahoma City, OK 73117
State office has had records since October 1908. Personal check or money order should be made payable to Vital Records Service. To verify current fees, the telephone number is (405) 271-4040 (recorded message). Information on how to obtain certified copies is also available via the internet at http://www.health.state.ok.us/program/vital/brec.html.

OREGON $15.00
Oregon Vital Records
P.O. Box 14050
Portland, OR 97293-0050
State office has had records since July 1903. Additional copies of the same record ordered at the same time are $12.00 each. Personal check or money order should be made payable to DHS/Vital Records. To verify current fees, the telephone number is (503) 731-4095 (recorded message). Information on how to obtain certified copies is also available via the internet at http://www.ohd.hr.state.or.us.

PENNSYLVANIA $4.00/ Wallet card $5.00
Division of Vital Records
101 South Mercer Street
Room 401
P.O. Box 1528
New Castle, PA 16101
State office has records since January 1906. All requests MUST include the signature and photo ID of the individual requesting the record. Personal check or money order should be made payable to Vital Records. To verify current fees, the telephone number is (724) 656-3100 (recorded message). Information on how to obtain certified copies is also available via the internet at http://webserver.health.state.pa.us/health/site.

PUERTO RICO $5.00
Department of Health
Demographic Registry
P.O. Box 11854
Fernández Juncos Station
San Juan, PR 00910
Central office has had records since July 22, 1931. Copies of earlier records may be obtained by writing to Local Registrar (Registrador Demografico) in municipality where event occurred or by writing to central office for information. Money order should be made payable to Secretary of the Treasury. Personal checks are not accepted. To verify current fees, the telephone number is (787) 728-7980. All applications must be accompanied by a photocopy of an identification card with picture. Example: Driver's license or Passport (not expired).

RHODE ISLAND $15.00
Office of Vital Records
Rhode Island Department of Health
3 Capitol Hill, Room 101
Providence, RI 02908-5097
State office keeps birth and marriage records for 100 years. Additional copies of the same record ordered at the same time are $10.00 each. Personal check or money order should be made payable to General Treasurer, State of Rhode Island. To verify current fees, the telephone number is (401) 222-2811 (recorded message). Information on how to obtain certified copies is also available via the internet at http://www.healthri.org/management/vital/home.htm.

SOUTH CAROLINA $12.00
Office of Vital Records
SC DHEC
2600 Bull Street
Columbia, SC 29201
State office has records since January 1915. Additional copies of the same birth records ordered at the same time of certification are $3.00. Personal check or money order should be made payable to Department of Health and Environmental Control. To verify current fees, call (803) 898-3630.

SOUTH DAKOTA $10.00
Vital Records
State Department of Health
600 East Capitol Avenue
Pierre, SD 57501-2536
State office has records filed after July 1905. Money order should be made payable to South Dakota Department of Health. Personal checks are accepted. To verify current fees the telephone number is (605) 773-4961 (recorded message). Information on how to obtain certified copies is also available via the internet at http://www.state.sd.us/doh/vitalrec/vital.htm. Submit a credit card order online or by phone at 605-773-4961. Additional $10 expedited fee per request for all credit card, online and phone orders.

TENNESSEE $12.00 long form/$7.00 short form
Tennessee Vital Records
Central Services Building
421 5th Avenue, North
Nashville, TN 37247
Additional copies of the same birth record requested at the same time are $4.00 each. Check or money order should be made payable to Tennessee Vital Records. Personal checks are accepted. To verify current fees, the telephone number is (615) 741-1763. Information on how to obtain certified copies is also available via the internet at http://www2.state.tn.us/health/vr/index.htm.

TEXAS $11.00
Bureau of Vital Statistics
Texas Department of Health
P.O. Box 12040
Austin, TX 78711-2040
State office has had birth and death records since 1903. Additional copies of the birth record ordered at same time are $11.00 each. Personal check or money order should be made payable to Texas Department of Health. To verify current fees, call (512) 458-7111 (recorded message). Information on how to obtain certified copies is also available via the Internet at http://www.tdh.state.tx.us/bvs.

UTAH $15.00
Office of Vital Records and Statistics
Utah Department of Health
288 North 1460 West
P.O. Box 141012
Salt Lake City, UT 84114-1012
State office has had records since 1905. Additional copies, when requested at the same time are $8.00 each. Personal check or money order should be made payable to Vital Records. To verify current fees, the telephone number is (801) 538-6105 (recorded message). Information on how to obtain certified copies is also available via the internet at http://www.health.utah.gov/vitalrecords.

VERMONT $7.00
Vermont Department of Health
Vital Records Section
P.O. Box 70
108 Cherry Street
Burlington, VT 05402-0070
State office has records for the latest 10 years. Check or money order
should be made payable to Vermont Department of Health. Personal
checks are accepted. To verify current fees, the telephone number is
(802) 863-7275 (recorded message). Information on how to obtain
certified copies is also available via the internet at
http://www.state.vt.us/health/_hs/vitals/records/obtain.htm.

VIRGINIA $10.00
Office of Vital Records
P.O. Box 1000
Richmond, VA 23218-1000
State office has had records 1912. Check or money order should be
made payable to State Health Department. Personal checks are accepted. To verify current fees, the telephone number is (804) 662-6200
(recorded message). Information on how to obtain certified copies is
also available via the internet at http://www.vdh.state.va.us.

VIRGIN ISLANDS $15.00 Mail request/$12.00 In person
Department of Health
Vital Statistics
Charles Harwood Memorial Hospital
St. Croix, VI 00820

St. Thomas and St. John $15.00 Mail request/$12.00 In person
Department of Health
Vital Statistics
Knud Hansen Complex
St. Thomas, VI 00802
Money order for birth and death records should be made payable to
Department of Health. Personal checks are not accepted. To verify cur-
rent fees, the telephone number is (340) 774-9000 ext. 4685 or 4686.

WASHINGTON $17.00
Department of Health
Center for Health Statistics
P.O. Box 9709
Olympia, WA 98507-9709
Must have exact information for births. For King, Pierce, and Spokane counties copies may also be obtained from county health departments. Personal check or money order should be made payable
to Department of Health. To verify current fees, the telephone number
is (360) 236-4300. Information on how to obtain certified copies is
also available via the internet at
http://www.doh.wa.gov/ehsphl/chs/cert.htm.

WEST VIRGINIA $5.00
Vital Registration Office
350 Capitol Street, Rm.165
Charleston, WV 25301-3701
State office has had records since January 1917. Check or money order should be made payable to Vital Registration. Personal checks are accepted. To verify current fees, the telephone number is (304) 558-2931. Information on how to obtain certified copies is also available via the internet at http://www.wvdhhr.org.

WISCONSIN $12.00
WI Vital Records
1 West Wilson Street
P.O. Box 309
Madison, WI 53701-0309
Additional copies of the same record ordered at the same time are $3.00 each. Personal check or money order should be made payable to State of Wisconsin Vital Records. A stamped, self-addressed business size (#10) envelope should be included with the request. To verify current fees, the telephone number is (608) 266-1371 (recorded message). Information on how to obtain certified copies is also available via the internet at
http://www.dhfs.state.wi.us/vitalrecords/index.htm

WYOMING $12.00
Vital Records Services
Hathaway Building
Cheyenne, WY 82002
State office has had records since July 1909. Personal check or money order should be made payable to Vital Records Services. To verify current fees, call (307) 777-7591. Information on how to obtain certified copies is also available via the Internet at
http://wdhfs.state.wy.us/vital_records.

SOCIAL SECURITY ADMINISTRATION
Application for a Social Security Card

Applying for a Social Security Card is easy <u>AND</u> it is free!

USE THIS APPLICATION TO APPLY FOR:
- An **original** Social Security card
- A **duplicate** Social Security card (same name and number)
- A **corrected** Social Security card (name change and same number)
- A **change of information** on your record other than your name (no card needed)

IMPORTANT: We CANNOT process this application unless you follow the instructions below and give us the evidence we need.

STEP 1 Read pages 1 through 3 which explain how to complete the application and what evidence we need.

STEP 2 Complete and sign the application using BLUE or BLACK ink. Do not use pencil or other colors of ink. Please print legibly.

STEP 3 Submit the completed and signed application with all required evidence to any Social Security office.

HOW TO COMPLETE THIS APPLICATION

Most items on the form are self-explanatory. Those that need explanation are discussed below. The numbers match the numbered items on the form. If you are completing this form for someone else, please complete the items as they apply to that person.

2. Show the address where you can receive your card 10 to 14 days from now.

3. If you check "Legal Alien **Not** Allowed to Work", you need to provide a document from the government agency requiring your Social Security number that explains why you need a number and that you meet all of the requirements for the benefit or service except for the number. A State or local agency requirement must conform with Federal law.

   If you check "Other", you need to provide proof you are entitled to a federally-funded benefit for which a Social Security number is required as a condition for you to receive payment.

5. Providing race/ethnic information is voluntary. However, if you do give us this information, it helps us prepare statistical reports on how Social Security programs affect people. We do not reveal the identities of individuals.

6. Show the month, day and full (4 digit) year of birth, for example, "1998" for year of birth.

8.B. Show the mother's Social Security number only if you are applying for an original Social Security card for a child under age 18. You may leave this item blank if the mother does not have a number or you do not know the mother's number. We will still be able to assign a number to the child.

9.B. Show the father's Social Security number only if you are applying for an original Social Security card for a child under age 18. You may leave this item blank if the father does not have a number or you do not know the father's number. We will still be able to assign a number to the child.

13. If the date of birth you show in item 6 is different from the date of birth you used on a prior application for a Social Security card, show the date of birth you used on the prior application and submit evidence of age to support the date of birth in item 6.

16. You **must** sign the application yourself if you are age 18 or older and are physically and mentally capable. If you are under age 18, you may also sign the application if you are physically and mentally capable. If you cannot sign your name, you should sign with an "X" mark and have two people sign as witnesses in the space beside the mark. If you are physically or mentally incapable of signing the application, generally a parent, close relative, or legal guardian may sign the application. Call us if you need clarification about who can sign.

ABOUT YOUR DOCUMENTS

- We need **ORIGINAL** documents or **copies certified by the custodian of the record.** We will return your documents after we have seen them.

- **We cannot accept photocopies or notarized copies of documents.**

- If your documents do not meet this requirement, we cannot process your application.

DOCUMENTS WE NEED

To apply for an **ORIGINAL CARD** (you have NEVER been assigned a Social Security number before), we need at least 2 documents as proof of:

- **Age,**
- **Identity, and**
- **U.S. citizenship or lawful alien status.**

To apply for a **DUPLICATE CARD** (same number, same name), we need proof of **identity.**

To apply for a **CORRECTED CARD** (same number, different name), we need proof of **identity.** We need one or more documents which identify you by the OLD NAME on our records and your NEW NAME. Examples include: a marriage certificate, divorce decree, or a court order that changes your name. Or we can accept two identity documents - one in your old name and one in your new name. (See IDENTITY, for examples of identity documents.)

IMPORTANT: If you are applying for a duplicate or corrected card and were **born outside the U.S.,** we also need proof of U.S. citizenship or lawful alien status. (See U.S. CITIZENSHIP or ALIEN STATUS for examples of documents you can submit.)

To **CHANGE INFORMATION** on your record other than your name, we need proof of:

- **Identity, and**
- **Another document which supports the change** (for example, a birth certificate to change your date and/or place of birth or parents' names).

AGE: We prefer to see your birth certificate. However, we can accept another document that shows your age if it is at least one year old. Some of the other documents we can accept are:

- Hospital record of your birth made before you were age 5
- Religious record showing your age made before you were 3 months old
- Passport
- Adoption record

Call us for advice if you cannot obtain one of these documents.

IDENTITY: We must see a document in the name you want shown on the card. The identity document must be of recent issuance so that we can determine your continued existence. We prefer to see a document with a photograph. However, we can generally accept a non-photo identity document if it has enough information to identify you (e.g., your name, as well as age, date of birth or parents' names). **WE CANNOT ACCEPT A BIRTH CERTIFICATE, HOSPITAL BIRTH RECORD, SOCIAL SECURITY CARD OR CARD STUB, OR SOCIAL SECURITY RECORD** as evidence of identity. Some documents we can accept are:

- Driver's license
- Employer ID card
- Passport

- Marriage or divorce record
- Adoption record
- Health insurance card (not a Medicare card)

- Military record
- Life insurance policy
- School ID card

As evidence of identity for infants and young children, we can accept :

- Doctor, clinic, hospital record
- Daycare center, school record
- Religious record (e.g., baptismal record)

IMPORTANT: If you are **applying for a card on behalf of someone else,** we must see proof of identity for both you and the person to whom the card will be issued.

U. S. CITIZENSHIP: We can accept most documents that show you were born in the U.S. If you are a U.S. citizen born outside the U.S., show us a U.S. consular report of birth, a U.S. passport, a Certificate of Citizenship, or a Certificate of Naturalization.

ALIEN STATUS: We need to see an unexpired document issued to you by the U.S. Immigration and Naturalization Service (INS), such as Form I-551, I-94, I-688B, or I-766. We CANNOT accept a receipt showing you applied for the document. If you are not authorized to work in the U.S., we can issue you a Social Security card if you are lawfully here and need the number for a valid nonwork reason. (See HOW TO COMPLETE THIS APPLICATION, Item 3.) Your card will be marked to show you cannot work. If you do work, we will notify INS.

HOW TO SUBMIT THIS APPLICATION

In most cases, you can mail this application with your evidence documents to any Social Security office. We will return your documents to you. If you do not want to mail your original documents, take them with this application to the nearest Social Security office.

EXCEPTION: If you are age 18 or older and have never been assigned a number before, you must apply in person.

If you have any questions about this form, or about the documents we need, please contact any Social Security office. A telephone call will help you make sure you have everything you need to apply for a card or change information on your record. You can find your nearest office in your local phone directory or on our website at www.ssa.gov.

THE PAPERWORK/PRIVACY ACT AND YOUR APPLICATION

The Privacy Act of 1974 requires us to give each person the following notice when applying for a Social Security number.

Sections 205(c) and 702 of the Social Security Act allow us to collect the facts we ask for on this form.

We use the facts you provide on this form to assign you a Social Security number and to issue you a Social Security card. You do not have to give us these facts, however, without them we cannot issue you a Social Security number or a card. Without a number, you may not be able to get a job and could lose Social Security benefits in the future.

The Social Security number is also used by the Internal Revenue Service for tax administration purposes as an identifier in processing tax returns of persons who have income which is reported to the Internal Revenue Service and by persons who are claimed as dependents on someone's Federal income tax return.

We may disclose information as necessary to administer Social Security programs, including to appropriate law enforcement agencies to investigate alleged violations of Social Security law; to other government agencies for administering entitlement, health, and welfare programs such as Medicaid, Medicare, veterans benefits, military pension, and civil service annuities, black lung, housing, student loans, railroad retirement benefits, and food stamps; to the Internal Revenue Service for Federal tax administration; and to employers and former employers to properly prepare wage reports. We may also disclose information as required by Federal law, for example, to the Department of Justice, Immigration and Naturalization Service, to identify and locate aliens in the U.S.; to the Selective Service System for draft registration; and to the Department of Health and Human Services for child support enforcement purposes. We may verify Social Security numbers for State motor vehicle agencies that use the number in issuing drivers licenses, as authorized by the Social Security Act. Finally, we may disclose information to your Congressional representative if they request information to answer questions you ask him or her.

We may use the information you give us when we match records by computer. Matching programs compare our records with those of other Federal, State, or local government agencies to determine whether a person qualifies for benefits paid by the Federal government. The law allows us to do this even if you do not agree to it.

Explanations about these and other reasons why information you provide us may be used or given out are available in Social Security offices. If you want to learn more about this, contact any Social Security office.

This information collection meets the clearance requirements of 44 U.S.C. §3507, as amended by section 2 of the **Paperwork Reduction Act of 1995.** You are not required to answer these questions unless we display a valid Office of Management and Budget control number. We estimate that it will take you about 8.5 to 9 minutes to read the instructions, gather the necessary facts, and answer the questions.

SOCIAL SECURITY ADMINISTRATION
Application for a Social Security Card

Form Approved
OMB No. 0960-0066

1

NAME → TO BE SHOWN ON CARD	First	Full Middle Name	Last
FULL NAME AT BIRTH IF OTHER THAN ABOVE	First	Full Middle Name	Last
OTHER NAMES USED			

2 MAILING ADDRESS → Do Not Abbreviate

Street Address, Apt. No., PO Box, Rural Route No.

City	State	Zip Code

3 CITIZENSHIP → (Check One)

☐ U.S. Citizen ☐ Legal Alien Allowed To Work ☐ Legal Alien **Not** Allowed To Work (See Instructions On Page 1) ☐ Other (See Instructions On Page 1)

4 SEX →

☐ Male ☐ Female

5 RACE/ETHNIC DESCRIPTION (Check One Only - Voluntary) →

☐ Asian, Asian-American or Pacific Islander ☐ Hispanic ☐ Black (Not Hispanic) ☐ North American Indian or Alaskan Native ☐ White (Not Hispanic)

6 DATE OF BIRTH _____ Month, Day, Year

7 PLACE OF BIRTH (Do Not Abbreviate) _____ City _____ State or Foreign Country _____ FCI

Office Use Only

8

A. MOTHER'S MAIDEN NAME →	First	Full Middle Name	Last Name At Her Birth

B. MOTHER'S SOCIAL SECURITY NUMBER → ☐☐☐ - ☐☐ - ☐☐☐☐

9

A. FATHER'S NAME →	First	Full Middle Name	Last

B. FATHER'S SOCIAL SECURITY NUMBER → ☐☐☐ - ☐☐ - ☐☐☐☐

10 Has the applicant or anyone acting on his/her behalf ever filed for or received a Social Security number card before?

☐ Yes (If "yes", answer questions 11-13.) ☐ No (If "no", go on to question 14.) ☐ Don't Know (If "don't know", go on to question 14.)

11 Enter the Social Security number previously assigned to the person listed in item 1. → ☐☐☐ - ☐☐ - ☐☐☐☐

12 Enter the name shown on the most recent Social Security card issued for the person listed in item 1. →

First	Middle Name	Last

13 Enter any different date of birth if used on an earlier application for a card. → _____ Month, Day, Year

14 TODAY'S DATE _____ Month, Day, Year

15 DAYTIME PHONE NUMBER ( ) _____ Area Code   Number

DELIBERATELY FURNISHING (OR CAUSING TO BE FURNISHED) FALSE INFORMATION ON THIS APPLICATION IS A CRIME PUNISHABLE BY FINE OR IMPRISONMENT, OR BOTH.

16 YOUR SIGNATURE ▶

17 YOUR RELATIONSHIP TO THE PERSON IN ITEM 1 IS:
☐ Self ☐ Natural Or Adoptive Parent ☐ Legal Guardian ☐ Other (Specify) _____

Request for Earnings and Benefit Estimate Statement

[ ] Please check this box if you want to get your statement in Spanish instead of English.

Please print or type your answers. When you have completed the form, fold it and mail it to us. (If you prefer to send your request using the Internet, contact us at http://www.ssa.gov)

1. Name shown on your Social Security card:

_____   _____
First Name   Middle Initial

_____
Last Name Only

2. Your Social Security number as shown on your card:

[ ][ ][ ] - [ ][ ] - [ ][ ][ ][ ]

3. Your date of birth (Mo.-Day-Yr.)

[ ][ ] - [ ][ ] - [ ][ ]

4. Other Social Security numbers you have used:

[ ][ ][ ] - [ ][ ] - [ ][ ][ ][ ]
[ ][ ][ ] - [ ][ ] - [ ][ ][ ][ ]

5. Your sex: [ ] Male   [ ] Female

For items 6 and 8 show only earnings covered by Social Security. Do NOT include wages from State, local or Federal Government employment that are NOT covered for Social Security or that are covered ONLY by Medicare.

6. Show your actual earnings (wages and/or net self-employment income) for last year and your estimated earnings for this year.

A. Last year's actual earnings: *(Dollars Only)*

$ [ ][ ][ ] , [ ][ ][ ] . 0 0

B. This year's estimated earnings: *(Dollars Only)*

$ [ ][ ][ ] , [ ][ ][ ] . 0 0

7. Show the age at which you plan to stop working.

[ ][ ]   *(Show only one age)*

8. Below, show the average yearly amount (not your total future lifetime earnings) that you think you will earn between now and when you plan to stop working. Include performance or scheduled pay increases or bonuses, but not cost-of-living increases.

If you expect to earn significantly more or less in the future due to promotions, job changes, part-time work, or an absence from the work force, enter the amount that most closely reflects your future average yearly earnings.

If you don't expect any significant changes, show the same amount you are earning now (the amount in 6B).

Future average yearly earnings: *(Dollars Only)*

$ [ ][ ][ ] , [ ][ ][ ] . 0 0

9. Do you want us to send the statement:
   • To you? Enter your name and mailing address.
   • To someone else (your accountant, pension plan, etc.)? Enter your name with "c/o" and the name and address of that person or organization.

_____
Name

_____
Street Address (Include Apt. No., P.O. Box, or Rural Route)

_____
City   State   Zip Code

Notice:
I am asking for information about my own Social Security record or the record of a person I am authorized to represent. I understand that if I deliberately request information under false pretenses, I may be guilty of a Federal crime and could be fined and/or imprisoned. I authorize you to use a contractor to send the statement of earnings and benefit estimates to the person named in item 9.

▲

Please sign your name (Do Not Print)

_____
Date   (Area Code) Daytime Telephone No.

Request for Earnings and Benefit Estimate Statement

Thank you for requesting this statement.

After you complete and return this form, we will--within 4 to 6 weeks--send you:

- a record of your earnings history and an estimate of how much you have paid in Social Security taxes, and
- estimates of benefits you (and your family) may be eligible for now and in the future.

We're pleased to furnish you with this information and we hope you'll find it useful in planning your financial future.

Social Security is more than just a program for retired people. It helps people of all ages in many ways. Whether you're young or old, male or female, single or with a family--Social Security can help you when you need it most. It can help support your family in the event of your death and pay you benefits if you become severly disabled.

If you have questions about Social Security or this form, please call our toll-free number, 1-800-772-1213.

Kenneth D. Apfel

Kenneth S. Apfel
Commissioner of Social Security

Mailing Address

Social Security Administration
Wilkes Barre Data Operations Center
PO Box 7004
Wilkes Barre PA 18767-7004

About The Privacy Act

Social Security is allowed to collect the facts on this form under Section 205 of the Social Security Act. We need them to quickly identify your record and prepare the earnings statement you asked us for. Giving us these facts is voluntary. However, without them we may not be able to give you an earnings and benefit estimate statement. Neither the Social Security Administration nor its contractor will use the information for any other purpose.

Paperwork Reduction Act Notice and Time It Takes Statement

The Paperwork Reduction Act of 1995 requires us to notify you that this information collection is in accordance with the clearance requirements of section 3507 of the Paperwork Reduction Act of 1995. We may not conduct or sponsor, and you are not required to respond to, a collection of information unless it displays a valid OMB control number. We estimate that it will take you about 5 minutes to complete this form. This includes the time it will take to read the instructions, gather the necessary facts and fill out the form.

U.S. Department of State

APPLICATION FOR U.S. PASSPORT OR REGISTRATION
HOW TO APPLY FOR A U.S. PASSPORT

OMB APPROVAL NO. 1405-0004
EXPIRATION DATE 03/31/2005
ESTIMATED BURDEN: 20 MINUTES
(See Page 4)

PLEASE DETACH AND RETAIN THIS INSTRUCTION SHEET FOR YOUR RECORDS

I applied:

Place: _____

Date *(mm-dd-yyyy)*: _____

FOR INFORMATION, QUESTIONS, AND INQUIRIES:

Please visit our website at travel.state.gov OR contact the National Passport Information Center at 1-900-225-5674, For TDD: 1-900-225-7778; or for credit card users: 1-888-362-8668, For TDD: 1-888-498-3648.

U.S. PASSPORTS ARE ISSUED ONLY TO U.S. CITIZENS OR NATIONALS. EACH PERSON MUST OBTAIN HIS OR HER OWN PASSPORT.

APPLICANTS WHO HAVE HAD A PREVIOUS U.S. PASSPORT:

If your most recent passport was issued less than 15 years ago and you were over 16 years old at the time of issuance, you may be eligible to use Form DS-82 (mail-in application). Please inquire about eligibility when you apply or visit our website as listed above. Address any requests for a passport amendment, extension of validity, or the addition of visa pages to a Passport Agency or a U.S. Consulate or Embassy abroad. In advance of your departure, check visa requirements with consular officials of the countries you will be visiting.

SPECIAL REQUIREMENTS FOR CHILDREN UNDER AGE 14 (As directed by Public Law 106-119.)

To submit an application for a child under age 14 both parents or the child's legal guardian(s) must appear and present all of the following:

- Evidence of child's U.S. citizenship,
- Evidence of child's relationship to parents or guardian(s), AND
- Parental identification

IF ONLY ONE PARENT APPEARS YOU MUST ALSO SUBMIT ONE OF THE FOLLOWING:

- Second parent's written statement consenting to passport issuance for the child,
- Primary evidence of sole authority to apply, OR
- A written statement (made under penalty of perjury) explaining the second parent's unavailability.

FIRST TIME APPLICANTS:

Please complete and submit this application in person. Each application must be accompanied by:

(1) PROOF OF U.S. CITIZENSHIP

(2) PROOF OF IDENTITY

(3) TWO PHOTOGRAPHS, AND

(4) FEES (as explained on reverse) to one of the following acceptance agents: a clerk of a Federal or State court of record or a judge or clerk of a probate court accepting applications, a designated municipal or county official, a designated postal employee at an authorized post office, an agent at a Passport Agency in Boston, Chicago, Honolulu, Houston, Los Angeles, Miami, New Orleans, New York, Norwalk CT, Philadelphia, San Francisco, Seattle, or Washington, DC, or a U.S. consular official at a U.S. Embassy or Consulate, if abroad. To find your nearest acceptance facility, visit our web site or contact the National Passport Information Center.

See Reverse Side for Detailed Information

PLEASE DETACH AND RETAIN THIS INSTRUCTION SHEET FOR YOUR RECORDS

DS-11
08-2002

1. PROOF OF U.S. CITIZENSHIP
   a. **APPLICANTS BORN IN THE UNITED STATES:** Submit previous U.S. passport or certified birth certificate. A birth certificate must include your given name and surname, date and place of birth, date the birth record was filed, and the seal or other certification of the official custodian of such records.
      (1) If the birth certificate was filed more than 1 year after the birth: It is acceptable if it is supported by evidence described in the next paragraph.
      (2) If no birth record exists: Submit registrar's notice to that effect. Also submit an early baptismal or circumcision certificate, hospital birth record, early census, school, or family Bible records, newspaper or insurance files, or notarized affidavits of persons having knowledge of your birth (preferably in addition to at least one record listed above). Evidence should include your given name and surname, date and place of birth, and seal or other certification of the issuing office (if customary) and signature of issuing official.

   b. **APPLICANTS BORN OUTSIDE THE UNITED STATES:** Submit a previous U.S. passport, Certificate of Naturalization, Certificate of Citizenship, Consular Report of Birth Abroad, or evidence described below.
      (1) If You Claim Citizenship Through Naturalization of Parent(s): Submit the Certificate(s) of Naturalization of your parent(s), your foreign birth certificate, and proof of your admission to the United States for permanent residence.
      (2) If You Claim Citizenship Through Birth Abroad to One U.S. Citizen Parent: Submit a Consular Report of Birth (Form FS-240), Certification of Birth (Form DS-1350 or FS-545), or your foreign birth certificate, proof of citizenship of your parent, and an affidavit of your U.S. citizen parent(s) showing all periods and places of residence or physical presence in the United States and abroad before your birth.
      (3) If You Claim Citizenship Through Birth Abroad to Two U.S. Citizen Parents: Submit a Consular Report of Birth (Form FS-240), Certification of Birth (Form DS-1350 or FS-545), or your foreign birth certificate, parent's marriage certificate, proof of citizenship of your parents and an affidavit of your U.S. citizen parent(s) showing all periods and places of residence or physical presence in the United States and abroad before your birth.
      (4) If You Claim Citizenship Through Adoption by a U.S. Citizen Parent(s): Submit evidence of your permanent residence status, full and final adoption, and your U.S. citizen parent(s) evidence of legal and physical custody.

2. PROOF OF IDENTITY
   You must establish your identity to the acceptance agent. You may submit items such as the following containing your signature AND physical description or photograph that is a good likeness of you: previous U.S. passport, Certificate of Naturalization, Certificate of Citizenship, driver's license (not temporary or learner's license), or government (Federal, State, municipal) employee identification card or pass. Temporary or altered documents are not acceptable

   IF YOU CANNOT PROVE YOUR IDENTITY as stated above, you must appear with an IDENTIFYING WITNESS who is a U.S. Citizen or permanent residnet alien who has known you for at least 2 years. Your witness must prove his or her identity and complete and sign an Affidavit of Identifying Witness (Form DS-71) before the acceptance agent. You must also submit some identification of your own.

3. TWO PHOTOGRAPHS
   Submit two identical photographs of you alone, sufficiently recent to be a good likeness of you (normally taken within the last 6 months), and 2 x 2 inches in size. The image size measured from the bottom of the chin to the top of the head (including hair) should not be less than 1 inch and not more than 1-3/8 inches. Photographs must be clear, front view, full face, taken in normal street attire without a hat or dark glasses, and printed on thin paper with a plain light (white or off-white) background. They may be in color or black and white. They must be capable of withstanding a mounting temperature of 225° Fahrenheit (107° Celsius). Photographs retouched so that your appearance is changed are unacceptable. Snapshots, most vending machine prints, and magazine or full-length photographs are unacceptable. Digitized photos must meet the previously stated qualifications and will be accepted for use at the discretion of Passport Services. (Visit our website for details)

4. FEES
   a. If you are 16 years of age or older: The passport processing fee is $55. In addition, a fee of $30 is charged for the execution of the application. Your passport will be valid for 10 years from the date of issue except where limited by the Secretary of State to a shorter period.
   b. If you are 15 years of age or younger: The passport processing fee is $40. In addition, a fee of $30 is charged for the execution of the application. Your passport will be valid for 5 years from the date of issue except where limited by the Secretary of State to a shorter period.

BY LAW, THE PASSPORT PROCESSING AND EXECUTION FEES ARE NON-REFUNDABLE

- **The passport processing and execution fees may be paid in one of the following forms:** Checks (personal, certified, traveler's), major credit card (Visa, Master Card, American Express, and Discover), bank draft or cashier's check, money order (U.S. Postal, international, currency exchange), or if abroad, the foreign currency equivalent, or a check drawn on a U.S. bank. All fees should be payable to the "U.S. Department of State" (except the $30 execution fee when applying at a designated acceptance facility), or if abroad, the appropriate Embassy or Consulate. NOTE: Some designated acceptance facilities do not accept credit cards as a form of payment.

- **For faster processing,** you may request Expedited Service. Expedited requests will be processed in three workdays from receipt at a Passport Agency. The additional fee for expedited service is $60. Expedited Service is available only in the United States.

- If you desire SPECIAL POSTAGE SERVICE (overnight mail, special delivery, etc.), include the appropriate postage fee with your payment.

- An additional $45 fee will be charged when, upon your request, the U.S. Department of State verifies issuance of a previous U.S. passport or Consular Report of Birth Abroad because you are unable to submit evidence of U.S. citizenship.

- For applicants with U.S. Government or military authorization for no-fee passports **no fees are charged, except the execution fee when applying at a designated acceptance facility.**

U.S. Department of State

APPLICATION FOR ☐ U.S. PASSPORT ☐ REGISTRATION
(Type or print all capital letters in blue or black ink in white areas only)

1. NAME (First and Middle)

LAST

2. MAIL PASSPORT TO: STREET / RFD # OR P.O. BOX **APT. #**

CITY **STATE**

ZIP CODE **COUNTRY / IN CARE OF (if applicable)**

☐ 5 Yr. ☐ 10 Yr. Issue Date _____

☐ R ☐ D ☐ O ☐ DP

End. # _____ Exp. _____

3. SEX ☐ M ☐ F

4. PLACE OF BIRTH (City & State or City & Country)

5. DATE OF BIRTH Month Day Year

6. SOCIAL SECURITY NUMBER (SEE FEDERAL TAX LAW NOTICE ON PAGE 4)

7. HEIGHT Feet Inches | **8. HAIR COLOR** | **9. EYE COLOR** | **10. HOME TELEPHONE** | **11. BUSINESS TELEPHONE** | **12. OCCUPATION**

13. PERMANENT ADDRESS (DO NOT LIST P.O. BOX) Street/R.F.D.# City State

14. FATHER'S FULL NAME Last First | BIRTHPLACE | BIRTHDATE | U.S. CITIZEN ☐ Yes ☐ No | **15. MOTHER'S FULL MAIDEN NAME** Last First | BIRTHPLACE | BIRTHDATE | U.S. CITIZEN ☐ Yes ☐ No

16. HAVE YOU EVER BEEN MARRIED? ☐ Yes ☐ No | **SPOUSE'S OR FORMER SPOUSE'S FULL NAME AT BIRTH** | BIRTHPLACE | BIRTHDATE | U.S. CITIZEN ☐ Yes ☐ No

DATE OF MOST RECENT MARRIAGE Month Day Year | **WIDOWED/DIVORCED?** ☐ Yes Give Date Month Day Year ☐ No | **17. OTHER NAMES YOU HAVE USED** (1) (2)

18. HAVE YOU EVER BEEN ISSUED A U.S. PASSPORT? ☐ Yes ☐ No **IF YES, COMPLETE NEXT LINE AND SUBMIT PASSPORT IF AVAILABLE.**

NAME IN WHICH ISSUED | MOST RECENT PASSPORT NUMBER | APPROXIMATE ISSUE DATE Month Day Year

DISPOSITION ☐ Submitted ☐ Stolen ☐ Lost ☐ Other _____

It is necessary to submit a statement with an application for a new passport when a previous valid or potentially valid passport cannot be presented. The statement must set forth in detail why the previous passport cannot be presented. Use Form DS-64.

STAPLE 2" x 2" STAPLE

SUBMIT TWO RECENT IDENTICAL PHOTOS

19. EMERGENCY CONTACT. If you wish, you may supply the name, address and telephone number of a person not traveling with you to be contacted in case of emergency.

NAME

STREET

CITY STATE ZIP CODE TELEPHONE

20. TRAVEL PLANS (not mandatory) Month Day Year

Date of Trip

Length of Trip

COUNTRIES TO BE VISITED:

21. STOP. DO NOT SIGN APPLICATION UNTIL REQUESTED TO DO SO BY PERSON ADMINISTERING OATH. I have not, since acquiring United States citizenship, performed any of the acts listed under "Acts or Conditions" on the reverse of this application form (unless explanatory statement is attached). I solemnly swear (or affirm) that the statements made on this application are true and the photograph attached is a true likeness of me.

X _____
Applicant's Signature - age 14 or older

X _____
Father's/Legal Guardian's Signature (if identifying minor)

X _____
Mother's/Legal Guardian's Signature (if identifying minor)

22. FOR ACCEPTANCE AGENT'S USE
Subscribed and sworn to (affirmed) before me Month Day Year

_____
(Signature of person authorized to accept application)

☐ Clerk of Court; Location _____
☐ PASSPORT Agent
☐ Postal Employee
☐ (Vice) Consul USA

23a. Applicant's or Father's Identifying Documents
☐ Driver's License ☐ Passport ☐ Other (Specify) _____
Issue Date: | Expiration Date: | Place of Issue:
Name _____ ID No. _____

23b. Mother's Identifying Documents
☐ Driver's License ☐ Passport ☐ Other (Specify) _____
Issue Date: | Expiration Date: | Place of Issue:
Name _____ ID No. _____

24. FOR ISSUING OFFICE USE ONLY (Applicant's evidence of citizenship)
☐ Birth Certificate ☐ SR ☐ CR ☐ City Filed/Issued:
☐ Passport Bearer's Name:
☐ Report of Birth:
☐ Naturalization/Citizenship Cert. No: Issued:
☐ Other:
☐ Seen & Returned:
☐ Attached:

APPLICATION APPROVAL

25. FEE _____ EXEC. _____ EF _____ OTHER _____

DS-11

OMB No. 1405-0004 Expires: 03/31/2005 Estimated Burden - 20 Minutes

Page 3 of 4

APPLICATION FOR U.S. PASSPORT OR REGISTRATION

FEDERAL TAX LAW

26 U.S.C. 6039E (Internal Revenue Code) requires a passport applicant to provide his or her name and social security number. If you have not been issued a social security number, enter zeros in box #6. The U.S. Department of State must provide this information to the Internal Revenue Service routinely. Any applicant who fails to provide the required information is subject to a **$500** penalty enforced by the IRS. All questions on this matter should be referred to the nearest IRS office.

ACTS OR CONDITIONS

(If any of the below-mentioned acts or conditions has been performed by or apply to the applicant, the portion which applies should be lined out, and a supplementary explanatory statement under oath (or affirmation) by the applicant should be attached and made a part of this application.) I have not, since acquiring United States citizenship, been naturalized as a citizen of a foreign state; taken an oath or made an affirmation or other formal declaration of allegiance to a foreign state; entered or served in the armed forces of a foreign state; accepted or performed the duties of any office, post, or employment under the government of a foreign state or political subdivision thereof; made a formal renunciation of nationality either in the United States, or before a diplomatic or consular officer of the United States in a foreign state; or been convicted by a court or court martial of competent jurisdiction of committing any act of treason against, or attempting by force to overthrow, or bearing arms against, the United States, or conspiring to overthrow, put down, or to destroy by force, the Government of the United States.

WARNING: False statements made knowingly and willfully in passport applications or in affidavits or other supporting documents submitted therewith are punishable by fine and/or imprisonment under provisions of 18 U.S.C. 1001 and/or 18 U.S.C. 1542. Alteration or mutilation of a passport issued pursuant to this application is punishable by fine and/or imprisonment under the provisions of 18 U.S.C. 1543. The use of a passport in violation of the restrictions contained therein or of the passport regulations is punishable by fine and/or imprisonment under 18 U.S.C. 1544. All statements and documents submitted are subject to verification.

PRIVACY ACT AND PAPERWORK REDUCTION ACT STATEMENTS

AUTHORITIES: The information solicited on this form is requested pursuant to provisions in Titles 8, 18, and 22 of the United States Code, whether or not codified, including specifically 22 U.S.C. 211a, 212, and 213, and all regulations issued pursuant to Executive Order 11295 (August 5, 1966), including Part 51, Title 22, Code of Federal Regulations (CFR). Also, as noted, 26 U.S.C. 6039E.

PURPOSE: The primary purpose for soliciting the information is to establish citizenship, identity, and entitlement to issuance of a U.S. passport. The information may also be used in connection with issuing other travel documents or evidence of citizenship, and in furtherance of the Secretary's responsibility for the protection of U.S. nationals abroad.

ROUTINE USES: The information solicited on this form may be made available as a routine use to other government agencies, to assist the U.S. Department of State in adjudicating passport applications, and for law enforcement and administration purposes. It may also be disclosed pursuant to court order. The information may be made available to foreign government agencies to fulfill passport control and immigration duties or to investigate or prosecute violations of law. The information may also be made available to private U.S. citizen 'wardens' designated by U.S. Embassies and Consulates.

Failure to provide the information requested on this form may result in the denial of a United States passport, related document, or service to the individual seeking such passport, document, or service.

Public reporting burden for this collection of information is estimated to average 20 minutes per response, including time required for searching existing data sources, gathering the necessary data, providing the information required, and reviewing the final collection. You do not have to provide the information unless this collection displays a currently valid OMB number. Send comments on the accuracy of this estimate of the burden and recommendations for reducing it to: U.S. Department of State (A/RPS/DIR) Washington, DC 20520.

U.S. Department of State
APPLICATION FOR U.S. PASSPORT BY MAIL

PLEASE DETACH AND RETAIN THIS INSTRUCTION SHEET FOR YOUR RECORDS.

Date of Application:

CAN I USE THIS FORM?

Complete this checklist to determine your eligibility to use this form.

1. I can submit my most recent U.S. passport. ☐ Yes ☐ No

2. I was at least 16 years old when my most recent U.S. passport was issued. ☐ Yes ☐ No

3. I was issued my most recent U.S. passport less than 15 years ago. ☐ Yes ☐ No

4. I use the same name as on my most recent U.S. passport; OR, I have had my name changed by marriage or court order and can submit proper documentation to reflect my name change. ☐ Yes ☐ No

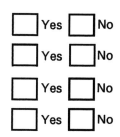

If you answered NO to any of the four statements above, <u>STOP</u> - You cannot use this form!!!
You must apply on application form DS-11 by making a personal appearance before a passport agent, postal clerk or clerk of court authorized to accept passport applications.

CAREFULLY FOLLOW THE INSTRUCTIONS ON THE REVERSE OF THIS PAGE
INCOMPLETE OR UNACCEPTABLE APPLICATIONS WILL DELAY THE ISSUANCE OF YOUR PASSPORT.

<u>**FOR INFORMATION, QUESTIONS, AND INQUIRIES:**</u> Please visit our website at **travel.state.gov** <u>OR</u> contact the National Passport Information Center at 1-900-225-5674, For TDD: 1-900-225-7778; or for credit card users: 1-888-362-8668, For TDD: 1-888-498-3648.

WHAT DO I NEED TO SEND WITH THE APPLICATION FORM?

1. Your most recent U.S. passport.
2. A marriage certificate or court order if your name has changed.
3. Passport processing fee of $55.
4. Two recent identical photographs with a light, plain background and taken within the last 6 months.

For detailed information on the items to be included, see below.

1. **YOUR MOST RECENT U.S. PASSPORT.** Issued at age 16 or older in your current name (or see item #2 below) and issued within the past 15 years. If your passport is damaged, you must apply on the DS-11 application form as specified below.

2. **A MARRIAGE CERTIFICATE OR COURT ORDER.** If the name you are currently using differs from the name on your most recent passport, you must submit a marriage certificate or court order showing the change of name. The name change document MUST bear the official seal of the issuing authority. Uncertified copies or notarized documents cannot be accepted. All documents will be returned to you with your passport. If you are unable to document your name change in this manner, you must apply on the DS-11 application form by making a personal appearance at (1) a passport agency; (2) any clerk of a Federal or State court of record or judge or clerk of a probate court accepting passport applications; or (3) a designated municipal or county official, or a designated postal employee at an authorized post office.

3. **THE PASSPORT PROCESSING FEE OF $55.** Enclose the $55 passport processing fee in the form of a personal check or money order.

MAKE CHECKS PAYABLE TO "U.S. DEPARTMENT OF STATE", THE FULL NAME AND DATE OF BIRTH OF THE APPLICANT MUST BE TYPED OR PRINTED ON THE FRONT OF THE CHECK. DO NOT SEND CASH. Passport Services cannot be responsible for cash sent through the mail. By law, the passport processing fee is non-refundable.

For faster processing, you may request Expedited Service. Expedited requests will be processed in 3 workdays from receipt at a Passport Agency. The additional fee for Expedited Service is $60. Expedited Service is available only in the United States.

If you desire **SPECIAL POSTAGE SERVICE** (registered, special delivery, etc.), include the appropriate postage fee on the check.

4. **TWO RECENT IDENTICAL PHOTOGRAPHS.** The photographs must have been taken within the past six months and be a good likeness of you. The photographs must be clear with a full front view of your face and taken on a light (white or off-white) background. Photographs may be in color or black and white and the image size must correspond to the dimensions on the diagram on page 3 of this form. Photographs must be taken in normal street attire, showing you without headcovering unless a signed statement is submitted that the headcovering is worn daily for religious or medical reasons. Dark glasses may not be worn in passport photographs unless a doctor's statement is submitted supporting the wearing of dark glasses for medical reasons.

MAIL THIS FORM TO:	DELIVERY - Other Than U.S. Postal Service	FOR INQUIRIES CONTACT:
National Passport Center P.O. Box 371971 Pittsburgh, PA. 15250-7971	Passport Services Lockbox Attn: Passport Supervisor, 371971 500 Ross Street, Room 154-0670 Pittsburgh, PA. 15250-9971	National Passport Information Center 1-900-225-5674 For TDD: 1-900-225-7778 For Credit Card Users: 1-888-362-8668 For TDD: 1-888-498-3648

NOTICE TO APPLICANTS RESIDING ABROAD

United States citizens residing abroad CANNOT submit this form to the Passport Facility listed above. Such applicants should contact the nearest United States Embassy or Consulate for procedures to be followed when applying overseas.

NOTICE TO APPLICANTS FOR OFFICIAL, DIPLOMATIC, OR NO-FEE PASSPORTS

You may use this application if you meet all of the provisions listed above. Submit your U.S. Government or military authorization for a no-fee passport with your application in lieu of the passport fee. CONSULT YOUR SPONSORING AGENCY FOR INSTRUCTIONS ON PROPER ROUTING PROCEDURES BEFORE FORWARDING THIS APPLICATION. Your completed passport will be released to your sponsoring agency for forwarding to you.

PLEASE DETACH AND RETAIN THIS INSTRUCTION SHEET FOR YOUR RECORDS.

U.S. Department of State
APPLICATION FOR U.S. PASSPORT BY MAIL

TYPE OR PRINT IN BLUE OR BLACK INK IN WHITE AREAS ONLY   USE BLOCK LETTERS/NUMBERS

NAME | FIRST | MIDDLE

LAST

MAIL PASSPORT TO

STREET / RFD #
OR P.O. BOX | APT. #

CITY | STATE | ZIP CODE

IN CARE OF *(IF APPLICABLE)*

Issue Date _____

R   D   O   DP

End. # _____   Exp. _____

FOLD

SEX
☐ Male
☐ Female

PLACE OF BIRTH
City & State or City & Country

DATE OF BIRTH
Month | Day | Year

SOCIAL SECURITY NUMBER
(SEE FEDERAL TAX LAW NOTICE ON REVERSE SIDE)

HEIGHT
Feet | Inches

HAIR COLOR

EYE COLOR

HOME TELEPHONE

BUSINESS TELEPHONE

NOTE: Most recent passport MUST be enclosed!

U.S. PASSPORT NUMBER

ISSUE DATE
Month | Day | Year

PLACE OF ISSUANCE

OCCUPATION *(Not Mandatory)*

DEPARTURE DATE

TRAVEL PLANS *(Not Mandatory)*
COUNTRIES TO BE VISITED

LENGTH OF STAY *(Not Mandatory)*

PERMANENT ADDRESS (Do not list P.O. Box)

STREET / R.F.D. # | CITY | STATE | ZIP CODE

Staple 2" x 2" Staple

Staple 2" x 2" Staple

SUBMIT TWO RECENT IDENTICAL PHOTOS WITH LIGHT, PLAIN BACKGROUND

EMERGENCY CONTACT. If you wish, you may supply the name, address, and telephone number of a person not traveling with you to be contacted in case of emergency.

NAME

STREET

CITY | STATE | ZIP CODE

TELEPHONE | RELATIONSHIP

OATH AND SIGNATURE

I have not, since acquiring United States Citizenship, performed any of the acts listed under "Acts or Conditions" on the reverse of this application form (unless explanatory statement is attached.)

I solemnly swear (or affirm) that the statements made on this application are true and the photograph attached is a true likeness of me, and that I have not been issued a passport subsequent to the one submitted herein.

NOTE: APPLICANT MUST SIGN & DATE

SIGNATURE | DATE

FOLD

DO NOT WRITE BELOW THIS SPACE - FOR PASSPORT SERVICES USE ONLY - DO NOT WRITE BELOW THIS SPACE

Application Approval

Evidence of Name Change
☐ Marriage Cert.   ☐ Court Order

Date _____
Place _____
From _____
To _____

Fees

OMB No. 1405-0020   Expires: 03/31/2005   Estimated Burden   15 Minutes   (See Page 4)

DS-82

In accordance with 5 CFR 1320 5(b), persons are not required to respond to the collection of this information unless this form displays a currently valid OMB control number.

APPLICATION FOR U.S. PASSPORT BY MAIL

FEDERAL TAX LAW

26 U.S.C. 6039E (Internal Revenue Code) requires a passport applicant to provide his or her name and social security number. If you have not been issued a social security number, enter zeros in the appropriate boxes. The U.S. Department of State must provide this information to the Internal Revenue Service routinely. Any applicant who fails to provide the required information is subject to a **$500** penalty enforced by the IRS. All questions on this matter should be referred to the nearest IRS office.

ACTS OR CONDITIONS

(If any of the below-mentioned acts or conditions has been performed by or apply to the applicant, the portion which applies should be lined out, and a supplementary explanatory statement under oath (or affirmation) by the applicant should be attached and made a part of this application.) I have not, since acquiring United States citizenship, been naturalized as a citizen of a foreign state; taken an oath or made an affirmation or other formal declaration of allegiance to a foreign state; entered or served in the armed forces of a foreign state; accepted or performed the duties of any office, post, or employment under the government of a foreign state or political subdivision thereof; made a formal renunciation of nationality either in the United States, or before a diplomatic or consular officer of the United States in a foreign state; or been convicted by a court or court martial of competent jurisdiction of committing any act of treason against, or attempting by force to overthrow, or bearing arms against, the United States, or conspiring to overthrow, put down, or to destroy by force, the Government of the United States.

WARNING: False statements made knowingly and willfully in passport applications or in affidavits or other supporting documents submitted therewith are punishable by fine and/or imprisonment under provisions of 18 U.S.C. 1001 and/or 18 U.S.C. 1542. Alteration or mutilation of a passport issued pursuant to this application is punishable by fine and/or imprisonment under the provisions of 18 U.S.C. 1543. The use of a passport in violation of the restrictions contained therein or of the passport regulations is punishable by fine and/or imprisonment under 18 U.S.C. 1544. All statements and documents submitted are subject to verification.

PRIVACY ACT AND PAPERWORK REDUCTION ACT STATEMENTS

AUTHORITIES: The information solicited on this form is requested pursuant to provisions in Titles 8, 18, and 22 of the United States Code, whether or not codified, including specifically 22 U.S.C. 211a, 212, and 213, and all regulations issued pursuant to Executive Order 11295 (August 5, 1966), including Part 51, Title 22, Code of Federal Regulations (CFR). Also, as noted, 26 U.S.C. 6039E.

PURPOSE: The primary purpose for soliciting the information is to establish citizenship, identity, and entitlement to issuance of a U.S. passport. The information may also be used in connection with issuing other travel documents or evidence of citizenship, and in furtherance of the Secretary's responsibility for the protection of U.S. nationals abroad.

ROUTINE USES: The information solicited on this form may be made available as a routine use to other government agencies, to assist the U.S. Department of State in adjudicating passport applications, and for law enforcement and administration purposes. It may also be disclosed pursuant to court order. The information may be made available to foreign government agencies to fulfill passport control and immigration duties or to investigate or prosecute violations of law. The information may also be made available to private U.S. citizen 'wardens' designated by U.S. Embassies and Consulates.

Failure to provide the information requested on this form may result in the denial of a United States passport, related document, or service to the individual seeking such passport, document or service.

Public reporting burden for this collection of information is estimated to average 15 minutes per response, including time required for searching existing data sources, gathering the necessary data, providing the information required, and reviewing the final collection. You do not have to provide the information unless this collection displays a currently valid OMB number. Send comments on the accuracy of this estimate of the burden and recommendations for reducing it to: U.S. Department of State (A/RPS/DIR) Washington, DC 20520.

RESUME WORKSHEET

Full Name: _____

Address: _____

_____

Phone: _____

(V/TDD)

E-mail: _____ (optional)

Professional Objective: _____

_____

_____ .

Degrees/Education:

Name of Institution: _____

City and State: _____

Degree and Year: _____

Name of Institution: _____

City and State: _____

Degree and Year: _____

-OR-

Name of High School: _____

City and State: _____

Type of Diploma: _____

Special Emphasis: _____

Year Graduated: _____

Name of College or University Where You Took Classes: _____

_____

City and State: _____

Special Emphasis: _____

Total Number of Credits Earned: _____

Dates Attended: _____

Certifications: (LIST ALL USING THIS SAME FORMAT)

Name of Certification: _____

Acronym: _____

Certified By (Name and Acronym): _____

Year Awarded: _____

Work Experience: (List most recent first)

Title: _____

Company or Agency: _____

Division or Department: _____

City and State: _____

Dates Employed: _____

Duties and Responsibilities: _____

_____

_____

_____

_____

_____

Title: _____

Company or Agency: _____

Division or Department: _____

City and State: _____

Dates Employed: _____

Duties and Responsibilities: _____

_____

_____

_____

_____

_____

References furnished upon request

REFERENCE WORKSHEET

Name: _____

Title: _____

Business/Agency: _____

Address: _____

Telephone/Fax: _____

E-mail: _____

Contacted re: Permission: _____ Date: _____ Letter on File: _____

Name: _____

Title: _____

Business/Agency: _____

Address: _____

Telephone/Fax: _____

E-mail: _____

Contacted re: Permission: _____ Date: _____ Letter on File: _____

Name: _____

Title: _____

Business/Agency: _____

Address: _____

Telephone/Fax: _____

E-mail: _____

Contacted re: Permission: _____ Date: _____ Letter on File: _____

Name: _____

Title: _____

Business/Agency: _____

Address: _____

Telephone/Fax: _____

E-mail: _____

Contacted re: Permission: _____ Date: _____ Letter on File: _____

ASSIGNMENT INTAKE INFORMATION

Today's Date & Time: _____

Caller: _____ Position: _____

Company/Agency Representing: _____

Telephone: _____ Fax: _____ E-mail:_____

ASSIGNMENT INFORMATION

Date(s): _____ Time(s): _____

Address: _____

Directions: _____

_____

Parking Provided: _____Yes _____ No   Where to Park: _____

Site Contact Person: _____ Telephone: _____

Person(s) Interpreting For: _____

Sign Language Preferences: _____

Description of Assignment: _____

_____

Partner: _____

BILLING

Cancellation

Price Quoted: _____ Per: _____ Policy: _____

PAYMENT EXPECTED IN 30 CALENDAR DAYS UNLESS OTHERWISE STATED

LATE FEE POLICY: $_____ PER 30 DAYS DELINQUENT

_____ Send Invoice to: _____

_____

Contact: _____ Telephone: _____

_____ Payment: On-Site Pickup   Location: _____

_____

Contact: _____ Telephone: _____

ASSIGNMENT COMPLETION DATE: _____

_____ ON-SITE PAYMENT RECEIVED   INVOICE MAILED: _____

PAYMENT RECEIVED:

Date:_____ Check#: _____

Amount: _____

TRAVEL/MILEAGE RECORD

Date	From	To	Odometer Reading Start	Finish	Miles	Gas	Parking

TOTALS: MILEAGE _____ **PARKING $** _____

ESTIMATED QUARTERLY TAXES WORKSHEET

Estimate the amount of money you will earn (gross) this year:
Gross = (A) $_____

APPROXIMATE PERCENTAGES

Federal Taxes = _____% of gross

Social Security Taxes = _____% of gross
(to be added to Federal Tax payments)

State Taxes = _____% of gross
(percent varies from state to state)

Approximation Formula for Estimated Quarterly Taxes Example:

"QUARTERLIES":

Federal Taxes: _____ % of (A) $_____ = $ _____ / 4 = $ _____ *

SS Taxes: _____ % of (A) $ _____ = $ _____ / 4 = $ _____ *

*Add Federal and SS "Quarterlies" to make the total Estimated Federal Tax Quarterly payment.

Total Estimated Federal Tax Quarterly Payment = $_____

PLUS

State Taxes: _____ % of (A) $_____ = $_____ / 4 = $_____

TOTAL AMOUNT DUE EACH QUARTER: $_____

Internal Revenue Service Centers

- Florida, Georgia, North Carolina, South Carolina,
West Virginia:
  Internal Revenue Service Center
  Atlanta, GA 39901-0002

- New Jersey, New York (New York City and counties of Nassau,
Rockland, Suffolk, and Westchester):
  Internal Revenue Service Center
  Holtsville, NY 00501-0002

- New York (all other counties), Massachusetts, Michigan,
Rhode Island:
  Internal Revenue Service Center
  Andover, MA 05501-0002

- Illinois, Iowa, Kansas, Minnesota, Missouri, Oklahoma, Utah,
Wisconsin:
  Internal Revenue Service Center
  Kansas City, MO 64999-0002

- Connecticut, Delaware, District of Columbia, Indiana, Maine,
Maryland, New Hampshire, Pennsylvania, Vermont:
  Internal Revenue Service Center
  Philadelphia, PA 19255-0002

- Ohio:
  Internal Revenue Service Center
  Cincinnati, OH 45999-0002

- Arizona, Colorado, Idaho, Montana, New Mexico, Texas,
Wyoming:
  Internal Revenue Service Center
  Austin, TX 73301-0002

- Nebraska, North Dakota, South Dakota, Washington:
  Internal Revenue Service Center
  Ogden, UT 84201-0002

- Alaska, California, Hawaii, Nevada, Oregon:
  Internal Revenue Service Center
  Fresno, CA 93888-0002

- Alabama, Arkansas, Kentucky, Louisiana, Mississippi,
Tennessee, Virginia:
  Internal Revenue Service Center
  Memphis, TN 37501-0002

- All APO and FPO addresses, American Samoa, non-permanent residents of Guam or the Virgin Islands*, Puerto Rico (or if excluding income under Internal Revenue Code section 933), a foreign country: U.S. citizens and those filing Form 2555, 2555-EZ, or 4563:

  > Internal Revenue Service Center
  > Philadelphia, PA 19255-0215
  > USA

- Permanent residents of Guam should use:

  > Department of Revenue and Taxation
  > Government of Guam
  > P.O. Box 23607
  > GMF, GU 96921

- *Permanent residents of Virgin Islands should use:

  > V.I. Bureau of Internal Revenue
  > 9601 Estate Thomas
  > Charlotte Amalie
  > St. Thomas, VI 00802

STATE TAX INFORMATION

ALABAMA
Alabama Department of Revenue
50 N. Ripley
Montgomery, Alabama
36132-7123
(334) 242-1170
www.ador.state.al.us

ALASKA
Alaska Department of Revenue
State Office Building
333 Willoughby Ave., 11th Floor
P.O. Box 110400
Juneau, AK 99811-0400
Tel: (907) 465-2300
Fax: (907) 465-2389
www.revenue.state.ak.us

ARIZONA
Arizona Department of Revenue
1600 W. Monroe
Phoenix, Arizona 85007
(602) 255-3381
(800) 352-4090 Statewide (outside
of Maricopa County)
www.revenue.state.az.us

ARKANSAS
Income Tax Administration
Room 112, Ledbetter Building
7th & Wolfe Streets
Little Rock, AR
(501) 682-1100
Mailing address:
P.O. Box 8110, Little Rock, AR
72203
www.state.ar.us/dfa

CALIFORNIA
Franchise Tax Board
P.O. Box 942840
Sacramento, CA 94240-0040
(800) 852-5711 - select option 5 for
operator assistance
TTY: (800) 822-6268 (follow
prompts)
www.ftb.ca.gov

COLORADO
Colorado Department of Revenue
1375 Sherman St.
Denver CO 80261-0005
(303) 238-SERV (7378)
www.revenue.state.co.us

CONNECTICUT
Department of Revenue Services
Taxpayer Services Division
25 Sigourney Street
Hartford, CT 06106-5032

(800) 382-9463 (in-state) or
(860) 297-5962
TTY: (860) 297-4911
www.drs.state.ct.us

DELAWARE
Carvel State Office Building
820 N. French Street
Wilmington, DE 19801
(800) 292-7826 (Delaware only)
Monday through Friday 8:00 a.m.
to 4:30 p.m. Eastern Time
www.state.de.us/revenue /
index.htm

DISTRICT OF COLUMBIA
Office of the Chief Financial Officer
1350 Pennsylvania Avenue, NW,
Room 209
Washington, DC 20004
(202) 727-2476
www.cfo.dc.gov/main.asp

FLORIDA
For a written response to questions, write:
Tax Information Services
Florida Department of Revenue
1379 Bloutstown Hwy.
Tallahassee, FL 32304-2716
Mail returns and payments to:
Florida Department of Revenue
5050 W. Tennessee St.
Tallahassee, FL 32399-0100
(800) 352-3671 (in Florida only)
(850) 488-6800 Monday through
Friday, 8 a.m. to 7 p.m., ET
TTY: (800) 367-8331 or
(850) 922-1115
www.state.fl.us/dor

GEORGIA
Georgia Department of Revenue
1800 Century Center Blvd., NE
Atlanta, GA 30345-3205
(404) 417-2300
www2.state.ga.US/Departments/
DOR

HAWAII
Department of Taxation
P.O. Box 833
Hilo, HI 96721-0833
(808) 974-6321
Fax: (808) 974-6300
TTY: (808) 587-1418 or
(800) 887-8974
www.state.hi.us/tax/tax.html

IDAHO
Idaho State Tax Commission
PO Box 56
Boise ID 83756-0056
(800) 972-7660
TTY: Use Idaho Relay Service
(800) 377-3529
www2.state.id.us/tax/index.html

ILLINOIS
Willard Ice Building
101 West Jefferson Street
Springfield, IL 62702
(800) 732-8866 or
(217) 782-3336 for Taxpayer Assistance
TTY: (800) 544-5304
Mailing address:
Illinois Department of Revenue
Springfield, IL 62719-0001
www.revenue.state.il.us

INDIANA
Department of Revenue
100 N Senate Ave.
Indianapolis, IN 46204
(317) 233-4018
TTY: (317) 232-4952
www.ai.org/dor/index.html

IOWA
Iowa Department of Revenue and
Finance
Taxpayer Services
P.O. Box 10457
Des Moines, IA 50306-0457
(515) 281-3114 from Des Moines or
out of state;
(800) 367-3388 from elsewhere
in Iowa or Rock Island, Moline or
Omaha
www.state.ia.us/tax

KANSAS
Kansas Department of Revenue
Docking State Office Building
915 SW Harrison Street, 1st Floor
Topeka, KS 66625-1712
(785) 368-8222 (Topeka) or
(877) 526-7738 (Toll-free)
7:00 AM - 5:45 PM Monday
through Friday
TTY: (785) 296-6461
www.ksrevenue.org

KENTUCKY
Kentucky Revenue Cabinet
200 Fair Oaks Lane
Frankfort, KY 40620
(502) 564-4581
revenue.state.ky.us

LOUISIANA
Louisiana Department of Revenue
P.O. Box 201
Baton Rouge, LA 70821-0201
(224) 219-2113
TTY: (225) 219-2114
www.rev.state.la.us

MAINE
Maine Revenue Services
24 State House Station
Augusta, ME 04333-0024
(207) 287-2076
(207) 624-9694 Fax
TTY: (907) 287-4477
www.state.me.us/revenue

MARYLAND
Comptroller of Maryland
Revenue Administration Division
Annapolis, Maryland 21411-0001
(410) 260-7980 from Central
Maryland
(800) MD-TAXES from elsewhere
www.comp.state.md.us

MASSACHUSETTS
51 Sleeper Street
Boston, MA 02205
(617) 887-MDOR (6367)
(800)392-6089 in Maine
Mailing address:
PO Box 7010, Boston, MA 02204
TTY: (617) 887-6140
www.dor.state.ma.us

MICHIGAN
Michigan Department of Treasury
Lansing, Michigan 48922
(517) 373-3200
(800) 487-7000
TTY: (517) 373-9419
www.michigan.gov/treasury

MINNESOTA
Minnesota Department of Revenue
Mail Station 5510
St. Paul, MN 55146-5510
Questions:
Minnesota Individual Income Tax
St. Paul, MN 55145-0010
(651) 296-3781
TTY: Call 711 for Minnesota Relay
www.taxes.state.mn.us/cont.html

MISSISSIPPI
Mississippi State Tax Commission
1577 Springridge Rd.
Raymond, MS 39154-9602
(601) 923-7000
Mailing address:
P.O. Box 1033, Jackson, MS
39215-1033
www.mstc.state.ms.us

MISSOURI
Department of Revenue
P.O. Box 329
Jefferson City, MO 65107-0329
(573) 751-3505 Monday through
Friday,
7:45 AM to 4:45 PM CST
TTY: (800) 735-2966
dor.state.mo.us

MONTANA
Department of Revenue
P.O. Box 5805
Helena, MT 59604-5805
(406) 444-6900
TTY: (406) 444-2830
www.state.mt.us/revenue/css/
default.asp

NEBRASKA
Nebraska Department of Revenue
301 Centennial Mall South
PO Box 94818
Lincoln, NE 68509-4818
(800) 742-7474 (NE & IA)
or (402)471-5729
TTY: (800) 382-9309
www.revenue.state.ne.us

NEVADA
Department of Taxation
Nevada does not impose a personal income tax nor corporate
tax. No filing is required.
tax.state.nv.us

NEW HAMPSHIRE
Department of Revenue Administration
45 Chenell Drive
PO Box 457
Concord, NH 03302-0457
(603) 271-2191
TTY: (800) 735-2964 (NH Relay)
www.state.nh.us/revenue

NEW JERSEY
New Jersey Division of Taxation
Office of Information and Publica-
tions
PO Box 281
Trenton, NJ 08695-0281

(609) 292-6400
TTY: (800) 286-6613 (within NJ,
NY, PA, DE, and MD);
(609) 984-7300 (anywhere)
www.state.nj.us/treasury/taxation

NEW MEXICO
Taxation and Revenue Department
1100 S. St. Francis Dr.
P.O. Box 630
Santa Fe, NM 87504-0630
(505) 827-0700
www.state.nm.us/tax

NEW YORK
New York State Tax Department
Taxpayer Assistance Bureau
W. A. Harriman Campus
Albany, NY 12227
(800) 225-5829
TTY: (800) 634-2110 (M-F 8:00 AM
to 6:00 PM)
www.tax.state.ny.us

NORTH CAROLINA
North Carolina Department of
Revenue
501 North Wilmington Street
Raleigh, North Carolina 27604
(919) 733-3991
Mailing address:
P.O. Box 25000
Raleigh, NC 27640-0640
www.dor.state.nc.us

NORTH DAKOTA
Office of State Tax Commissioner
State Capitol
600 East Boulevard Avenue
Bismarck, ND 58505-0599
(701) 328-2770
TTY: (800) 366-6888 (ask for
(800) 638-2901)
www.state.nd.us/taxdpt/

OHIO
Ohio Department of Taxation
Taxpayer Services Division
800 Freeway Drive North
Columbus, OH 43229
(800) 282-1780
TTY: (800) 750-0750 (Ohio Relay)
www.state.oh.us/tax

OKLAHOMA
Oklahoma Tax Commission
Taxpayer Assistance
PO Box 53248
Oklahoma City, OK 73152-3248.
(405) 521-3160
(800) 522-8165 ext: 13160 (in state)
www.oktax.state.ok.us/faq.html

OREGON
Oregon Department of Revenue
955 Center Street NE
Salem, OR 97301-2555
(503) 378-4988
(800) 356-4222 (in Oregon only)
www.dor.state.or.us

PENNSYLVANIA
Bureau of Individual Taxes
DEPT 280403
Harrisburg PA 17128-0403
(888) PATAXES (prerecorded
answers)
(717) 787-8201 for individual tax-
payers
TTY: (800) 447-3020
www.revenue.state.pa.us/revenue/
site/default.asp

RHODE ISLAND
Rhode Island Division of Taxation
One Capitol Hill
Providence, RI 02908
(401) 222-1040
TTY: (401) 222-6287
www.tax.state.ri.us

SOUTH CAROLINA
South Carolina Department of
Revenue
Taxable Processing Center
PO Box 101105
Columbia, SC 29211-0105
(800) 763-1295
TTY: (803) 898-5656
www.sctax.org

SOUTH DAKOTA
South Dakota Department of
Revenue
445 East Capitol Avenue
Pierre, SD 57501
(800) TAX-9188
www.state.sd.us/revenue/
revenue.html

TENNESSEE
Tennessee Department of Rev-
enue
Taxpayer Services
500 Deaderick Street
Nashville, Tennessee 37242

(615) 253-0600 or (615) 741-4465
(800) 342-1003 (Tennessee only)
www.state.tn.us/revenue

TEXAS
Texas Comptroller of Public Ac-
counts
Lyndon B. Johnson State Office
Building
111 East 17th Street
Austin, Texas 78774
(800) 252-5555
Mailing address:
Texas Comptroller of Public Ac-
counts
Post Office Box 13528
Capitol Station
Austin, Texas 78711-3528
TTY: (800) 248-4099; 463-4621
(Austin)
www.cpa.state.tx.us

UTAH
Utah State Tax Commission
210 N. 1950 West
Salt Lake City, Utah 84134
(801) 297-2200
(800) 662-4335
www.tax.ex.state.ut.us

VERMONT
Vermont Department of Taxes
109 State Street
Montpelier, Vermont 05609-1401
(866) 828-2865 (toll-free in-state)
(802) 828-2865 (local)
TTY: (800) 253-0191 or
(802) 828-2515
www.state.vt.us/tax

VIRGINIA
Virginia Department of Taxation
Office of Customer Services
Post Office Box 1115
Richmond, VA 23218-1115
(804) 367-8031 from 8:30 a.m. to
4:30 p.m.
(888) 268-2829 (outside Richmond,
VA)
TTY: (804) 367-8329
www.tax.state.va.us

WASHINGTON
Washington State Department of
Revenue
PO Box 47450
Olympia, WA 98504-7450
(800) 647-7706 (M, T, Th and F
7:30 AM to 5:00 PM;
W 9:00 AM to 5:00 PM (Pacific
Time))
TTY: (800) 451-7985
dor.wa.gov

WEST VIRGINIA
West Virginia Department of Tax
and Revenues
Tax Payer Services Division
P.O. Box 2389
Charleston, WV 25328-2389
(304) 558-3333
(800) 982-8297 (toll free in WV
only:
M-F 8:30-4:30 EST)
TTY: (304) 344-2068 or
(800) 422-2075
www.state.wv.us/taxdiv

WISCONSIN
Wisconsin Department of Revenue
Individual Income Tax Assistance
P.O. Box 8949
Madison, WI 53708-8949
(608) 266-2772
(608) 266-2486
TTY: (608) 267-1049
www.dor.state.wi.us

WYOMING
Wyoming Department of Revenue
Wyoming does not levy a person-
al or corporate income tax.
DOR@state.wy.us

"TOOL KIT" FOR INTERPRETERS WORKSHEET

My kit should include the following:

_____
_____
_____
_____
_____
_____
_____
_____
_____
_____
_____
_____
_____
_____
_____
_____
_____
_____
_____
_____
_____
_____
_____
_____
_____
_____
_____
_____
_____
_____
_____

Things I need to get:

_____   _____
_____   _____
_____   _____
_____   _____
_____   _____
_____   _____
_____   _____

EMERGENCY ESSENTIALS

SURVIVAL BASICS

- Water (minimum 2 quarts per person per day)

- First aid kit

- First aid book

- Food (vegetarian/kosher/others)

- Can opener (non-electric)

- Emergency blanket

- Flashlights, radio and spare batteries

- Fire extinguisher (a-b-c type)

- Whistle

- Swiss Army knife

- Tent

- Food bars

- Out of state contact information cards

YOU MAY WANT TO ADD THE FOLLOWING ITEMS:
Sturdy shoes
Jogging Suit
$$$$$CASH$$$$$
Coins
Toothpaste and brush
Hygiene supplies
Toilet paper
Hand towelettes
Pencil & memo pad
Local area map
Postcards (pre-stamped & addressed)
Spare change of clothes
Prescription medicine for 3 days
Sweater
Spare pair of prescription glasses
Infant supplies (if applicable)
Sunglasses
Always have at least ½ of a tank of gas in car

Used with permission from "THE EARTHQUAKE STORE", Los Angeles, California

ALCOHOLICS ANONYMOUS PREAMBLE

Alcoholics Anonymous is a fellowship of men and women who share their experience, strength and hope with each other that they may solve their common problem and help others to recover from alcoholism.

The only requirement for membership is a desire to stop drinking. There are no dues or fees for A.A. membership; we are self-supporting through our own contributions. A.A. is not allied with any sect, denomination, politics, organization or institution; does not wish to engage in any controversy, neither endorses nor opposes any causes. Our primary purpose is to stay sober and help other alcoholics to achieve sobriety.

Copyright @ by the AA Grapevine, Inc.; Reprinted with permission

SERENITY PRAYER
(ABBREVIATED)

God, grant me the serenity to accept the things
I cannot change,

Courage to change the things I can,

And the wisdom to know the difference.

Prayer attributed to St. Francis of Assisi

THE TWELVE STEPS OF ALCOHOLICS ANONYMOUS

1. We admitted we are powerless over alcohol – that our lives had become unmanageable.

2. Came to believe that a Power greater than ourselves could restore us to sanity.

3. Made a decision to turn our will and our lives over to the care of God *as we understood HIM.*

4. Made a searching and fearless moral inventory of ourselves.

5. Admitted to God, to ourselves and to another human being the exact nature of our wrongs.

6. Were entirely ready to have God remove all these defects of character.

7. Humbly asked Him to remove our shortcomings.

8. Made a list of all persons we had harmed, and became willing to make amends to them all.

9. Made direct amends to such people wherever possible, except when to do so would injure them or others.

10. Continued to take personal inventory and when we were wrong promptly admitted it.

11. Sought through prayer and meditation to improve our conscious contact with God, *as we understood Him,* praying only for knowledge of His will for us and the power to carry that out.

12. Having a spiritual awakening as the result of these steps, we tried to carry this message to alcoholics, and to practice these principles in all our affairs.

THE TWELVE TRADITIONS OF ALCOHOLICS ANONYMOUS

1. Our common welfare should come first; personal recovery depends on A.A. unity.

2. For our group purpose, there is but one ultimate authority – a loving God as He may express Himself in our group conscience. Our leaders are but trusted servants; they do not govern.

3. The only requirement for A.A. membership is a desire to stop drinking.

4. Each group should be autonomous except in matters affecting other groups or A.A. as a whole.

5. Each group has but one primary purpose – to carry its message to the alcoholic who still suffers.

6. An A.A. group ought never endorse, finance, or lend the A.A. name to any related facility or outside enterprise, lest problems of money, property, and prestige divert us from our primary purpose.

7. Every A.A. group ought to be fully self-supporting, declining outside contributions.

8. Alcoholics Anonymous should remain forever nonprofessional, but our service centers may employ special workers.

9. A.A., as such, ought never be organized; but we may create service boards or committees directly responsible to those they serve.

10. Alcoholics Anonymous has no opinion on outside issues; hence the A.A. name ought never be drawn into public controversy.

11. Our public relations policy is based on attraction rather than promotion; we need always maintain personal anonymity at the level of press, radio, and films.

12. Anonymity is the spiritual foundation of all our traditions, ever reminding us to place principles before personalities.

"SIGNER-CISES"

GENERAL CONSIDERATIONS:

- Avoid signing when hands are cold.

- Exercise and stretch in non-painful ranges. Know the difference between "stretch" and pain.

- There should be no pain after stretching or exercising.

WARM-UP EXERCISES:

- Open and close fists rapidly 5 - 10 times.

- Circle wrists counterclockwise and clockwise 5-10 times in each direction.

- Spread and close fingers 5 - 10 times each hand.

- Sign alphabet at moderate speed once.

- Shake hands out. **This should be done anytime hands feel tight.**

STRETCHING EXERCISES:

- Place hands in prayer position with only finger tips touching. Lift elbows and press fingers in backward direction. Hold for 5 seconds and repeat 5 times.

- Arm out straight, palm down, bend at wrist and push down on back of hand with opposite hand. Hold for 5 seconds and repeat 5 times. Change hands.

- Arm out straight. Palm up. Push fingers downward with opposite hand (wrist should bend backward). Repeat 5 times with 5–second hold. Change hands.

REMEMBER: IF AN EXERCISE OR ACTIVITY CAUSES PAIN— OMIT IT!

Developed by: Vanet Yapp, R.P.T. California State University, Northridge, Student Health Center, 1/12/84.

CARPAL TUNNEL SYNDROME/
REPETITIVE MOTION DISORDERS
REFERENCES

"Carpal Tunnel Syndrome: The Risk to Educational Interpreters". Joe D. Stedt, Ph.D., AAD, July,1989, pp. 223-226.

Other references for CTS:
Article: "Overuse Syndromes of the Upper Extremity in Interpreters for the Deaf. Lester Cohn, MD, Rhonda M. Lowry, Sandra Hart. Orthopedics, February, 1990, Vol. 13, No.2, pp. 207-209.

Gary R. Sanderson, National Center on Deafness, California State University, Northridge,18111 Nordhoff Street, Northridge, California 91330-8267. Telephone: (818) 677-2611 (TTY/Voice); FAX: (818) 677-4899.

Sample Worksheet

DONATIONS
200__

DATE:

ORGANIZATION NAME:

ADDRESS:

DONATION DESCRIPTION:

VALUE:

CONTACT: **TELEPHONE:**

RECEIPT: **E-MAIL:**

DATE:

ORGANIZATION NAME:

ADDRESS:

DONATION DESCRIPTION:

VALUE:

CONTACT: **TELEPHONE:**

RECEIPT: **E-MAIL:**

DATE:

ORGANIZATION NAME:

ADDRESS:

DONATION DESCRIPTION:

VALUE:

CONTACT: **TELEPHONE:**

RECEIPT: **E-MAIL:**

DATE:

ORGANIZATION NAME:

ADDRESS:

DONATION DESCRIPTION:

VALUE:

CONTACT: **TELEPHONE:**

RECEIPT: **E-MAIL:**

RESOURCES

- Directory of National Organizations of and for Deaf and Hard of Hearing People

- Workers' Compensation Administrators Directory (United States, Other U.S. Areas and Canada)

- Registry of Interpreters for the Deaf (RID) Information

- Associate, Certification, and Continuing Education Programs (U.S. and Canada)

- Bachelor's and Graduate Degree Programs

- Annual Membership Application (SAMPLE)

- Explanation of Certificates

- National Testing System Computer-Based Testing Application (SAMPLE)

- National Testing System Comprehensive Application (SAMPLE)

- Certification Maintenance Program (CMP)

- Associate Continuing Education Tracking (ACET) Program

- Approved CMP and ACET Sponsors

- RID Affiliate Chapters and Regions

- National Association of the Deaf (NAD) Certifications

- Americans With Disabilities Act (ADA) Handbook Information

DIRECTORY OF NATIONAL ORGANIZATIONS OF AND FOR DEAF AND HARD OF HEARING PEOPLE

This directory was developed with information provided by each organization. All of the organizations are national and nonprofit and provide information on deaf and hard of hearing people and/or specific professional or consumer areas of interest.

Each organization was asked to identify up to four descriptors that best describe the organization's focus. The codes are:

C	Consumer and/or Advocacy
E	Educational
F	Funding Source
I	Information and/or Referral
M	Medical
P	Professional
Rc	Recreational
R	Religious
Rs	Research
S	Self-help/Support
So	Social

ABLEDATA

8630 Fenton Street, Suite 930
Silver Spring, MD 20910
Voice: (800) 227-0216
Voice: (301) 608-8998
TTY: (301) 608-8912
FAX: (301) 608-8958
E-mail: ABLEDATA@orcmacro.com
Web: http://www.abledata.com
ABLEDATA provides information on assistive technology, rehabilitation equipment and other products for people with disabilities. Project staff maintains a database containing information on approximately 30,000 assistive technology products from over 3,000 domestic and foreign manufacturers and distributors. The database can be searched at the ABLEDATA website. ABLEDATA also produces publications on a variety of assistive products. These publications and other interactive resources are available on the website with hundreds of links to assistive technology manufacturers, distributors, and other disability-related websites. ABLEDATA staff are available Monday - Friday, 8:30 a.m.-5:30 p.m. Eastern Time. The National Institute on Disability and Rehabilitation Research of the U.S. Department of Education funds ABLEDATA.

I

ADARA: Professionals Networking for Excellence in Service Delivery with Individuals who are Deaf or Hard of Hearing
(Formerly AMERICAN DEAFNESS AND REHABILITATION ASSOCIATION)
P.O. Box 480
Myersville, MD 21773
E-mail: ADARAorgn@aol.com
Web: http://www.adara.org
PUBLICATION: **JADARA**: A Journal for Professionals Networking for Excellence in Service Delivery with Individuals Who Are Deaf and Hard of Hearing, **ADARA UPDATE** (newsletter)
Promotes and participates in quality human service delivery to deaf and hard of hearing people through agencies and individuals. ADARA is a partnership of national organizations, local affiliates, professional sections, and individual members working together to support social services and rehabilitation delivery for deaf and hard of hearing people.
P

ALEXANDER GRAHAM BELL ASSOCIATION FOR THE DEAF, INC.
3417 Volta Place NW
Washington, DC 20007
Voice: (202) 337-5220
TTY: (202) 337-5221
FAX: (202) 337-8314
Web: http://www.agbell.org
PUBLICATIONS: **The Volta Review** (journal), **Volta Voices** (magazine)
A membership organization and information center on pediatric hearing loss and spoken language approach. AG Bell emphasizes the use of technology, in conjunction with spoken speech and speechreading. The association focuses specifically on children with hearing loss, providing ongoing support and advocacy for parents, professionals and other interested parties. AG Bell provides scholarships, financial and parent-infant awards, publishes books on deafness, and advocates for the rights of children who are deaf or hard of hearing.
E F I P S

AMERICAN ACADEMY OF AUDIOLOGY
11730 Plaza America Drive, #300
Reston, VA 20190
Voice/TTY: (703) 790-8466
Voice/TTY: (800) AAA-2336
FAX: (703) 790-8631
Web: http://www.audiology.org
PUBLICATIONS: **Audiology Today** (magazine), **Journal of AAA** (journal),

The American Academy of Audiology, the world's largest professional organization of audiologists, is dedicated to providing quality hearing care services through professional development, education, research and increased public awareness of hearing disorders. To learn more about the audiology profession and how audiologists are helping the 28 million Americans who suffer from hearing loss contact the website. Americans who suffer from hearing loss, please visit http://www.audiology.org
E P I

AMERICAN ACADEMY OF OTOLARYNGOLOGY-HEAD AND NECK SURGERY
1 Prince Street
Alexandria, VA 22314-3357
Voice: (703) 836-4444
TTY: (703) 519-1585
FAX: (703) 683-5100
Web: http://www.entnet.org
PUBLICATIONS: Otolaryngology-Head and Neck Surgery (journal), The Bulletin (membership publication)
Promotes the art and science of medicine related to otolaryngology-head and neck surgery, including providing continuing medical education courses and publications. Distributes patient leaflets relating to ear, nose and throat problems and makes referrals to physicians.
M P

AMERICAN ASSOCIATION OF THE DEAF-BLIND
814 Thayer Avenue, Room 302
Silver spring, MD 20910-4500
TTY: (301) 495-4402
Voice (301) 495-4403
FAX: (301) 495-4404
Web: http://www.aadb.org
PUBLICAITON: **Deaf-Blind American**
Promotes better opportunities and services for deaf-blind people. Mission is to assure that a comprehensive, coordinated system of services is accessible to all deaf-blind people, enabling them to achieve their maximum potential through increased independence, productivity, and integration into the community. The biennial conventions provide a week of workshops, meetings, tours, and recreational activities.
C I

AMERICAN HEARING RESEARCH FOUNDATION

8 South Michigan Avenue, Suite 814
Chicago, IL 60603-4539
Voice: (312) 726-9670
FAX: (312) 726-9695
Web: http://www.american-hearing.org
PUBLICATION: **Newsletter**
Supports medical research and education into the causes, prevention, and cures of deafness, hearing losses, and balance disorders. Also keeps physicians and the public informed of the latest developments in hearing research and education.
Rs

AMERICAN SOCIETY FOR DEAF CHILDREN

P.O. Box 3355
Gettysburg, PA 17325
Voice/TTY: (800) 942-ASDC (Parent Hotline)
Voice/TTY: (717) 334-7922 (Business)
FAX: (717) 334-8808
E-mail: ASDC1@aol.com
Web: http://www.deafchildren.org/
PUBLICATION: The Endeavor
ASDC is a nonprofit parent-helping-parent organization promoting a positive attitude toward signing and deaf culture. Also provides support, encouragement, and current information about deafness to families with deaf and hard of hearing children.
C I S E

AMERICAN SPEECH-LANGUAGE-HEARING ASSOCIATION

10801 Rockville Pike
Rockville, MD 20852
HELPLINE: (800) 638-8255 (V/TTY)
TTY: (301) 897-5700
FAX: (301) 571-0457
Web: http://www.asha.org
PUBLICATION: **Journal of Speech-Language-Hearing Research; American Journal of Audiology; American Journal of Speech Language pathology; Language Speech and Hearing Services in the Schools; ASHA Magazine; ASHA Leader**
A professional and scientific organization for speech-language pathologists and audiologists concerned with communication disorders. Provides informational materials and a toll-free HELPLINE number for consumers to inquire about speech, language, or hearing problems. Also provides referrals to audiologists and speech-language pathologists in the United States.
C I P Rs

AMERICAN TINNITUS ASSOCIATION

P.O. Box 5
Portland, OR 97207-0005
Voice: (800) 634-8978
Voice: (503) 248-9985
FAX: (503) 248-0024
Web: http://www.ata.org
PUBLICAITON: **Tinnitus Today**

The American Tinnitus Association (ATA) is a nonprofit, voluntary, human health, and welfare agency dedicated to providing support of scientific research leading to the elimination of tinnitus as a health problems. It also provides education, information, self-help, and hearing-health resources to millions of American who have tinnitus.

C E F I P S

ARKANSAS REHABILITATION RESEARCH AND TRAINING CENTER FOR PERSONS WHO ARE DEAF AND HARD OF HEARING

University of Arkansas
4601 W. Markham St.
Little Rock, AR 72205
Voice/TTY: (501) 686-9691
FAX: (501) 686-9698
Web: http://www.uark.edu/deafrtc

The center focuses on issues affecting the employability of deaf and hard of hearing rehabilitation clients—career assessment, career preparation, placement, career mobility, and advancement. Provides information and/or databases related to the rehabilitation of deaf and hard of hearing people served by the Federal/state Vocational Rehabilitation Program.

E I P Rs

ASSOCIATION OF LATE-DEAFENED ADULTS (ALDA)

1131 Lake Street #204
Oak Park, IL 60301
Voice/FAX: 877-907-1738
TTY: (708) 358-0135
E-mail: President@alda.org
Web: http://www.alda.org/
PUBLICAITON: **ALDA NEWS**

Supports the empowerment of people who are deafened. Provides resources and information and promotes advocacy and awareness of the needs of deafened adults.

C I S So

AUDITORY-VERBAL INTERNATIONAL, INC.
2121 Eisenhower Ave., Suite 402
Alexandria, VA 23314
Voice (703) 739-1049
TTY: (703) 739-0874
FAX: (703) 739-0395
E-mail: audiverb@aol.com
Web: http://www.auditory-verbal.org
PUBLICATION: **The AURICLE**
To provide the choice of listening and speaking as the way of life, for children and adults who are deaf or hard of hearing. Through the use of assistive technology such as digital hearing aids or cochlear implants and auditory-verbal therapy, many deaf and hard of hearing children can learn to listen and speak.
C E F I M P S So

BEGINNINGS for Parents of Hearing Impaired Children, Inc.
P.O. Box 17646
Raleigh, NC 27619
Voice/TTY: (919) 5850-2746
Voice/TTY: (800) 541-4327 (NC residents only)
Web: http://www.beginningssvcs.com
PUBLICATIONS: **Newsletter, Parent Manual,** brochures and videotapes
Nonprofit organization provides emotional support and access to information as a central resource for families with deaf or hard of hearing children, age birth through 21 years. Provides an impartial approach to meeting the diverse needs of these families and the professionals who serve them. These services are also available to deaf parents who have hearing children. The mission of BEGINNINGS is to help parents be informed, empowered and supported as they make decisions about their child. In addition, BEGINNINGS is committed to providing technical assistance to professionals who work with these families to help the children achieve full participation in society.
C I E

BETTER HEARING INSTITUTE
515 King Street, Suite 420
Alexandria, VA 22314
Voice/TTY: (703) 684-3391
Voice/TTY: (888) HEAR HELP BHI (Office)
Voice/TTY: (800) EAR-WELL (Hearing Helpline)
FAX: (703) 684-6048
E-mail: DDEnston@clarionmr.com
Web: http://www.betterhearing.org /
BHI is a nonprofit educational organization that implements national public information programs on hearing loss and available medical, surgical, hearing aid, and rehabilitation assistance for millions with uncorrected hearing problems.

Promotes awareness of hearing loss through television, radio, and print media public service messages. BHI maintains a toll-free "Hearing HelpLine" telephone service that provides information on hearing loss, sources of assistance, lists of local hearing professionals, and other available hearing help to callers anywhere in the United States and Canada.
E I

BOYS TOWN NATIONAL RESEARCH HOSPITAL
555 N. 30th Street
Omaha, NE 68131
Voice: (402) 498-6511
TTY: (402) 498-6543
FAX: (402) 498-6638
Web: http://www.boystownhospital.org
Boys Town National Research Hospital is an international leader in research, diagnosis, and treatment of children with hearing loss and communication disorders. Highly trained physicians work closely clinicians and researchers, creating a rapid transfer of research advances from the laboratory to clinic, classroom and bedside. Early intervention programs, modeled around the world, are an equally important aspect of the hospital's work.
E I M Rs

CAPTIONED MEDIA PROGRAM
(Formerly Captioned Films/Videos Program)
National Association of the Deaf
1447 E. Main Street
Spartanburg, SC 29307
Voice: (800) 237-6213
TTY: (800) 237-6819
FAX: (800) 538-5636
Web: http://www.cfv.org
PUBLICATION: **Free-Loan Open-Captioned Media Catalog**
The CMP is a free-loan open-captioned media program. Several hundred titles are also streamed on the CMP web site. Deaf and hard of hearing persons, teachers, parents, and others may borrow these materials. Materials include educational videos (for preschool through college) and general-interest, which will benefit a deaf or hard of hearing person (classical movies and special-interest topics such as travel, hobbies, recreation, and others). Some titles are available in CD-Rom or DVD.
C E I

COCHLEAR IMPLANT ASSOCIATION, INC.
5335 Wisconsin Avenue, NW, Suite 440
Washington, DC 20015-2034
Voice/TTY: (202) 895-2781
PUBLICATION: **CONTACT**
E-mail: pwms.cici@worldnet.att.net
Web: http://www.cici.org
Cochlear Implant Association (CIAI), formerly Cochlear Implant Club International, provides information and support to cochlear implant users and their families, professionals, and the general public.
C E I

CISS INTERNATIONAL COMMITTEE OF SPORTS FOR THE DEAF
7310 Grove Road, Suite #106
Frederick, MD 21704
FAX: 301-620-2990
E-mail: info@ciss.org
Web: http://www.ciss.org
The Comité International des Sports des Sourds (CISS) was founded in Paris, France on the 24th of August 1924. CISS celebrates the spirit of Deaf Sports where Deaf athletes come together as members of a cultural and linguistic minority to strive to reach the pinnacle of competition, the CISS adopted a motto: PER LUDOS AEQUALITIAS (Equal through sport).
I E Rc So

CONFERENCE OF EDUCATIONAL ADMINISTRATORS OF SCHOOLS AND PROGRAMS FOR THE DEAF, INC.
P.O. Box 1778
St. Augustine, FL 32085-1778
Voice/TTY: (904) 810-5200
FAX: (904) 810-5525
E-mail: innceasd@aug.com
Web: http://www.ceasd.org
PUBLICAITONS: **American Annals of the Deaf**
Gallaudet University Press
800 Florida Avenue, NE
Washington, DC 20002-3695
Voice/TTY: (202) 651-5488
FAX: (202) 651-5489
Focuses on improvements in the education of deaf and hard of hearing people through research, personnel development, advocacy, and training.
C E P S

COUNCIL OF AMERICAN INSTRUCTORS OF THE DEAF
P.O. Box 377
Bedford, TX 76095-0377
Voice/TTY: (817) 354-8414
E-mail: caid@swbell.net
Web: http://www.caid.org
PUBLICATION: **American Annals of the Deaf, News n Notes**
An organization that promotes professional development, communication, and information among educators of deaf and hard of hearing individuals and other interested people. Host of national convention and regional meetings.
P

DEAFNESS AND COMMUNICATIVE DISORDERS BRANCH
Rehabilitation Services Administration
Office of Special Education and Rehabilitative Services
Department of Education
330 C Street SW, Room 3228
Washington, DC 20202-2736
Voice: (202) 205-9152
TTY: (202) 205-8352
FAX: (202) 205-9340
Web: http://www.ed.gov/offices/OSERS/RSA/People/dcdb.html
Promotes improved and expanded rehabilitation services for deaf and hard of hearing people and individuals with speech or language impairments. Provides technical assistance to RSA staff, state rehabilitation agencies, other public and private agencies, and individuals. Also provides funding for interpreter training and administers the projects.
I F

DEAFNESS RESEARCH FOUNDATION
1050 17th St., N.W Suite 701
Washington, D.C. 20036
Voice: (800) 535-3323/(202) 289-5850
FAX: (202) 293-1805
Web: http://www.drf.org
PUBLICATION: **Hearing Health Advocate**
DRF is the leading source of private funding for basic and clinical research in hearing science. It also sponsors the National Campaign for Hearing Health, a public education and advocacy effort that promotes lifetime of hearing health for all.
F I M Rs

THE EAR FOUNDATION
1817 Patterson Street
Nashville, TN 37203
Voice/TTY: (615) 284-7807
Voice/TTY: (800) 545-HEAR
FAX: (615) 284-7935
Web: http://www.earfoundation.org
A national, not-for-profit organization committed to integrating the hearing and balance impaired person into the mainstream of society through public awareness and medical education. Also administers The Meniere's Network, a national network of patient support groups providing people with the opportunity to share experiences and coping strategies.
I S E

EPISCOPAL CONFERENCE OF THE DEAF
P.O. Box 27685
Philadelphia, PA 19118-0069
Voice: (205) 967-1437
TTY: (205) 967-1430
E-mail: JLCroft@juno.com
PUBLICATION: **The Deaf Episcopalian**
Promotes ministry for deaf people throughout the Episcopal Church. Affiliated with approximately 65 congregations in the United States.
R I

GALLAUDET UNIVERSITY
PRESIDENT: I. King. Jordan, Ph.D.
800 Florida Avenue NE
Washington, DC 20002-3695
Voice/TTY: (202) 651-5000
Web: http://pr.gallaudet.edu
PUBLICATION: **Gallaudet Today**
Gallaudet University, the world's only four-year liberal arts university for students who are deaf or hard of hearing. Established in 1864 by an act of Congress, Gallaudet offers more than 50 undergraduate and graduate degree programs and numerous continuing education and summer courses. The University disseminates information through such units as the Gallaudet Bookstore, Gallaudet University Press, Gallaudet Research Institute and the Laurent Clerc National Deaf Education Center's National Deaf Education Network and Clearinghouse.
E I C Rs

GALLAUDET UNIVERSITY ALUMNI ASSOCIATION

Peikoff Alumni House ("Ole Jim")
Gallaudet University
800 Florida Avenue NE
Washington, DC 20002-3695
Voice: (202) 651-5060
TTY: (202) 651-5061
FAX: (202) 651-5062
Web: http://alumni.gallaudet.edu
PUBLICATION: **Gallaudet Today**
Represents more than 14,000 alumni of Gallaudet University across the United States and around the world. The GUAA, which is governed by an elected board of directors, provides a variety of services that support and benefit the University, the alumni, and the general deaf community.
C F So

HEARING EDUCATION AND AWARENESS FOR ROCKERS - H.E.A.R.

P.O. Box 460847
San Francisco, CA 94146
Voice: (415) 773-9590 (hotline)
Web: http://www.hearnet.com
Educates the public about the real dangers of hearing loss resulting from repeated exposure to excessive noise levels. Offers information about hearing protection, hearing aids, assistive listening devices, ear monitor systems, testing and other information about hearing loss and tinnitus. Operates a 24-hour hotline information, referral, and support network services and conducts a hearing screening program in the San Francisco Bay area. Also launches public hearing awareness campaigns, provides programs for schools and seminars, and distributes earplugs to club and concertgoers. Initiated H.E.A.R. affiliates via hearnet websites in other cities worldwide. H.E.A.R. records fundraising CD's with Public Service Announcements. Sponsorship opportunities available in each program.
C E I M S

HEAR NOW

6700 Washington Avenue
Eden Praire, MN 55344
Voice: (800) 648-HEAR (4327)
FAX: (952) 828-6946
E-mail: nonprofit@starkey.com
A private, non-profit organization that provides hearing aids for adults and children who are legal residents of the United States, who are deaf or hard of hearing and who have limited income. HEAR Now is a provider of last resort. All other options for service must be used before benefit can be approved.

Services are distributed through a nationwide network of hearing professionals. Providers are asked to waive fitting and follow-up fees for the first year of warranty coverage. Clients pay for their hearing evaluations and plus a non-refundable HEAR Now processing fee of $39.00 per aide. The organization provided more than 7,800 hearing aides to people in need last year. HEAR Now also collects old hearing aids for recycling. Donated aides should be packaged and mailed. Donations are tax deductible and will be acknowledged. People who qualify to receive hearing aides receive NEW aides.
C F I P

The George Washington University
HEATH RESOURCE CENTER
The National Clearinghouse on Postsecondary Education for Individuals with Disabilities, a program of the George Washington University.
2121 K Street, NW Suite 220
Washington, DC 20037
Voice/TTY: (202) 973-0904
Voice: (800) 544-3284
FAX: (202) 973-0908
Web: http://www.heath.gwu.org
HEATH disseminates information nationally about disability issues in postsecondary education. It offers publications and a telephone service of use to administrators, service providers, teachers, instructors, rehabilitation counselors, health professionals, and to individuals with disabilities and their families.
I E

HELEN KELLER NATIONAL CENTER FOR DEAF-BLIND YOUTHS AND ADULTS
111 Middle Neck Road
Sands Point, NY 11050
Voice: (516) 944-8900
TTY: (516) 944-8637
FAX: (516) 944-7302
E-mail: hkncinfo@rcn.org
Web: http://www.helenkeller.org
PUBLICATIONS: **The Nat-Cent News**
The national center and its 10 regional offices provide diagnostic evaluations, comprehensive vocational and personal adjustment training, and job preparation and placement for people who are deaf-blind from every state and territory. Field services include information and referral and advocacy and technical assistance to professionals, consumers, and families. The Center also maintains a national registry of deaf-blind persons.
C E I

HOUSE EAR INSTITUTE
2100 W. Third Street, 5th Floor
Los Angeles, CA 90057
Voice: (213) 483-4431
TTY: (213) 483-2642
FAX: (213) 483-8789
Web: http://www.hei.org/
PUBLICATION: **House Calls**
The House Ear Institute is dedicated to advancing hearing science through research and education to improve quality of life. Scientist explore the causes of auditory disorders on the cellular and molecular level and refine the development and application of diagnostic devices, auditory implants and hearing aids. Children's Auditory Research and Education (CARE) Center addresses the special hearing health issues and assistive device needs of infants and children with a full spectrum of research, diagnostic, reatment and educational services.
E I M Rs

INTERNATIONAL CATHOLIC DEAF ASSOCIATION
United States Section
1030 S. Lagrange Rd #9
Lagrange, IL 60525-2893
TTY: (708) 579-5817
FAX: (708) 579-5847
E-mail:. ICDAUS@Ameritech.net
Web: http://www.icda-us.org
PUBLICATION: **The Deaf Catholic**
Promotes ministry for Catholic deaf people. Chapters are encouraged to arrange Sunday masses for deaf people in their local areas with the liturgy presented in sign language. Responds to spiritual-related requests worldwide.
C E I R So

INTERNATIONAL HEARING SOCIETY
16880 Middlebelt Road
Livonia, MI 48154
Voice: (734) 522-7200
Voice: (800) 521-5247 Hearing Aid (Helpline)
FAX: (734) 522-0200
Web: http://www.ihsinfo.org
PUBLICATION: **The Hearing Professional**
Professional associations of specialists who test hearing aid select, it, and dispense hearing instruments. The society conducts programs of competence qualifications, education, and training, and promotes specialty-level accreditation. The Hearing Aid Helpline provides consumer information and referral.
C M P

JEWISH DEAF CONGRESS
(Formerly National Congress of Jewish Deaf)
214-11 85th Avenue
Hollis Hills, New York 11427
TTY: (718) 740-0470
FAX: (718) 740-4994
E-mail: mflorsheim@conf2003jdc.com
PUBLICAITON: **J.D.C. QUARTERLY**
Advocates for religious, educational, and cultural ideals and fellowship for Jewish deaf people. Conducts workshops for rabbis, parents of deaf children, and interpreters. Works with 20 affiliates and maintains a Hall of Fame.
C F I R

JOHN TRACEY CLINIC
806 W. Adams Blvd.
Los Angeles, CA 90007
Voice: (213) 748-5481
TTY: (213) 747-2924
Voice/TTY: (800) 522-4582
FAX: (213) 749-1651
Web: http://www.jtc.org
John Tracey Clinic is an educational facility for parents of infants and preschool-age children with hearing losses. In addition to on-site services, worldwide correspondence courses in English and Spanish are offered to parents whose children are of preschool age and are hard of hearing, deaf, or deaf-blind. All services of JTC are free of charge to the families.
E I S

JUNIOR NATIONAL ASSOCIATION OF THE DEAF
814 Thayer Avenue
Silver Spring, MD 20910-4500
TTY: (301) 587-4875
Voice: (301) 587-1788
FAX: (301) 587-1791
Web site: http://www.nad.org/JRNAD
PUBLICATION: **Junior NAD** magazine
Develops and promotes citizenship, scholarship, and leadership skills in deaf and hard of hearing students (grades 7-12) through chapter projects, national conventions, contests, and other activities. The NAD also sponsors a month-long Youth Leadership Camp program each summer on Oregon.
E Rc So

LEAGUE FOR THE HARD OF HEARING
71 West 23rd Street
New York, NY 10010-4162
Voice: (917) 305-7700
TTY: (917) 305-7999
FAX: (917) 305-7888
Web: http://www.lhh.org
PUBLICATION: **League Newsletter**
The League for the Hard of hearing mission is to improve the quality of life for infants, children, and adults with all degrees of hearing loss. We accomplish our mission by providing hearing rehabilitation and human services for people who are hard of hearing or deaf, and their families, regardless of age, ability to pay, or mode of communication, and by striving to empower consumers to achieve their potential. Our leadership is exemplified by adhering to the highest clinical standards, conducting extensive hearing conservation and public education programs about hearing, and developing best practice models for disciplines that related to hearing and research.
C E I M P Rs S

MEDIA ACCESS GROUP AT WGBH
125 Western Avenue
Boston, MA 02134
Voice/TTY: (617) 300-3600
FAX: (617) 300-1020
Web: http://access.wgbh.org
PUBLICATIONS: **Media Access Group Newsletter, MAG Guides** on topics of interest to caption viewers, video description viewers, and the television and film industry.
The Media Access Group at WGBH is a nonprofit service of the WGBH Educational Foundation. Our mission is to make all forms of media accessible to people who are deaf, hard of hearing, blind or visually impaired. With offices in Boston, Los Angeles, and New York, we produce captions and video description for every segment of the television, video and film industry.
C I Rs

NATIONAL ASSOCIATION OF SCHOOL PSYCHOLOGISTS
Interest Group on Deaf and Hard of Hearing Students and their Families
4340 East West Highway, Suite 402
Bethesda, MD 20814
Voice: (301) 657-0270
TTY: (301) 657-4155
FAX: (301) 657-0275
Web: http://www.naspweb.org
PUBLICATIONS: **School Psychology Review, Communiqué**
The mission of the National Association of School Psycholo-

gists (NASP) is to promote educationally and psychologically healthy environments for all students by implementing research-based effective programs that prevent problems, enhance independence, and promote optimal learning. This is accomplished through state-of-the-art research and training, advocacy, ongoing program forum, website, and listserv where members can network, share resources, and support each other in providing school based psychological services to students who are deaf or hard of hearing.
E I P Rs

NATIONAL ASSOCIATION OF THE DEAF
814 Thayer Avenue, Suite 250
Silver Spring, MD 20910-4500
Voice: (301) 587-1788
TTY: (301) 587-1789
FAX: (301) 587-1791
Web: http://www.nad.org
PUBLICATIONS: **NAD** magazine
National Association of the Deaf - Nation's largest organization safeguarding the accessibility and civil rights of 28 million deaf and hard of hearing Americans in education, employment, health care, and telecommunications. Focuses on grassroots advocacy and empowerment, captioned media, deafness-related information and publications, legal assistance, policy development and research, public awareness, and youth leadership development.
C I

NATIONAL BLACK DEAF ADVOCATES
P.O. Box 22846
Rochester, NY 14692-2846
Web: http://ww.nbda.org
PUBLICATION: **NBDA News**
Promotes leadership, deaf awareness, and active participation in the political, educational, and economic processes that affect the lives of black deaf citizens. Programs include YES (Youth Employment Summit) for deaf youth. Currently has 28 chapters in the United States and the Virgin Islands.
C E I P So

NATIONAL CAPTIONING INSTITUTE
1900 Gallows Road, Suite 3000
Vienna, VA 22182
Voice/TTY: (703) 917-7600
FAX: (703) 917-9878
Web: http://www.ncicap.org
PUBLICATION: **Caption**
NCI, a nonprofit corporation founded in 1979, is the world's

largest provider of closed-captioned television services for the broadcast, cable and home video industry.

I

NATIONAL CATHOLIC OFFICE OF THE DEAF
7202 Buchanan Street
Landover Hills, MD 20784-2236
Voice: (301)577-1684
TTY: (301) 577-4184
FAX: (301) 577-1690
E-mail: NCOD@Erols.com
Web: http://www.ncod.org/
PUBLICAITONS: **Vision**

Assists in the coordination of the efforts of people and organizations involved in the church's ministry with deaf and hard of hearing people; serves as a resource center for information concerning spiritual needs and religious educational materials; and assists bishops and pastors with their pastoral responsibilities to people who are deaf or hard of hearing.

C I P R

CPB/WGBH NATIONAL CENTER FOR ACCESSIBLE MEDIA
WGBH Educational Foundation
125 Western Avenue
Boston, MA 02134
Voice: (617) 300-3400
TTY: (617) 300-2489
FAX: (617) 300-1035
Web: http://ncam.wgbh.org
PUBLICAITON: **Media Access**

The CPB/WGBH National Center for Accessible Media aims to increase access to public mass media (television, radio, print, movies, multimedia) for underserved consumers, such as disabled people or speakers of other languages. NCAM researches and develops media access technologies that make them more inclusive or expand their use. And acts as a resource to broadcasters, producers, educators, and consumers through consulting, training, journal articles, and conferences.

C I Rs

NATIONAL CUED SPEECH ASSOCIATION
DEAF CHILDREN'S LITERACY PROJECT
Information Service/Bookstore
23970 Hermitage Road
Cleveland, OH 44122-4008
Voice/TTY: (800) 459-3529
Voice/TTY: (216) 292-6213
E-mail: cuedspdisc@aol.com
Web: http://www.cuedspeech.org
PUBLICATION: Cued Speech Journal, On Cue Newsletter

NCSA and its affiliate centers and chapters support and promote the effective use of Cued Speech for communication, language acquisition, and literacy. NCSA offers information about Cued Speech use with children and adults with hearing, speech, and language needs. Supports family camps and provides instructor certification, bookstore catalog, Cued Speech charts in more than 50 languages, and referrals/networking. Cued Speech provides the appropriate phonemic language base for literacy.
C E I P S So

NATIONAL FRATERNAL SOCIETY OF THE DEAF
1118 S. 6th Street
Springfield, IL 62703
Voice: (217) 789-7429
TTY: (217) 789-7438
FAX: (217) 789-7489
Web: http://www.nfsd.com
PUBLICATION: **The Frat**
Works in the area of life insurance and advocacy for deaf people and has 60 divisions across the country.
C E I S So

NATIONAL INFORMATION CENTER FOR CHILDREN AND YOUTH WITH DISABILITIES (NICHCY)
P.O. Box 1492
Washington, DC 20013-1492
Voice/TTY: (800) 695-0285
Voice/TTY: (202) 884-8200
FAX: (202) 884-8441
E-mail: nichcy@aed.org
Web: http://www.nichcy.org
PUBLICATIONS: **NICHCY News Digest, Transition Summary, Parent's Guide**
NICHCY provides fact sheets, state resource sheets, and general information to assist parents, educators, caregivers, advocates, and others in helping children and youth with disabilities participate as fully as possible in their community. The Web site offers all publications in full text as well as a comprehensive database of specialized organizations and agencies. NICHCY information is available in English and Spanish.
E I

NATIONAL INFORMATION CLEARINGHOUSE ON CHILDREN WHO ARE DEAF-BLIND (DB-LINK)
Teaching Research
345 Monmouth Avenue
Monmouth, OR 97361
Voice: (800) 438-9376
TTY: (800) 854-7013

FAX: (503) 838-8150
Web: http://www.tr.wou.edu/dblink/
PUBLICATION: **Deaf-Blind Perspectives**
Collects, organizes, and disseminates information related to children and youth (ages 0-21) who are deaf-blind and connects consumers of deaf-blind information to sources of information about deaf blindness, assistive technology, and deaf-blind people, education, and all other areas related to deaf-blindness. DB-LINK is a collaborative effort involving the Helen Keller National Center, Perkins School for the blind, and Teaching Research.
C E I M P Rs

NATIONAL INSTITUTE ON DEAFNESS AND OTHER COMMUNICATION DISORDERS INFORMATION CLEARINGHOUSE
1 Communication Avenue
Bethesda, MD 20892-3456
Voice: (800) 241-1044
TTY: (800) 241-1055
FAX: (301) 770- 8977
Web: http://www.nidcd.nih.gov
PUBLICATION: **INSIDE**
The NIDCD Information Clearinghouse is a national resource center for information about hearing, balance, smell, taste, voice, speech, and language. The clearinghouse serves health professionals, patients, industry, and the public.
I F P Rs

THE NATIONAL REHABILITATION INFORMATION CENTER
4200 Forbes Boulevard
Lanham, MD 20910
Voice: (301) 459-5900
Voice: (800) 346-2742
TTY: (301) 459-4263
FAX: (301) 459-4263
E-mail: naricinfo@heitechservices.com
Web: http://www.naric.com
PUBLICATIONS: **NIDRR Program Directory, Compendium**
Provides information and referral services on disability and rehabilitation, including quick information and referral, data base searches of the bibliographic data base REHABDATA, and document delivery. NARIC also provides the NIDRR Program Directory and the Compendium of Products by NIDRR Grantees and Contractors.
I

NATIONAL TECHNICAL INSTITUTE FOR THE DEAF

Rochester Institute of Technology
52 Lomb Memorial Drive,
Rochester, NY 14623-5604
Voice/TTY: (585) 475-6400
FAX: (585) 475-5623
Web: http://www.rit.edu/NTID
Provides deaf and hard-of-hearing students with outstanding state-of-the art technical and professional education programs, complemented by a strong arts and sciences curriculum.
E I

THE NATIONAL THEATRE OF THE DEAF

55 Van Dyke Avenue, Suite 312
Hartford, CT 06106
Voice/TTY: (860) 724-5179
Toll free: (800) 300-5179
FAX: (860) 550-7974
Web: http://www.ntd.org
Concentrates on artistic and theatrical professional development of deaf actors. Tours the United States and abroad. Also presents Little Theatre of the Deaf productions in schools, theaters, museums, and libraries. Sponsors a professional school, and Deaf Theatre Conference for everyone. Recruiting and outreach.
C E F I P Rc Rs So

PUBLICATIONS AND INFORMATION DISSEMINATION (PID)

(Formerly National Deaf Education Network and Clearinghouse)
Laurent Clerc National Deaf Education Center
Gallaudet University
KDES PAS-6
800 Florida Avenue, NE
Washington, DC 20002-3695
V/TTY: (202) 651-5051 (information)
FAX: (202) 651-5708
E-mail: Clearinghouse.Infotogo@gallaudet.edu (information)
Voice/TTY: (202) 651-5340 (products)
E-mail: Products.ClercCenter@Gallaudet.edu (products)
Web: http://clerccenter.gallaudet.edu/InfoToGo/index.html
The Publications and Information Dissemination office performs a number of functions related to information dissemination at the Gallaudet University Laurent Clerc National Deaf Education Center. The Clearinghouse responds to inquiries about a diverse range of topics related to deaf and hard of hearing children in the age group of 0-21. PID also collaborates with authors from within the Gallaudet community and around the nation to design, produce, and disseminate books, videotapes, periodicals, and other information related to deaf

and hard of hearing children, their families, and the professionals who serve them.
I

RAINBOW ALLIANCE OF THE DEAF
Barbara Hathaway c/o Karen L. Rosenthal
2424 S. Cottonwood Lane, Lot #10
Tucson, AZ 85713
Web: http://www.rad.org
E-group: RADChapters@egroups.com
RAD is a national organization serving gay, lesbian and bisexual people who are deaf and hard of hearing. Plus friends of our family are included. Represents approximately 24 chapters throughout the United States and Canada.
E C I S So

REGISTRY OF INTERPRETERS FOR THE DEAF, INC.
333 Commerce Street
Alexandra, VA 22314
Voice: (703) 838-0030
TTY: (703) 838-0459
FAX: (703) 838-0454
Web site: http://rid.org
PUBLICATION: **Views**
RID strives to increase the quality, and qualifications of sign language and oral interpreters through their National Testing System, Certification Maintenance Program, and Ethical Practices Systems. A professional organization for interpreters provides information on interpreting to the general public, publishes a national directory of certified interpreters, and makes referral to interpreter agencies.
E I P

REHABILITATION ENGINEERING RESEARCH CENTER ON HEARING ENHANCEMENT AND ASSISTIVE DEVICES (RERC)
Kendall Green
800 Florida Ave, NE
Washington DC 20002
Voice/TTY/FAX: (202) 651-5335
E-mail: Matthew.bakke@gallaudet.edu
Contact person: Lois O'Neill
Voice: (718) 350-3203
FAX: (718) 899-3433
E-mail: Loneill@lexnyc.org
Web: http://www.hearingresearch.org
PUBLICATION: hearingresearch.org (bi-annual newsletter)
The RERC on Hearing Enhancement promotes and develops technological solutions to problems confronting individuals with hearing loss. Projects include automatic speech recognition, directional microphones, digital hearing aids, assistive

listening system assessment, electromagnetic interference issues, child-friendly audiometry, and technology training for rehabilitation counselors. The Gallaudet RERC also provides training in the use of hearing assistance technology to hearing health professionals, consumers and other stakeholders.
E Rs

REHABILITATION RESEARCH & TRAINING CENTER FOR PERSONS WHO ARE HARD OF HEARING OR LATE DEAFENED

CSPP Research and Service Foundation
Alliant University-San Diego
6160 Cornerstone Court East
San Diego, CA 92121-3725
Voice: (858) 623-2777 x388
TTY: (858) 554-1540
Voice/TTY: (800) 432-7619
FAX: (858) 642-0266
Web: http://www.cspp.edu
A federally funded Rehabilitation and Training Center (RRTC) that focuses on conducting research and developing training programs related to maintaining employment status and personal adjustment needs of individuals who are hard of hearing or late deafened. The new funding, awarded in September 1997, supports a program that broadens the RRTC's mandate from its former primary focus on mental health issues related to hearing loss to also include workplace issues for hard of hearing and late deafened. This objective is promoted through research, educational workshops, self-help groups, dissemination of materials and training sessions for hard of hearing and late deafened consumers, service providers, employers and all other interested persons.
E I Rs S

THE SEE CENTER FOR THE ADVANCEMENT OF DEAF CHILDREN

Main Office: P.O. Box 1181
Los Alamitos, CA 90720
Voice/TTY: (562) 430-1467
FAX: (562) 795-6614
E-mail: seectr@aol.com
Web: http://www.seecenter.org/
Information and referral for parents and educators of deafness-related topics and signing Exact English (SEE). Provides evaluation of sign skills, workshops, and consulting services related to communication in general and SEE in particular.
E I S

SELF HELP FOR HARD OF HEARING PEOPLE, INC.
7910 Woodmont Ave., Suite 1200
Bethesda, MD 20814
Voice: (301) 657-2248
TTY: (301) 657-2249
FAX: (301) 913-9413
Web: http://www.hearingloss.org
PUBLICATION: **Hearing Loss: The Journal of Self Help for Hard of Hearing People**
Promotes awareness and information about hearing loss, communication, assistive devices, and alternative communication skills through publications, exhibits, and presentations.
C E I S

TELECOMMUNICATIONS FOR THE DEAF, INC.
8630 Fenton Street, Suite 604
Silver Spring, MD 20910-3803
Voice: (301) 589-3786
TTY: (301) 589-3006
FAX: (301) 589-3797
Web: http://www.tdi-online.org
PUBLICATIONS: **GA-SK** (quarterly), **National Directory & Guide** (annual)
A nonprofit consumer advocacy organization promoting equal access to telecommunications and media for people who are deaf, hard of hearing, late deafened or deaf-blind. Conducts consumer education and involvement, technical assistance and consulting, application of existing and emerging technologies, networking and collaboration, uniformity of standards, national policy development and advocacy.
C E I

TRIPOD
1727 West Burbank Boulevard
Burbank, CA 91506-1312
Voice/TTY: (818) 972-2080
FAX: (818) 972-2090
Web: http://www.tripod.org
TRIPOD facilitates and supports communication and education programs that empower deaf and hard of hearing children and their families through gathering and disseminating information through fundraising, outreach, creative collaboration and family advocacy.
C E Rs S

USA DEAF SPORTS FEDERATION
911 Tierra Linda Drive
Frankfort, NY 40601-4633
Web: http://www.usadsf.org
PUBLICATION: **USADSF Bulletin, Deaf Sports Review**
Governing body for all deaf sports and recreation in the United States. Sponsors U.S. team to the World Games for the Deaf and other regional, national, and international competitions.
C I Rc So

VESTIBULAR DISORDERS ASSOCIATION
P.O. Box 4467
Portland, OR 97208-4467
Voice: (503) 229-7705
Voice: (800) 837-8428
FAX: (503) 229-8064
Web: http://www.vestibular.org
PUBLICATION: **On the Level**
Provides information and support for people with inner-ear vestibular disorders and develops awareness of the issues surrounding these disorders.
I M S

WORLD RECREATION ASSOCIATION OF THE DEAF, INC./USA
P.O. Box 3211
Quartz Hill, CA 93586
TTY/FAX: (661) 943-8879
PUBLICATION: **WRAD NEWS**
Web: http://www.wrad.org
Established to foster the development of innovation in recreational and cultural activities for the deaf and hard of hearing community.
I E P Rc So

Reprinted with permission

WORKERS' COMPENSATION ADMINISTRATORS DIRECTORY UNITED STATES, OTHER US AREAS AND CANADA

This Workers' Compensation Administrators Directory was compiled by Robert W. McDowell for the North Carolina Industrial Commission, 4319 Mail Service Center, Raleigh, North Carolina 27699-4319.

If you are looking for an overview of State Workers' Compensation Laws, the U.S. Department of Labor (http://www.dol.gov/) provides one in PDF (Portable Document Format). (Note: You must download and install a free Adobe Acrobat Reader to view and print PDF files.)

TABLE OF CONTENTS
U.S. Department of Labor
OWCP Regionals
United States and D.C.:
Other U.S. Areas: American Samoa Guam Navajo Nation Northern Mariana Islands Puerto Rico Virgin Islands
Canada

U.S. DEPARTMENT OF LABOR
U.S. Department of Labor (DOL) — http://www.dol.gov/
200 Constitution Avenue NW
Washington, District of Columbia 20210
DOL's Employment Standards Administration (ESA) — http://www.dol.gov/dol/esa/
(202) 219-6692, Fax: (202) 219-8568
ESA's Office of Workers' Compensation Programs (OWCP) — http://www.dol.gov/dol/esa/public/owcp_org.htm
(202) 219-6191

Contacts for Longshore and Harbor Workers' Compensation -http://www.dol.gov/dol/esa/public/contacts/owcp/lscontac.htm
Compensation — http://www.dol.gov/dol/esa/public/contacts/owcp/fecacont.htm
Contacts for Coal Mine Workers' Compensation —http://www.dol.gov/dol/esa/public/contacts/owcp/blcontac.htm

OWCP Regionals
Northeast Region (consists of New York and Boston offices)
201 Varick Street, Room 750
New York, New York 10014
(212) 337-2033

Boston Subregion
JFK Federal Building
Room E-260
Boston, Massachusetts 02203
(617) 565-2102

Region 3—Philadelphia
Curtis Center
Suite 780 West
170 S. Independence Mall West
Philadelphia, Pennsylvania 19106-3313
(215) 861-5401, Fax: (215) 861-5400

Region 4—Atlanta (Jacksonville, FL) —http://www.dol.gov/dol/esa/public/contacts/owcp/6do.htm
OWCP Region 4 covers Alabama, Florida, Georgia, Kentucky, Mississippi, North Carolina, South Carolina, and Tennessee.
   214 North Hogan Street, Room 1026
   Jacksonville, Florida 32202
   (904) 357-4725

Region 5—Chicago
   230 South Dearborn Street
   8th Floor
   Chicago, Illinois 60604
   (312) 596-7131

Region 6—Dallas
—http://www2.dol.gov/dol/esa/public/contacts/owcp/dallas/dallash.htm
OWCP Region 6 covers Arkansas, Louisiana, New Mexico, Oklahoma, and Texas.
   Federal Building
   525 South Griffin Street
   Room 407
   Dallas, Texas 75202
   (214) 767-4312

Region 7—Kansas City
   City Center Square Building
   1100 Main Street, Suite 750
   Kansas City, Missouri 64105
   (816) 426-2195

Region 8—Denver
   1999 Broadway, Suite 600
   Post Office Box 46550
   Denver, Colorado 80201-6550
   (720) 264-3160, Fax: (720) 264-3111

Region 9—San Francisco
—http://www.dol.gov/dol/esa/public/contacts/owcp/9sf.htm
OWCP Region 9 covers Arizona, California, Hawaii, Nevada, Guam, and Trust Territories of the Pacific.
   71 Stevenson Street
   Second Floor
   San Francisco, California 94105
   (415) 975-4160

Region 10—Seattle
   1111 Third Avenue, Suite 615
   Seattle, Washington 98101-3212
   (206) 553-5521

National Operations Office
   800 North Capitol Street, N.W., Room 800
   Washington, D.C. 20211
   (202) 219-4275

UNITED STATES AND D.C.

ALABAMA
State of Alabama—http://www.state.al.us/2k1/
Department of Industrial Relations—http://www.dir.state.al.us/
Workers' Compensation Division—http://www.dir.state.al.us/wc.htm
Industrial Relations Building
649 Monroe Street
Montgomery, Alabama 36131
(800) 528-5166, (334) 242-2868; Fax: (334) 261-3143; Fraud: (800) 923-2533;
Ombudsman: (800) 528-5166, (334) 242-2868 (in Montgomery area)

ALASKA
State of Alaska—http://www.state.ak.us/
Department of Labor and Workforce Development
http://www.labor.state.ak.us/home.htm
Workers' Compensation Division
http://www.labor.state.ak.us/wc/wc.htm
Post Office Box 25512
Juneau, Alaska 99802-5512
(907) 465-2790; Fax: (907) 465-2797

Workers' Compensation Board
http://www.gov.state.ak.us/boards/factsheet/fact110.html
Department of Labor
Post Office Box 25512
M/S 0700
Juneau, Alaska 99802-5512
(907) 465-2790, Fax: (907) 465-2797
Commissioner_Labor@labor.state.ak.us

ARIZONA
State of Arizona—http://www.state.az.us/
Industrial Commission of Arizona—http://www.ica.state.az.us/
800 West Washington
Phoenix, Arizona 85007
    or
Post Office Box 19070
Phoenix, Arizona 85005-9070
(602) 542-4411, Fax: (602) 542-7889; Ombudsman: (602) 542-4538,
Fax: (602) 542-4350
Download free PDF (Portable Document Format) versions of Arizona
workers' compensation forms courtesy Interface Technologies
http://www.interfacetec.com/

Industrial Commission Review Board
State Compensation Fund— http://www.statefund.com/
3031 North Second Street
Phoenix, Arizona 85012
(602) 631-2000; Fax: (602) 631-2213

ARKANSAS
State of Arkansas— http://www.state.ar.us/
Workers' Compensation Commission— http://www.awcc.state.ar.us/
4th & Spring Streets
Post Office Box 950
Little Rock, Arkansas 72203-0950
(800) 622-4472, (501) 682-3930; Fax: (501) 682-2777; Legal Advisor Direct:
(800) 250-2511; TDD: (800) 285-1131
Arkansas Relay System TDD: (800) 285-1131

CALIFORNIA

State of California—http://www.ca.gov/s/
Department of Industrial Relations—http://www.dir.ca.gov/
Commission on Health and Safety and Workers' Compensation
(CHSWC)—http://www.dir.ca.gov/CHSWC/chswc.html
455 Golden Gate Avenue, 10th Floor
San Francisco, California 94102
(415) 557-1304, Fax: (415) 703-4234, E-mail: chswc@hq.dir.ca.gov
Division of Workers' Compensation (DWC)
http://www.dir.ca.gov/DWC/dwc_home_page.htm
455 Golden Gate Avenue, 9th Floor
San Francisco, California 94102-3660
    or
Post Office Box 420603
San Francisco, California 94142
E-mail: dwc@dir.ca.gov
(800) 736-7401, (415) 703-4600 ; Fax: (415) 703-3971
Download free PDF (Portable Document Format) versions of California
workers' compensation forms courtesy Interface Technologies
http://www.interfacetec.com/

Industrial Medical Council (IMC)—http://www.dir.ca.gov/IMC/imchp.html
Post Office Box 8888
San Francisco, California 994128-8888
(800) 794-6900 (in California), (650) 737-2000
Workers' Compensation Appeals Board (WCAB)—http://www.dir.ca.gov/
WCAB/wcab.htm
455 Golden Gate Avenue, 2nd Floor
San Francisco, California 94102-3660
    or
Post Office Box 429459
San Francisco, California 94142-9459
(415) 975-0700

Self-Insurance Plans (SIP)—http://www.dir.ca.gov/SIP/sip.html
2265 Watt Avenue, Suite 1
Sacramento, California 95825
(916) 483-3392; Fax: (916) 483-1535, E-mail: SIP@dir.ca.gov

State Compensation Insurance Fund (SCIF)—http://www.scif.com/
1275 Market Street
San Francisco, California 94103
(415) 565-1234, Claims Reporting Service (toll free): (888) 222-3211

COLORADO

State of Colorado—http://www.state.co.us/
Department of Labor & Employment—http://www.coworkforce.com/
Division of Workers' Compensation
http://www.coworkforce.com/DWC/
1515 Arapahoe Street
Tower 2, Suite 500
Denver, Colorado 80202-2117
(888) 390-7936, (800) 685-0891 (Spanish), (303) 575-8700, Fax: (303) 318-8710, E-mail: workers.comp@state.co.us
Download free PDF (Portable Document Format) versions of Colorado
workers' compensation forms courtesy Interface Technologies— http://www.interfacetec.com/

Industrial Claims Appeals Office
    Workers' Compensation: (303) 620-4277
    Unemployment Insurance: (303) 620-4272

1515 Arapahoe Street
Tower 2, Suite 350
Denver, Colorado 80202
(303) 894-2378

CONNECTICUT
State of Connecticut—http://www.state.ct.us/index.asp
Workers' Compensation Commission—http://wcc.state.ct.us/
Capitol Place
21 Oak Street, Fourth Floor
Hartford, Connecticut 06106
(860) 493-1500, Fax: (860) 247-1361
Download free PDF (Portable Document Format) versions of Connecticut workers' compensation forms courtesy Interface Technologies— http://www.interfacetec.com/

Compensation Review Board (CRB)—http://wcc.state.ct.us/index2.htm
Capitol Place
21 Oak Street, Fourth Floor
Hartford, Connecticut 06106
(203) 493-1500, Fax: (203) 247-1361

DELAWARE
State of Delaware—http://www.state.de.us/
Department of Labor—http://www.delawareworks.com/
4425 North Market Street
Wilmington, Delaware 19802
Division of Industrial Affairs
http://www.delawareworks.com/divisions/industaffairs/diaindex.html
4425 North Market Street
Wilmington, Delaware 19802
Office of Workers' Compensation
http://www.delawareworks.com/divisions/industaffairs/
workers.comp.htm
State Office Building, Sixth Floor
820 North French Street
Wilmington, Delaware 19801
(302) 761-8200, Fax: (302) 577-3750

DISTRICT OF COLUMBIA
District of Columbia—http://www.ci.washington.dc.us/
Department of Employment Services—http://does.ci.washington.dc.us/
Office of Workers' Compensation
http://does.ci.washington.dc.us/services/wkr_comp.shtm
1200 Upshur Street, NW
Post Office Box 56098
Washington, District of Columbia 20011
(202) 576-6265, Fax: (202) 541-3595

FLORIDA
State of Florida—http://www.state.fl.us/
Department of Labor and Employment Security
http://www2.myflorida.com/les/
Division of Workers' Compensation
http://www2.myflorida.com/les/wc/
301 Forrest Building
2728 Centerview Drive
Tallahassee, Florida 32399-0680
(850) 488-2514; Fax: (850) 922-6779; Fraud: (800) 742-2214 (in Florida) (Department of Insurance Bureau of Workers' Compensation Fraud: (850) 922-3116); Safety: (800) 367-4378 (in Florida), (850) 488-3044

Download free PDF (Portable Document Format) versions of Florida workers' compensation forms courtesy Interface Technologies
http://www.interfacetec.com/

Workers' Compensation Oversight Board
http://www2.myflorida.com/les/wc/board.html
100 Marathon Building
2574 Seagate Drive
Tallahassee, Florida 32399-2152
(850) 487-2613, SunCom: 277-2613; Fax: (850) 487-3232

Office of Judges of Compensation Claims
http://www2.myflorida.com/les/jcc/jccjdg.html
180 Rhyne Building
2740 Centerview Drive
Tallahassee, Florida 32399-0655
(850) 488-2043, Fax: (850) 922-3661

GEORGIA
State of Georgia—http://www.state.ga.us/
Georgia State Board of Workers' Compensation
http://www.ganet.org/sbwc/
270 Peachtree Street, NW
Atlanta, Georgia 30303-1299
(800) 533-0682, (404) 656-3875, Fax: (404) 656-7768, Fraud/Compliance: (404) 657-1391, Safety Library: (404) 656-9057
Download free PDF (Portable Document Format) versions of Georgia workers' compensation forms courtesy Interface Technologies
http://www.interfacetec.com/

Georgia Subsequent Injury Trust Fund—http://www.ganet.org/sitf/
Suite 500, North Tower
1720 Peachtree Street, NW
Atlanta, Georgia 30309-2420
(404) 206-6360, Fax: (404) 206-6363, TDD: (404) 206-5053

HAWAII
State of Hawaii—http://www.hawaii.gov/
Department of Labor & Industrial Relations (DLIR)—http://dlir.state.hi.us/
830 Punchbowl Street
Honolulu, HI 96813
Disability Compensation Division—http://dlir.state.hi.us/dc_1.pdf
830 Punchbowl Street, Room 209
Honolulu, Hawaii 96813
(808) 586-9151, Fax: (808) 586-9219

Labor & Industrial Relations Appeals Board
888 Mililani Street, Room 400
Honolulu, Hawaii 96813
(808) 586-8600

IDAHO
State of Idaho—http://www2.state.id.us/
Industrial Commission—http://www2.state.id.us/iic/index.html
317 Main Street
Post Office Box 83720
Boise, Idaho 83720-0041
(800) 950-2110, (208) 334-6000; Fax: (208) 334-2321; TDD: (800) 950-2110

State Insurance Fund—http://www.state.id.us/isif/index.htm
1215 West State Street
Post Office Box 83720
Boise, Idaho 83720-0044
(800) 334-2370, (208) 334-2370 (in the Boise area); Fax: (208) 334-2262
(Policyholder Services,
Administration, Management Services, Legal), (208) 334-3253 (Claims),
(208) 334-3254 (Underwriting); Fraud: (800) 448-ISIF (4743)
E-mail addresses:
   Claims: Claims@isif.state.id.us
   Customer Service Center: CustomerService@isif.state.id.us
   Fraud: Claims@isif.state.id.us
   General Information/News Media Inquiries: abunch@isif.state.id.us
   Management Services: ManagementServices@isif.state.id.us
   Manager's Office: Administration@isif.state..id.us
   Policyholder Services: PHS@isif.state.id.us
   Underwriting: Underwriting@isif.state.id.us

ILLINOIS
State of Illinois—http://www.state.il.us/
Industrial Commission—http://www.state.il.us/agency/iic/
100 West Randolph Street, Suite 8-200
Chicago, Illinois 60601
(312) 814-6611, Fax: (312) 814-6523
Download free PDF (Portable Document Format) versions of Illinois workers' compensation forms courtesy Interface Technologies
http://www.interfacetec.com/

Office of Self-Insurance Administration
701 South Second Street
Springfield, Illinois 62704
(217) 785-7084, Fax: (217) 785-6557

INDIANA
State of Indiana—http://www.state.in.us/
Workers' Compensation Board of Indiana
http://www.state.in.us/wkcomp/index.html
Government Center South
402 West Washington Street, Room W-196
Indianapolis, Indiana 46204
(317) 232-3808; Claims/Statistics: (317) 233-4930; Fax: (317) 233-5493;
Insurance: (317) 233-3910; Ombudsman: (800) 824-COMP (2667),
(317) 232-5922

IOWA
State of Iowa—http://www.state.ia.us/
Iowa Workforce Development—http://www.iowaworkforce.org/
1000 East Grand Avenue
Des Moines, Iowa 50319-0209
(800) JOB-IOWA, (515) 281-5387
Iowa Division of Workers' Compensation
http://www.state.ia.us/iwd/wc/index.html
1000 East Grand Avenue
Des Moines, Iowa 50319-0209
(800) JOB-IOWA (562-4692), (515) 281-5387; Fax: (515) 281-6501
E-mail: IWD.DWC@iwd.state.ia.us

KANSAS
State of Kansas—http://www.state.ks.us/
Department of Human Resources—http://www.hr.state.ks.us/
Kansas Workers' Compensation

http://www.hr.state.ks.us/wc/html/wc.htm
800 SW Jackson, Suite 600
Topeka, Kansas 66612-1227
(800) 332-0353, (785) 296-3441; Fax: (785) 296-0839; Fraud:
(800) 332-0353, (785) 296-6392; Industrial Safety & Health: (800) 332-0353,
(785) 296-4386; Ombudsman: (800) 332-0353, (785) 296-2996

KENTUCKY
Commonwealth of Kentucky—http://www.kydirect.net/
Kentucky Labor Cabinet
http://www.state.ky.us/agencies/labor/labrhome.htm
1047 U.S. 127S, Suite 4
Frankfort, Kentucky 40601
(502) 564-3070
Department of Workers' Claims—http://dwc.state.ky.us/
Perimeter Park West, Building C
1270 Louisville Road
Frankfort, Kentucky 40601
(502) 564-5550 (Administrative Services, Open Records);
Fax: (502) 564-8250 (Administrative Services), (502) 564-9533 (Ombuds-
man), (502) 564-5732 (Open Records), (502) 564-0916 (Security and
Compliance); Ombudsman: (800) 554-8601 (Frankfort), (800) 554-8603
(Paducah); Security and Compliance: (502) 564-0905
E-mail: kywc.ombudsman@mail.state.ky.us
Download free PDF (Portable Document Format) versions of Kentucky
workers' compensation forms courtesy Interface Technologies
http://www.interfacetec.com/

Workers' Compensation Funding Commission
#42 Millcreek Park
Post Office Box 1220
Frankfort, Kentucky 40602-1220
(502) 573-3505, Fax: (502) 573-4923

Kentucky Workers' Compensation Law (via CompEd, Inc.)
http://www.comped.net/

LOUISIANA
State of Louisiana—http://www.state.la.us/
Department of Labor—http://www.laworks.net/
Mailing Address:
Post Office Box 94094
Baton Rouge, Louisiana 70804-9094
Street Address:
1001 North 23rd Street
Baton Rouge, Louisiana 70804
(225) 342-3111
Office of Workers' Compensation Administration
http://www.laworks.net/Sec2OWCA.asp
Mailing Address:
Post Office Box 94040
Baton Rouge, Louisiana 70804-9040
Street Address:
1001 North 23rd Street
Baton Rouge, Louisiana 70802
(225) 342-7555, Fax: (225) 342-5665, Fraud: (800) 201-3362, Safety:
(800) 201-2497
E-mail: owca@ldol.state.la.us

MAINE
State of Maine—http://www.state.me.us/
Workers' Compensation Board—http://www.state.me.us/wcb/
27 State House Station
Augusta, Maine 04333
(207) 287-7096; Fax: (207) 287-7198
Download free PDF (Portable Document Format) versions of Maine workers' compensation forms courtesy Interface Technologies
http://www.interfacetec.com/

MARYLAND
State of Maryland—http://www.state.md.us/
Maryland Workers' Compensation Commission
http://www.charm.net/~wcc/
10 East Baltimore Street
Baltimore, Maryland 21202
(800) 492-0479, (410) 864-5100; Fax: (410) 333-8122

Download free PDF (Portable Document Format) versions of Maryland workers' compensation forms courtesy Interface Technologies
http://www.interfacetec.com/

Insured Workers' Insurance Fund—http://www.iwif.com/
8722 Loch Raven Boulevard
Towson, Maryland 21286-2235
(800) 492-0197, (410) 494-2200 Fax: (410) 494-2001

MASSACHUSETTS
Commonwealth of Massachusetts—http://www.state.ma.us/
Department of Industrial Accidents—http://www.state.ma.us/dia/
600 Washington Street, 7th Floor
Boston, Massachusetts 02111
(800) 323-3249, (617) 727-4900; Fax: (617) 727-6477; TTY: (800) 224-6196
Download free PDF (Portable Document Format) versions of Massachusetts workers' compensation forms courtesy Interface Technologies
http://www.interfacetec.com/

Massachusetts Workers' Compensation Advisory Council
http://www.state.ma.us/wcac/wcac.html
600 Washington Street, Seventh Floor
Boston, Massachusetts 02111
(617) 727-4900 x378, Fax: (617) 727-7122

MICHIGAN
State of Michigan
http://www.migov.state.mi.us/MichiganGovernor.htm
Department of Consumer & Industry Services—http://www.cis.state.mi.us/home.htm
G. Mennen William Building
525 W. Ottawa
Post Office Box 30004
Lansing, Michigan 48909
(517) 373-1820
Bureau of Workers' Disability Compensation
http://www.cis.state.mi.us/wkrcomp/bwdc/home.htm
7150 Harris Drive
Post Office Box 30016
Lansing, Michigan 48909
(517) 322-1296, Fax: (517) 322-1808, TDD in Lansing: (517) 322-5987
Download free PDF (Portable Document Format) versions of Michigan

workers' compensation forms courtesy Interface Technologies
http://www.interfacetec.com/

Board of Magistrates
http://www.cis.state.mi.us/wkrcomp/bmag/home.htm
Post Office Box 30016
Lansing, Michigan 48909
(517) 241-9380, Fax: (517) 241-9379, TDD in Lansing: (517) 322-5987

Workers' Compensation Appellate Commission
http://www.cis.state.mi.us/wkrcomp/wcac/home.htm
Victor Office Center, Third Floor
201 North Washington Square
Post Office Box 30468
Lansing, Michigan 48909-7968
(517) 335-5828, Fax: (517) 335-5829

Michigan Economic Development Corporation
http://medc.michigan.org/
300 North Washington Square
Lansing, Michigan 48913
(517) 373-9808
Compensation—http://medc.michigan.org/services/workerscomp/
Compensation Cost Control Service
Victor Office Center, Fourth Floor
201 North Washington Square
Lansing, Michigan 48909-7968
(517) 373-9809, Fax: (517) 241-3689

MINNESOTA

State of Minnesota—http://www.state.mn.us/
Department of Labor & Industry—http://www.doli.state.mn.us/
443 Lafayette Road North
St. Paul, Minnesota 55155-4307
(800) DIAL-DLI (342-5354), (651) 284-5000; TTY: (612) 297-4198

Workers' Compensation Division
http://www.doli.state.mn.us/workcomp.html
443 Lafayette Road North
St. Paul, Minnesota 55155
(800) DIAL-DLI (342-5354) in Greater Minnesota, (800) 342-5354 or
(651) 284-5005 in the St. Paul area, (800) 365-4584 or (218) 723-4670 in the
Duluth area; Fax: (651) 282-5405; Fraud: (888) 372-8366, (651) 297-5797,
TDD: (651) 297-4198
E-mail: DLI.Workcomp@state.mn.us; Fraud: DLI.ISU @state.mn.us
Download free PDF (Portable Document Format) versions of Minnesota
workers' compensation forms courtesy Interface Technologies
http://www.interfacetec.com/

Workers' Compensation Court of Appeals—http://www.workerscomp.st
ate.mn.us/
405 Minnesota Judicial Center
25 Constitution Avenue
St. Paul, Minnesota 55155
(651) 296-6526, Fax: (651) 297-2520, TTY/TDD: (800) 627-3529

MISSISSIPPI

State of Mississippi—http://www.state.ms.us
Mississippi Workers' Compensation Commission
http://www.mwcc.state.ms.us/
STREET ADDRESS:
   1428 Lakeland Drive
   Jackson, Mississippi 39216
MAILING ADDRESS:
   Post Office Box 5300
   Jackson, Mississippi 39296-5300
(601) 987-4200, Fraud: (601) 359-4250

MISSOURI

State of Missouri—http://www.state.mo.us/
Department of Labor and Industrial Relations
http://www.dolir.state.mo.us/dolir1a.htm
3315 West Truman Boulevard
Jefferson City, Missouri 65102
   or
Post Office Box 504
Jefferson City, Missouri 65102-0504
(573) 751-9691, Fax: (573) 751-4135

Division of Workers' Compensation
http://www.dolir.state.mo.us/wc/index.htm
STREET ADDRESS:
   3315 West Truman Boulevard
   Jefferson City, Missouri 65102
MAILING ADDRESS:
   Post Office Box 58
Jefferson City, Missouri 65102-0058
(573) 751-4231, Fax: (573) 751-2012, Employee Hotline: (800) 775-2667,
Fraud and Noncompliance: (800)-592-6003, (573)-526-6630
Download free PDF (Portable Document Format) versions of Missouri
workers' compensation forms courtesy Interface Technologies
http://www.interfacetec.com/

Labor and Industrial Relations Commission
http://www.dolir.state.mo.us/lirc/index.htm
STREET ADDRESS:
   3315 West Truman Boulevard
   Jefferson City, Missouri 65102
MAILING ADDRESS:
   Post Office Box 599
   Jefferson City, Missouri 65102-0599
(573) 751-2461, Fax: (573) 751-7806

MONTANA

State of Montana—http://www.state.mt.us/
Montana State Compensation Insurance Fund
http://stfund.state.mt.us/
STREET ADDRESS:
   5 South Last Chance Gulch
   Helena, Montana 59601
MAILING ADDRESS:
   Post Office Box 4759
   Helena, Montana 59604-4759
(406) 444-6500, Customer Service: (800) 332-6102, Claim Reporting: (800)
243-9121, Fraud Reporting: (888) 682-7463

Workers' Compensation Court—http://wcc.dli.state.mt.us/
STREET ADDRESS:
  1625 11th Avenue
  Helena, Montana
MAILING ADDRESS:
  Post Office Box 537
  Helena, Montana 59624-0537
(406) 444-7794, Fax: (406) 444-7798

Employment Relations Division—http://erd.dli.state.mt.us/
Department of Labor & Industry—http://dli.state.mt.us/
Post Office Box 8011
Helena, Montana 59624
(406) 444-6530, Fax: (406) 444-4140, Fraud: (800) 922-2873

Self Insurers' Guaranty Fund
Post Office Box 4133
Missoula, Montana 59806
(406) 549-8849

NEBRASKA

State of Nebraska—http://www.state.ne.us/
Workers' Compensation Court—http://www.nol.org/home/WC/
State House, 13th Floor
Post Office Box 98908
Lincoln, Nebraska 68509-8908
(800) 599-5155 (in Nebraska only), (402) 471-6468 (Lincoln and out of state), Fax: (402) 471-2700

NEVADA

State of Nevada — http://silver.state.nv.us/
Department of Business & Industry
http://www.state.nv.us/b&i/index.htm
In Northern Nevada:
788 Fairview Avenue, Suite 100
Carson City, Nevada 89701-5491
(775) 687-4250, Fax: (775) 687-4266

In Southern Nevada:
555 E. Washington Avenue, Suite 4900
Las Vegas, Nevada 89101
(702) 486-2750, Fax: 702-486-2758

Division of Industrial Relations — http://dirweb.state.nv.us/
400 West King Street, Suite 400
Carson City, Nevada 89703
(775) 687-3032, Fax: (775) 687-6305

Industrial Insurance Regulation Section
http://dirweb.state.nv.us/iirs.htm
400 West King Street, Suite 400
Carson City, Nevada 89703
(775) 687-3033, Fax: (775) 687-6305

1301 North Green Valley Parkway, Suite 200
Henderson, Nevada 89014
(702) 486-9080, Fax: (702) 990-0364

Nevada Attorney for Injured Workers — http://www.state.nv.us/b&i/aiw/
1000 East William Street, Suite 213
Carson City, Nevada 89710
(775) 687-4076, Fax: (775) 687-4134
E-mail: NAIW@govmail.state.nv.us

Employers Insurance Company of Nevada
http://www.employersinsco.com/
515 East Musser Street
Carson City, Nevada 89714
(775) 886-1000; Claim Reporting: (888) 900-1455, Fax: (775) 327-2701;
Underwriting/Insurance Services:
(888) 682-6671
E-mail: info@eicn.com

NEW HAMPSHIRE
State of New Hampshire—http://www.state.nh.us/
Department of Labor—http://www.state.nh.us/dol/index.html
95 Pleasant Street
Concord, New Hampshire 03301
(603) 271-3177
Workers' Compensation Division
http://www.state.nh.us/dol/dol-wc/index.html
95 Pleasant Street
Concord, New Hampshire 03301
(603) 271-3174 (claims), (603) 271-2042 (coverage), (603) 271-6172
(self-insurance), (603) 271-3328 (vocational rehabilitation)
Download free PDF (Portable Document Format) versions of New
Hampshire workers' compensation forms courtesy Interface Technologies— http://www.interfacetec.com/

NEW JERSEY
State of New Jersey—http://www.state.nj.us/
Department of Labor—http://www.state.nj.us/labor/
John Fitch Plaza
Post Office Box 110
Trenton, New Jersey 08625
(609) 292-2323, Fax: (609) 633-9271
Division of Workers' Compensation
http://www.state.nj.us/labor/wc/Default.htm
Post Office Box 381
Trenton, New Jersey 08625-0381
(609) 292-2414, Fax: (609) 984-2515
Download free PDF (Portable Document Format) versions of New Jersey
workers' compensation forms courtesy Interface Technologies
http://www.interfacetec.com/

N.J. Compensation Rating and Inspection Bureau
http://www.njcrib.com/
60 Park Place
Newark, New Jersey 07102
(973) 622-6014, Fax: (973) 622-6110

NEW MEXICO
State of New Mexico—http://www.state.nm.us/
Workers' Compensation Administration—http://www.state.nm.us/wca/
Post Office Box 27198
Albuquerque, New Mexico 87125-7198
E-mail: WCAHotline@state.nm.us
(800) 255-7965, (505) 841-6000, Fax: (505) 841-6009, Help Line/Hot Line:
(866) WORKOMP (967-5667)

NEW YORK

State of New York—http://www.state.ny.us/
New York State Workers' Compensation Board
http://www.wcb.state.ny.us/
100 Broadway-Menands
Albany, New York 12241
(518) 474-6670, Fax: (518) 473-1415
Download free PDF (Portable Document Format) versions of New York
workers' compensation forms courtesy Interface Technologies
http://www.interfacetec.com/

New York State Insurance Fund—http://www.nysif.com/
199 Church Street
New York, New York 10007
(212) 312-9000, Fax: (212) 385-2073

NORTH CAROLINA

State of North Carolina—http://www.sips.state.nc.us/
Department of Commerce—http://www.nccommerce.com/
Mailing Address:
4301 Mail Service Center
Raleigh, North Carolina 27699-4301
Street Address:
301 North Wilmington Street
Raleigh, NC 27020-0571
(919) 733-4151
E-mail: info@mail.commerce.state.nc.us

North Carolina Industrial Commission—http://www.comp.state.nc.us/
Mailing Address:
4319 Mail Service Center
Raleigh, North Carolina 27699-4319
Street Address:
Dobbs Building (sixth floor)
430 North Salisbury Street
Raleigh, North Carolina 27603-5937
(919) 807-2500, Fax: (919) 715-0282

Fraud Investigations Section: (888) 891-4895 (in North Carolina)
http://www.comp.state.nc.us/ncic/pages/fraud.htm
Ombudsman Section: (800) 688-8349
http://www.comp.state.nc.us/ncic/pages/ombudsmn.htm
Safety Education Section: (919) 807-2603
http://www.comp.state.nc.us/ncic/pages/safety.htm
Download free PDF (Portable Document Format) versions of North Carolina workers' compensation forms courtesy Interface Technologies
http://www.interfacetec.com/

NORTH DAKOTA

State of North Dakota—http://discovernd.com/
North Dakota Workers' Compensation
http://www.ndworkerscomp.com/
500 East Front Avenue
Bismark, North Dakota 58504-5685
(800) 777-5033, (701) 328-3800, Fax: (701) 328-3820

OHIO

State of Ohio—http://www.state.oh.us/
Ohio Bureau of Workers' Compensation—http://www.ohiobwc.com/
30 West Spring Street
Columbus, Ohio 43215-2256
E-mail: Feedback@bwc.state.oh.us
(800) OHIOBWC, (614) 644-6292, Fax: (614) 752-9021
Download free PDF (Portable Document Format) versions of Ohio workers' compensation forms courtesy Interface Technologies
http://www.interfacetec.com/

Industrial Commission of Ohio—http://www.ohioic.com/index.jsp
30 West Spring Street
Columbus, Ohio 43215-2256
(800) 521-2691, (614) 466-6136, Fax: (614) 752-8304

OKLAHOMA

State of Oklahoma—http://www.state.ok.us/
Department of Labor—http://www.okdol.state.ok.us/
4001 North Lincoln Boulevard
Oklahoma City, Oklahoma 73105-5212
(888) 269-5353, (405) 528-1500 Fax: (405) 528-5751
Workers' Enforcement Compensation Division
http://www.okdol.state.ok.us/workcomp/index.htm

Oklahoma Workers' Compensation Court—http://www.owcc.state.ok.us/
Denver N. Davison Court Building
1915 North Stiles Avenue
Oklahoma City, Oklahoma 73105
(800) 522-8210 (statewide), (405) 522-8600, Fax: (405) 522-8683 (2nd floor offices), (405) 522-8651 (records department), (405) 522-8687 (administration)

CompSource Oklahoma—http://www.compsourceok.com/
(formerly the Oklahoma State Insurance Fund)
Mailing Address:
Post Office Box 53505
Oklahoma City, Oklahoma 73152-3505
Street Addresses:
(Administration, Claims, Financial Services, Special Investigations)
1901 North Walnut Avenue
Oklahoma City, Oklahoma 73105
(Policyholder Services, Information Systems)
410 North Walnut Avenue
Oklahoma City, Oklahoma 73104
(800) 872-7015 (Report an Injury), (405) 232-7663, Fax: (405) 552-5800, Fraud: (800) 899-1847.

OREGON

State of Oregon—http://www.state.or.us/
Department of Consumer & Business Services
http://www.cbs.state.or.us/
350 Winter Street NE
Salem, Oregon 97301-3878
(503) 378-4100, Fax: (503) 378-6444

Workers' Compensation Division —http://www.cbs.state.or.us/wcd/
350 Winter Street NE, Room 27
Salem, Oregon 97301-3879
(800) 452-0288 (Workers' Compensation Infoline); (503) 947-7810, Fax: (503) 947-7514; TTY: (503) 947-7993; Fraud Hotline: (800) 422-8778 (in

Oregon); Small Business Ombudsman: (503) 378-4209, Fax: (503) 373-7639; Ombudsman for Injured Workers: (800) 927-1271, (503) 378-3351, Fax: (503) 373-7639
dcbs.wcdmail@state.or.us

Workers' Compensation Board—http://www.cbs.state.or.us/wcb/
2601 25th Street SE, Suite 150
Salem, Oregon 97302-1282
(503) 378-3308

Workers' Compensation Management-Labor Advisory Committee—http://www.cbs.state.or.us/mlac/
Department of Consumer & Business Services
350 Winter Street, Room 200
Salem, Oregon 97301-3878
(503) 947-7867; Fax: (503) 378-6444

Ombudsman for Injured Workers—http://www.cbs.state.or.us/external/wco/index.html
350 Winter Street NE, Room 160
Salem, Oregon 97310
(800) 927-1271, (503) 378-3351
Ombudsman for Small Business— http://www.cbs.state.or.us/external/sbo/index.html
350 Winter Street NE
Salem, Oregon 97301-3878
(503) 378-4209, V/TTY: (503) 378-4100

SAIF Corporation—http://www.saif.com/
400 High Street SE
Salem, Oregon 97312-1000
(800) 285-8525, (503) 373-8000

PENNSYLVANIA
State of Pennsylvania—http://www.state.pa.us/PAPower/
Department of Labor and Industry— http://www.dli.state.pa.us/landi/site/default.asp
Labor & Industry Building
Room 1700
7th and Forster Streets
Harrisburg, Pennsylvania 17120
(717) 787-5279
Bureau of Workers' Compensation— http://www.dli.state.pa.us
1171 South Cameron Street, Room 324
Harrisburg, Pennsylvania 17104-2501
(800) 482-2383 (inside Pennsylvania), (717) 772-4447 (local/out of state), TTY: (800) 362-4228 (for hearing and speech impaired only)
E-mail: ra-li-bwc-helpline@state.pa.us
Download free PDF (Portable Document Format) versions of Pennsylvania workers' compensation forms courtesy Interface Technologies— http://www.interfacetec.com/

State Workmen's Insurance Fund
100 Lackawanna Avenue
Scranton, Pennsylvania 18503
(570) 941-1600

Workmen's Compensation Appeal Board
1171 South Cameron Street, Room 305
Harrisburg, Pennsylvania 17104-2511
(717) 783-7838

RHODE ISLAND

State of Rhode Island—http://www.state.ri.us/
Workers' Compensation Court
One Dorrance Plaza
Providence, Rhode Island 02903
(401) 277-3097, Fax: (401) 421-3123

Department of Labor and Training—http://www.dlt.state.ri.us/
1511 Pontiac Avenue
Cranston, Rhode Island 02920-4407
(401) 462-8000
Workers' Compensation Division
1511 Pontiac Avenue
Cranston, Rhode Island 02920-0942
Post Office Box 20190
Cranston, Rhode Island 02920-0190
(401) 462-8100, Fax: (401) 462-8105, TDD: (401) 462-8084
Download free PDF (Portable Document Format) versions of Rhode Island workers' compensation forms courtesy Interface Technologies http://www.interfacetec.com/

SOUTH CAROLINA

State of South Carolina—http://www.state.sc.us/
Workers' Compensation Commission—http://www.state.sc.us/wcc/
Post Office Box 1715
1612 Marion Street
Columbia, South Carolina 29202-1715
(803) 737-5700, Fax: (803) 737-5768
executivedirector@infoave.net
Download free fillable PDF (Portable Document Format) versions of South Carolina workers' compensation forms courtesy Interface Technologies— http://www.interfacetec.com/

S.C. State Accident Fund
Post Office Box 102100
800 Dutch Square Boulevard
Columbia, South Carolina 29221-5000
(800) 521-6576, (803) 896-5800

S.C. Second Injury Fund
22 Koger Center
Winthrop Building, Suite 119220
Executive Center Drive
Columbia, South Carolina 29210
(803) 798-2722, Fax: (803) 798-5290

S.C. Workers' Compensation Uninsured Employers' Fund
22 Koger Center
Winthrop Building, Suite 119220
Executive Center Drive
Columbia, South Carolina 29210
(803) 798-2722, Fax: (803) 798-5290

SOUTH DAKOTA

State of South Dakota—http://www.state.sd.us/
Department of Labor
http://www.state.sd.us/state/executive/dol/dol.htm
Division of Labor and Management
http://www.state.sd.us/state/executive/dol/dlm/dlm-home.htm
Kneip Building, Third Floor
700 Governors Drive

Pierre, South Dakota 57501-2291
E-mail: labor@dol-pr.state.sd.us
(605) 773-3681, Fax: (605) 773-4211

TENNESSEE

State of Tennessee—http://www.state.tn.us/
Department of Labor and Workforce Development
http://www.state.tn.us/labor-wfd/
Workers' Compensation Division—
http://www.state.tn.us/labor-wfd/wcomp.html
710 James Robertson Parkway
Gateway Plaza, Second Floor
Nashville, Tennessee 37243-0665
(800) 332-2667 (within Tennessee), (615) 532-4812, Fax: (615) 532-1468
Download free PDF (Portable Document Format) versions of Tennessee
workers' compensation forms courtesy Interface Technologies
http://www.interfacetec.com/

TEXAS

State of Texas—http://www.state.tx.us/
Texas Workers' Compensation Commission (TWCC)
http://www.twcc.state.tx.us/
Southfield Building, MS-3
4000 South IH-35
Austin, Texas 78704-7491
(512) 804-4100 or 804-4636, Fax: (512) 804-4101, Fraud Hotline:
(888) 327-8818, Injured Worker
Hotline/Ombudsman: (800) 252-7031
executive.director@twcc.state.tx.us
Download free PDF (Portable Document Format) versions of Texas workers' compensation forms courtesy Interface Technologies
http://www.interfacetec.com/

Research and Oversight Council on Workers' Compensation
http://www.roc.capnet.state.tx.us/
9800 North Lamar Boulevard, Suite 260
Austin, Texas 78753
E-mail: roc@mail.capnet.state.tx.us
(512) 469-7811 Fax: (512) 469-7481, TTD: (800) 736-2989

UTAH

State of Utah—http://www.state.ut.us/
Labor Commission—http://www.labor.state.ut.us/
Industrial Accidents Division
http://www.labor.state.ut.us/indacc/indacc.htm
Post Office Box 146610
Salt Lake City, Utah 84114-6610
(801) 530-6800, Fax: (801) 530-6804

VERMONT

State of Vermont—http://www.state.vt.us/
Department of Labor & Industry—http://www.state.vt.us/labind/
National Life Building
Drawer 20
Montpelier, Vermont 05620-3401
(802) 828-2288, Fax: (802) 828-2195

Workers' Compensation Division
http://www.state.vt.us/labind/wcindex.htm
National Life Building

Drawer 20
Montpelier, Vermont 05620-3401
(802) 828-2286, Fax: (802) 828-2195
Download free PDF (Portable Document Format) versions of Vermont
workers' compensation forms courtesy Interface Technologies
http://www.interfacetec.com/

VIRGINIA
Commonwealth of Virginia—http://www.state.va.us/
Virginia Workers' Compensation Commission
http://www.vwc.state.va.us
1000 DMV Drive
Richmond, Virginia 23220
(804) 367-8600, Fax: (804) 367-9740, TDD: (804) 367-8600
Download free PDF (Portable Document Format) versions of Virginia
workers' compensation forms courtesy Interface Technologies
http://www.interfacetec.com/

WASHINGTON
State of Washington—http://access.wa.gov/
Department of Labor and Industries—http://www.wa.gov/lni/
Labor and Industries Building
Post Office Box 44001
Olympia, Washington 98504-4001
(360) 902-4213, Fax: (360) 902-4202

Board of Industrial Insurance Appeals—http://www.wa.gov/biia/
2430 Chandler Court, SW
Post Office Box 42401
Olympia, Washington 98504-2401
(800) 442-0447, (360) 753-9646, Fax: (360) 586-5611
Download free PDF (Portable Document Format) versions of Washington
workers' compensation forms courtesy Interface Technologies
http://www.interfacetec.com/

Workers' Compensation Information—http://www.wa.gov/lni/insurance/

WEST VIRGINIA
West Virginia—http://www.state.wv.us/
Bureau of Employment Programs—http://www.state.wv.us/bep/
Post Office Box 3824
Charleston, West Virginia 25338-3824
(304) 558-2630 Fax: (304) 558-2992

Workers' Compensation Division
http://www.state.wv.us/bep/wc/default.HTM
Post Office Box 3824
Charleston, West Virginia 25338-3824
(800) 628-4265, (304) 926-5048 Fax: (304) 926-5372

Office of Judges —http://www.state.wv.us/bep/WC/OOJ/DEFAULT.HTM
Post Office Box 2233
Charleston West Virginia 25328-2233
(304) 558-1686 Fax: (304) 558-1021

Workers' Compensation Appeal Board
Post Office Box 2628
Charleston, West Virginia 25329-2628
(304) 558-3375, Fax: (304) 558-1322

WISCONSIN

State of Wisconsin—http://www.wisconsin.gov/state/home
Department of Workforce Development—http://www.dwd.state.wi.us/
Workers' Compensation Division
http://www.dwd.state.wi.us/wc/default.htm
Mailing Address:
Post Office Box 7901
Madison, Wisconsin 53707-7901
Street Address:
Room C100
201 East Washington Avenue
Madison, Wisconsin 53703
(608) 266-1340; Fax: (608) 267-0394; Fraud (608) 261-8486
Download free PDF (Portable Document Format) versions of Wisconsin
workers' compensation forms courtesy of Interface Technologies
http://www.interfacetec.com/

Workers' Compensation Advisory Council
http://www.dwd.state.wi.us/notespub/wcadvcou/
(608) 266-6841

Wisconsin Compensation Rating Bureau—http://www.wcrb.org/
Mailing Address:
Post Office Box 3080
Milwaukee, WI 53201-3080
Street Address:
20700 Swenson Drive, Suite 100
Waukesha, Wisconsin 53186
(262) 796-4540, Fax: (262) 796-4400

Wisconsin Labor and Industry Review Commission
http://www.dwd.state.wi.us/lirc/
Mailing Address:
Post Office Box 8126
Madison, Wisconsin 53708-8126
Street Address:
Wisconsin Public Broadcasting Building
3319 West Beltline Highway
Madison, Wisconsin
(608) 266-9850 Fax: (608) 267-4409

WYOMING

State of Wyoming—http://www.state.wy.us/
Department of Employment—http://wydoe.state.wy.us/
122 West 25th Street
Herschler Building 2 East
Cheyenne, Wyoming 82002
(307) 777-7672, Fax: (307) 777-5805

Workers' Safety and Compensation Division
http://wydoe.state.wy.us/doe.asp?ID=9
122 West 25th Street
Herschler Building 2 East
Cheyenne, Wyoming 82002
(307) 777-7159, Fax: (307) 777-6552.
    To Report an Injury: (800) 870-8883 or (307) 777-7441,
    Fax: (307) 777-6552.
    To Report Fraud: (888) 996-9226 or (307)777-7677, Fax: (307) 777-3581.

Employment Tax Division—http://wydoe.state.wy.us/doe.asp?ID=10
Post Office Box 2760
Casper, Wyoming 82602-2760
(307) 235-3201 (Casper) or (307) 777-7471 (Cheyenne)

OTHER U.S. AREAS

AMERICAN SAMOA
American Samoa—http://members.aol.com/pologa/welcome.html
Workmen's Compensation Commission
Office of the Governor
Pago Pago, American Samoa 96799

GUAM
Guam—http://www.gov.gu/
Department of Labor
Workers' Compensation Commission
Government of Guam
Post Office Box 9970
Tamuning, Guam 96931-9970
(671) 647-4205, Fax: (671) 649-4922

NAVAJO NATION
Navajo Nation—http://www.navajo.org/
Workers' Compensation Program
Post Office Box 2489
Window Rock, Arizona 86515
(928) 871-6389, Fax: (928) 871-6087

NORTHERN MARIANA ISLANDS

PUERTO RICO
Puerto Rico—http://fortaleza.govpr.org/ingles/govwel.htm
Industrial Commissioner's Office
G.P.O. Box 364466
San Juan, Puerto Rico 00936
(787) 783-3808, Fax: (787) 783-5610

State Insurance Fund
G.P.O. Box 5028
San Juan, Puerto Rico 00936

VIRGIN ISLANDS
Virgin Islands—http://www.gov.vi/
Department of Labor—http://www.gov.vi/vild/
21-31 Hospital Street
Christiansted
St. Croix, U.S. Virgin Islands 00802
(340) 776-3700 or (340) 773-1994, Fax: (340) 774-5908, (340) 773-0094, or
(340) 776-0529
Workers' Compensation Division
3012 Vitraco Mall, Golden Rock
Christiansted
St. Croix, Virgin Islands 00820-4666
(809) 692-9390, Fax: (809) 773-4338

CANADA

FEDERAL JURISDICTION
Government of Canada—http://canada.gc.ca/
Labour Program
Human Resources Development Canada
http://labour-travail.hrdc-drhc.gc.ca/
Human Resources Development Canada
11 Prince of Wales Drive
Ottawa, Ontario K2C 3T2
(800) 463-2493 (in Canada), (416) 954-5900 (Metro Toronto Area),
(519) 645-4424 (London Area)

ALBERTA
Government of Alberta—http://www.gov.ab.ca/index2.html
Department of Labour—http://www.gov.ab.ca/~lab/
9940 - 106 Street
Edmonton, Alberta T5K 2N2
(403) 427-8848, (403) 297-2222 (Calgary)
Workers' Compensation Board-Alberta—http://www.wcb.ab.ca/
Box 2415, 9912 - 107 Street
Edmonton, Alberta~T5J 2S5
(403) 498-4000, (403) 498-4950 (Government Relations Office-Edmonton),
Fax: (403) 422-2889 TTY: (403) 422-2716
E-mail: geninfo.wcb.ab@ibm.net

BRITISH COLUMBIA
Government of British Columbia—http://www.gov.bc.ca/
Workers' Compensation Board of British Columbia
http://www.worksafebc.com/
6951 Westminster Highway
Post Office Box 5350 STN Terminal
Richmond, British Columbia V6B 5L5
(800) 661-2112 (in British Columbia only), (604) 273-2266, (604) 273-7711
(after hours safety and health emergency reporting) Fax: (604) 276-3151

MANITOBA
Government of Manitoba—http://www.gov.mb.ca/
Department of Labour
Workplace Safety and Health Division
http://www.gov.mb.ca/labour/safety/index.html
200 - 401 York Avenue
Winnipeg, Manitoba R3C 0P8
(800) 282-8069, (204) 945-3446 Fax: (204) 945-4556
Workers' Compensation Board of Manitoba—http://www.wcb.mb.ca/
E-mail: wcb@wcb.mb.ca

NEW BRUNSWICK
Government of New Brunswick—http://www.gov.nb.ca/
New Brunswick Workplace Health, Safety and Compensation
Commission—http://www.gov.nb.ca/whscc/index.htm
1 Portland Street
Post Office Box 160
Saint John, New Brunswick E2L 3X9
(800) 222-9775 (in New Brunswick only), (506) 632-2200
Fax: (506) 738-4229

NEWFOUNDLAND and LABRADOR
Government of Newfoundland—http://www.gov.nf.ca/
Department of Environment and Labour—http://www.gov.nf.ca/env
Occupational Health and Safety Division
Confederation Building, 4th Floor, West Block
Post Office Box 8700
St John's, Newfoundland A1B 4J6
(800) 563-5471 (in Newfoundland only), (709) 729-1932
Fax: (709) 729-6639
Workers' Compensation Commission of Newfoundland and Labrador
http://www.wcb.nf.ca/

NORTHWEST TERRITORIES
Government of the Northwest Territories —http://www.gov.nt.ca/
Northwest Territories Workers' Compensation Board
Post Office Box 8888
Yellowknife, Northwest Territories X1A 2R3
(800) 661-0792 (in North America), (867) 920-3888 Fax: (867) 873-4596

NOVA SCOTIA
Government of Nova Scotia—http://www.gov.ns.ca/
Occupational Health & Safety Division
Department of Labour
5151 Terminal Road, 6th floor
Post Office Box 697
Halifax, Nova Scotia B3J 2T8
(800) 9-LABOUR or (800) 952-2687 (in Nova Scotia only), (902) 424-5400
Fax: (902) 424-3239
Workers' Compensation Board of Nova Scotia—http://www.wcb.ns.ca/

ONTARIO
Government of Ontario—http://www.gov.on.ca/
Occupational Health & Safety Branch
http://www.gov.on.ca/LAB/ohs/ohse.htm
Ministry of Labour—http://www.gov.on.ca/LAB/
400 University Avenue, 8th Floor
Toronto, Ontario M7A 1T7
(800) 268-8013 (in Ontario only), (416) 326-7770 Fax: (416) 326-7761
Workplace Safety & Insurance Board (formerly Workers' Compensation
Board)—http://www.wcb.on.ca/wcb/wcb.nsf/public/homepage (new site
available soon: http://www.wsib.on.ca)
200 Front Street West
Toronto, Ontario
(800) 387-5540, (416) 344-1000 Fax: (416) 344-4684 TTY: (800) 387-0050
E-mail: wsibcomm@wsib.on.ca
Workplace Safety and Insurance Appeals Tribunal
http://www.wcat.on.ca/engindex.htm
505 University Avenue, 7th Floor
Toronto, Ontario M5G 1X4
(416) 598-4638 Fax: (416) 326-5164
Occupational Health and Safety Branch
Ministry of Labour—http://www.gov.on.ca/LAB/ohs/
400 University Avenue, 8th Floor
Toronto, Ontario M7A 1T7
(800) 268-8013 (in Ontario only), (416) 326-7770 Fax: (416) 326-7761

PRINCE EDWARD ISLAND

Government of Prince Edward Island—http://www.gov.pe.ca/
Occupational Health and Safety Division
Workers' Compensation Commission
P.O. Box 757
Charlottetown, Prince Edward Island C1A 7L7
(800) 237-5049 (in Prince Edward Island only), (902) 368-5680
Fax: (902) 368-5696

QUEBEC

Province of Québec—http://www.gouv.qc.ca/
Commission de la santé et de la sécurité du travail du Québec
http://www.csst.qc.ca/
(Occupational Health and Safety Commission)
C P 6056, Succursale Centre-ville
Montréal, Québec H3C 4E1
(800) 667-7585 (in Québec only), (514) 864-9362 Fax: (514) 864-9214

SASKATCHEWAN

Government of Saskatchewan—http://www.gov.sk.ca/
Department of Labour—http://www.gov.sk.ca/govt/labour/
Occupational Health and Safety Division
1870 Albert Street
Regina, Saskatchewan S4P 3V7
(800) 567-7233, (306) 787-4496 Fax: (306) 787-2208 ~
Saskatoon Office: (306) 933-5042; 1-800-667-5051
FAX: (306) 933-7339

YUKON TERRITORY

Government of Yukon—http://www.gov.yk.ca/
Workers' Compensation, Health and Safety Board
Occupational Health and Safety Branch
401 Strickland Street
Whitehorse, Yukon Territory Y1A 5N8
(800) 661-0443, (867) 667-5450 Fax: (867) 393-6279

REGISTRY OF INTERPRETERS FOR THE DEAF INFORMATION ASSOCIATE, CERTIFICATE, AND CONTINUING EDUCATION PROGRAMS UNITED STATES AND U.S. TERRITORIES

ALABAMA

ALABAMA INSTITUTE FOR THE DEAF AND BLIND
PO Box 698 - EH Gentry
Talladega, AL 35161
(256) 761-3492 V/TTY
(256) 761-3454 Fax
www.aidb.state.al.us

BISHOP STATE COMMUNITY COLLEGE
351 N Broad St
Mobile, AL 36609
(251) 690-6450 V/TTY
(251) 690-6892 Fax
www.bscc.cc.al.us

ARIZONA

PHOENIX COLLEGE
1202 W. Thomas Rd.
Phoenix, AZ 85013-4234
(602) 285-7190 V/TTY
(602) 285-7596 Fax
www.phoenixcollege.edu

PIMA COMMUNITY COLLEGE
2202 W. Anklam Rd
Tucson, AZ 85709
(520) 206-6652
(520) 206-6020 Fax
www.pimacc.pima.edu

ARKANSAS

UNIVERSITY OF ARKANSAS AT LITTLE ROCK
2801 S. University Avenue
Little Rock, AR 72204-1099
(501) 569-3169 V/TTY
(501) 569-8129 Fax
www.ualr.edu/~rehdept/int-ed/front_page.htm

CALIFORNIA

AMERICAN RIVER COLLEGE
4700 College Oak Dr.
Sacramento, CA 95841
(916) 484-8653
(916) 484-8366 Fax
(916) 484-8270 TTY
www.arc.losrios.edu

BAKERSFIELD COLLEGE
1801 Panorama Dr.
Bakersfield, CA 93305
(661) 395-4595
(661) 395-4434 Fax
www.bakersfieldcollege.edu

CALIFORNIA STATE UNIVERSITY AT NORTHRIDGE
18111 Nordhoff St.
Northridge, CA 91330-8265
(818) 667-5116
(818) 677-5717 Fax
(818) 677-4973 TTY
www.csun.edu/~sch_educ/dfst/dfst.html

EL CAMINO COLLEGE
16007 Crenshaw Blvd
Torrance, CA 90506
(310) 660-6754
(310) 660-3922 Fax
www.elcamino.edu

GOLDEN WEST COLLEGE
15744 Golden West St.
Huntington Beach, CA 92647
(714) 895-8907
(714) 895-8989 Fax
www.gwc.cccd.edu

LOS ANGELES PIERCE COLLEGE
6201 Winnetka Ave
Woodland Hills, CA 91371
(818) 719-6471 V/TTY
(818) 710-9844 Fax
www.lapc.cc.ca.us

MOUNT SAN ANTONIO COLLEGE
1100 N Grand Ave
Walnut, CA 91789
(909) 594-5611 ext.4443
(909) 594-7777 Fax
www.mtsac.edu

OHLONE COLLEGE
Interpreter Preparation Program
43600 Mission Blvd.
PO Box 3909
Fremont, CA 94539
(510) 659-6275
(510) 659-6032 Fax
(510) 659-6112 TTY
www.ohlone.cc.ca.us

OXNARD COLLEGE
4000 South Rose Ave.
Oxnard, CA 93033
(805) 986-5800 ext.7661
www.oxnard.cc.ca.us

PALOMAR COMMUNITY COLLEGE
1140 W. Mission Rd
San Marcos, CA 92069
(760) 744-1150
www.palomar.edu

RIVERSIDE COMMUNITY COLLEGE
4800 Magnolia Avenue
Riverside, CA 92506-1299
(909) 222-8832
(909) 222-8149 Fax
(909) 222-8682 TTY
www.rccd.cc.ca.us

SAN DIEGO MESA COLLEGE
Interpreter Training Program
Supervisor, Room F-204
7250 Mesa College Dr.
San Diego, CA 92111-4998
(619) 627-2743

(619) 624-0931 Fax
(619) 627-2923 TTY
www.mesacollege.net

COLORADO

FRONT RANGE COMMUNITY COLLEGE
3645 W 112th Ave.
Westminster, CO 80031
(303) 404-5061 V/TTY
(303) 466-1623 Fax
www.frcc.cc.co.us/programs/w/ipp

PIKES PEAK COMMUNITY COLLEGE
5675 S. Academy Blvd.
Colorado Springs, CO 80906
(719) 540-7091
(719) 540-7075 Fax
(719) 540-7131 TTY
www.ppcc.cccoes.edu

UNIVERSITY OF COLORADO - BOULDER
Project TIEM (Teaching Interpreter Educators
and Mentors)
SLHS Dept UCB 409
2501 Kittredge Loop Rd.
Boulder, CO 80309
(877) 613-9458 V
(303) 492-3274 Fax
(877) 613-9457 TTY
www.colorado.edu/slhs/tiem.online

CONNECTICUT

NORTHWESTERN CONNECTICUT COMMU-
NITY COLLEGE
Park Place East
Winsted, CT 06098-1798
(860) 738-6375
(860) 738-6439 Fax
www.nwcc.commnet.edu

DISTRICT OF COLUMBIA

CAPITAL COMMUNITY INSTITUTE
1720 Minnesota Ave., SE
Washington, DC 20020
(202) 889-3395
(202) 889-6312 Fax
omecci@aol.com

GALLAUDET UNIVERSITY
RSA Interpreter Training Grant
GUKCC Room 3123
800 Florida Ave NE
Kellogg Conference Center
Washington, DC 20002
(202) 651-6056 V/TTY
(202) 651-6019 Fax
www.gradschool.gallaudet.edu/slps

FLORIDA

DAYTONA BEACH COMMUNITY COLLEGE
PO Box 2811
1200 W. International Speedway Blvd
Daytona Beach, FL 32120-2811
(386) 255-8131 ext. 3208
(386) 226-2903 Fax
www.dbcc.cc.fl.us

FLORIDA COMMUNITY COLLEGE AT JACK-
SONVILLE
11901 Beach Blvd
Box 60
Jacksonville, FL 32246
(904) 646-2406
(904) 646-2396 Fax
www1.fccj.org/rmcdavid

HILLSBOROUGH COMMUNITY COLLEGE
Interpreter Training Program
PO Box 30030
Tampa, FL 33630
(813) 253-7240 V/TTY
(813) 253-7504 Fax
www.hcc.cc.fl.us/services/departments/
interptrain/index.htm

MIAMI- DADE COMMUNITY COLLEGE
11380 NW 27th Ave., Rm. 1354
Miami, FL 33167
(305) 237-1274
(305) 237-1560 Fax
www.mdcc.edu

ST. PETERSBURG COLLEGE
2465 Drew St.
Clearwater, FL 33765
(727) 791-2759 V/TTY
(727) 791-2776 Fax
www.spjc.edu/webcentral/acad/itp/index.htm

GEORGIA

FLOYD COLLEGE
ASL Immersion Training Program for Interpreters
PO Box 1864
3175 Highway 27 S
Rome, GA 30162-1864
(706) 295-6307 V/TTY
(706) 295-6610 Fax
www.fc.peachnet.edu

GEORGIA PERIMETER COLLEGE
555 N. Indian Creek Dr.
Clarkston, GA 30021
(404) 299-4360 V/TTY
(404) 299-4364 Fax
www.gpc.peachnet.edu/~csmith/intp.php

HAWAII

KAPIOLANI COMMUNITY COLLEGE
ASL/Interpreter Education Program
4303 Diamond Head Rd
Manono Bldg #116
Honolulu, HI 96816
(808) 734-9154 V/TTY
(808) 734-9893 Fax
www.kcc.hawaii.edu

IDAHO

COLLEGE OF SOUTHERN IDAHO
315 Falls Ave.
PO Box 1238
Twin Falls, ID 83303-1238
(208) 733-9554 ext. 2181
www.csi.edu

IDAHO STATE UNIVERSITY
Campus Box 8116
Pocatello, ID 83209
(208) 282-4350 V/TTY
(208) 282-4571 Fax
www.isu.edu

ILLINOIS

ILLINOIS CENTRAL COLLEGE
1 College Dr.
East Peoria, IL 61635-0001
(309) 694-8439
(309) 694-5260 TTY
www.icc.cc.il.us

JOHN A. LOGAN COLLEGE
700 Logan College Rd.
Carterville, IL 62918
(618) 985-3741 ext. 8456
(618) 985-4654 Fax
(618) 985-8870 TTY
www.jal.cc.il.us/ipp

MACMURRAY COLLEGE
447 East College Ave.
Jacksonville, IL 62650
(217) 479-7164 TTY
www.mac.edu

SOUTHWESTERN ILLINOIS COLLEGE
Interpreter Studies Program
2500 Carlyle Ave.
Belleville Campus
Belleville, IL 62221
(618) 235-2700 ext. 5144
(618) 235-2052 Fax
(618) 614-5145 TTY
www.southwestern.cc.il.us

WAUBONSEE COMMUNITY COLLEGE
Interpreter Training Program
5 E. Glena Blvd.
Aurora, IL 60506
(630) 801-7900
www.wcc.cc.il.us

WAUBONSEE COMMUNITY COLLEGE
Route 47 at Waubonsee Dr.
Sugar Grove, IL 60554
(630) 466-7900 ext. 2925
www.waubonsee.edu

WILLIAM RAINEY HARPER COLLEGE
1200 W. Algonquin Rd
Palatine, IL 60067-7398
(847) 925-6415
(847) 925-6048 Fax
(847) 925-6772 TTY
www.harpercollege.com

INDIANA

BETHEL COLLEGE
ASL/English Interpreter Training Prgm.
1001 W. McKinley Ave.
Mishawaka, IN 46545
(219) 257-7615 V/TTY
www.bethelcollege.edu

INDIANA UNIVERSITY PURDUE UNIVERSITY
INDIANAPOLIS (IUPUI)
425 University Boulevard
Indianapolis, IN 46202
(317) 274-8930 V/TTY
(317) 278-1287 Fax
www.iupui.edu/~interprt

VINCENNES UNIVERSITY
1200 E. 42nd St.
Indianapolis, IN 46205
(317) 923-2305
(317) 924-2609 Fax
(317) 923-2307 TTY
www.vinu.edu

IOWA

IOWA WESTERN COMMUNITY COLLEGE
2700 College Rd., Box 4C
Council Bluffs, IA 51502
(712) 325-3203
(712) 329-4748 Fax
(712) 325-3495 TTY
www.iwcc.cc.ia.us

KIRKWOOD COMMUNITY COLLEGE
6301 Kirkwood Blvd. SW
Cedar Rapids, IA 52406
(319) 398-5480
(319) 398-1021 Fax
(319) 398-5480 TTY
www.kirkwood.cc.ia.us

SCOTT COMMUNITY COLLEGE
500 Belmont Rd.
Bettendorf, IA 52722
(563) 441-4240
(563) 441-4204 Fax
(563) 441-4204 TTY
www.eicc.edu

KANSAS

COWLEY COUNTY COMMUNITY COLLEGE
4501 E 47th St. S
Southside Education Center
Wichita, KS 67210
(316) 978-8166 TTY
(800) 766-3777 (Kansas Relay for voice callers; then give TTY #)
www.cowley.cc.ks.us/programs/itp

JOHNSON COUNTY COMMUNITY COLLEGE
12345 College Blvd Box 31
Overland Park, KS 66210
(913) 469-8500
(913) 469-2358 Fax
(913) 469-4478 TTY
www.jccc.net/acad/liberal_arts/it/index.htm

LOUISIANA

DELGADO COMMUNITY COLLEGE
615 City Park Ave.
New Orleans, LA 70119
(504) 483-4553
(504) 483-1953 Fax
www.dcc.edu

LOUISIANA COMMISSION FOR THE DEAF
8225 Florida Blvd.
Baton Rouge, LA 70806
(800) 256-1523
(800) 543-2099 TTY
www.dss.state.la.us
kclausen@lrs.dss.state.la.us

MARYLAND

COMMUNITY COLLEGE OF BALTIMORE COUNTY
Catonsville Campus
800 S. Rolling Rd.
Catonsville, MD 21228
(410) 455-4474 V/TTY
(410) 455-5134 Fax
www.ccbc.cc.jd.us/campuses/cat/academics/careers/c_itr.htm

MASSACHUSETTS

NORTHEASTERN UNIVERSITY
400 Meserve Hall
360 Huntington Ave.
Boston, MA 02115
(617) 373-3064
(617) 373-3065 Fax
(617) 373-3067 TTY
www.asl.neu.edu

NORTHERN ESSEX COMMUNITY COLLEGE
100 Elliott Way
Haverhill, MA 01830
(978) 556-3610
(978) 556-3611 TTY
www.necc.mass.edu

MICHIGAN

LANSING COMMUNITY COLLEGE
5200 Communication Dept.
PO Box 40010
Lansing, MI 48150
(517) 483-1040 V/TTY
(517) 483-5247 Fax
(517) 483-1031 TTY
www.lansing.cc.mi.us/careers/signlanguage

MADONNA UNIVERSITY
36600 Schoolcraft Rd.
Livonia, MI 48150
(734) 432-5617 V/TTY
(734) 432-5393 Fax
ww2.munet.edu/rust2/default.htm

MOTT COMMUNITY COLLEGE
1401 E. Court St.
Flint, MI 48502
(810) 762-0470
(810) 232-9478 Fax
(810) 762-0272 TTY
www.mcc.edu

MINNESOTA

COLLEGE OF ST. CATHERINE
Interpreting Program
601 25th Ave. South
Minneapolis, MN 55454
(651) 690-7862 V/TTY
(651) 690-7849 Fax
www.stkate.edu

MINNESOTA COURT INTERPRETER PRO-GRAM
25 Constitution Ave. Ste. 105
St. Paul, MN 55155
cip@courts.state.mn.us

ST. PAUL TECHNICAL COLLEGE
235 Marshall Ave.
St Paul, MN 55102
(651) 846-1327 V/TTY
(651) 221-1339 Fax
www.sptc.mnscu.edu

MISSISSIPPI

HINDS COMMUNITY COLLEGE
Interpreter Training Program
Box 10423
Raymond, MS 39154
(601) 857-3487
(601) 857-3647 Fax
www.hinds.cc.ms.us

MISSISSIPPI GULF COAST COMMUNITY COLLEGE
2226 Switzer Rd.
Gulfport, MS 39507
(228) 896-2542
(228) 896-2528 Fax
www.mgccc.edu

MISSOURI

MAPLE WOODS COMMUNITY COLLEGE
2601 NE Barry Rd
Kansas City, MO 64156
(816) 437-3331
(816) 437-3441 Fax
www.kcmetro.edu

ST. LOUIS COMMUNITY COLLEGE AT FLORISSANT VALLEY
3400 Pershall
Ferguson, MO 63135
(314) 595-4470
(314) 595-4217 Fax
(314) 595-2120 TTY

WILLIAM WOODS UNIVERSITY
One University Avenue
Fulton, MO 65251-1098
(573) 592-1123
(573) 592-1139 Fax
(573) 592-1140 TTY
www.williamwoods.edu

NEBRASKA

METROPOLITAN COMMUNITY COLLEGE
PO Box 3777
Omaha, NE 68103
(402) 547-2786 T
www. metropo.mccneb.edu
cmanning@metropo.mccneb.edu

NEVADA

COMMUNITY COLLEGE OF SOUTHERN
NEVADA
3200 E Cheyenne Ave N2C
N. Las Vegas, NV 89030-4296
(702) 651-2633
(702) 651-4760 Fax
www.ccsn.nevada.edu

NEW HAMPSHIRE

UNIVERSITY OF NEW HAMPSHIRE
Sign Language Interpreting Prgm.
400 Commercial St
Manchaster, NH 03101
(603) 641-4143
(603) 641-4303 Fax
(603) 662-4511 TTY
www.unh.edu

NEW JERSEY

BURLINGTON COUNTY COLLEGE
County Route 530
Pemberton, NJ 08068
(609) 894-4900
www.bcc.edu

CAMDEN COUNTY COLLEGE
Interpreter Training Program
P.O. Box 200
Blackwood, NJ 08012
(609) 227-7200 ext.4948
(609) 374-4884 Fax
(609) 374-4948 TTY
www.camdencc.edu

UNION COUNTY COLLEGE
1033 Springfield Ave
Cranford, NJ 07016
(908) 709-0349
(908) 709-0827 Fax
(908) 412-0294 TTY
www.ucc.edu

NEW MEXICO

SANTA FE COMMUNITY COLLEGE
6401 Richards Ave
Santa Fe, NM 87505-4887
(505) 428-1622
www.santa-fe.cc.nm.us

UNIVERSITY OF NEW MEXICO
Department of Linguistics
Building #112
Albuquerque, NM 87131
(505) 277-0928 V/TTY
(505) 277-1754 Fax
www.unm.edu/~sign/
sign@unm.edu

NEW YORK

CORNING COMMUNITY COLLEGE
One Academic Dr
Corning, NY 14830-3297
(607) 962-9125
(607) 962-9131 Fax
(607) 962-9576 TTY
www.corning-cc.edu/PROGRAMS/61.htm

LAGUARDIA COMMUNITY COLLEGE
Interpreter Education Project
31-10 Thomson Ave.
Room C-239
Long Island City, NY 11101
(718) 482-5313 V/TTY
(718) 609-2005 Fax
www.lagcc.cuny/IEP

NATIONAL TECHNICAL INSTITUTE FOR THE
DEAF (NTID)
52 Lomb Memorial Dr.
LBJ Building
Rochester, NY 14623-5604
(716) 475-6431 V/TTY
(716) 475-6500 Fax
www.ntidweb.rit.edu

SEYMOUR JOSEPH INSTITUTE OF
AMERICAN SIGN LANGUAGE
43 Ramona Ave
Staten Island, NY 10312
(718) 984-8200 V
(718) 608-9155 Fax
(718) 608-9156 TTY
mbacheller@sjiasl.org

SUFFOLK COUNTY COMMUNITY COLLEGE
533 College Rd. R106
Selden, NY 11784
(631) 451-4651 V/TTY
(631) 451-4671 Fax
www.sunysuffolk.edu

NORTH CAROLINA

BLUE RIDGE COMMUNITY COLLEGE
Interpreter Education Program
College Dr.
Flat Rock, NC 28731
(828) 692-3572 ext. 326
(828) 692-2441 Fax
(828) 692-4515 TTY
www.blueridge.cc.nc.us

CENTRAL PIEDMONT COMMUNITY
COLLEGE
P.O. Box 35009
Charlotte, NC 28235
(704) 330-6829
(704) 330-6677 Fax
www.cpcc.edu

GARDNER WEBB UNIVERSITY
110 South Main Street
Boiling Springs, NC 28017
(704) 406-4418

(704) 406-4329 Fax
(704) 406-2371 TTY
www.gardner-webb.edu

WILSON TECHNICAL COMMUNITY COLLEGE
Interpreter Education Program
PO Box 4305
902 Herring Ave
Wilson, NC 27893
(252) 246-1331
(252) 243-7148 Fax
www.wilsontech.cc.nc.us

NORTH DAKOTA

LAKE REGION STATE COLLEGE
1801 North College Dr.
Devils Lake, ND 58301
(701) 662-9000 V/TTY
(701) 662-9009 Fax
www.lrsc.nodak.edu

OHIO

CINCINNATI STATE TECHNICAL AND
COMMUNITY COLLEGE
3520 Central Parkway
Cincinnati, OH 45223-2690
(513) 569-1829 V/TTY
(513) 569-5770 Fax
www/cinstate.cc.oh.us

COLUMBUS STATE COMMUNITY COLLEGE
Union Hall Room 210, CSCC
550 E Spring St
Columbus, OH 43215
(614) 287-5616
(614) 287-6007 Fax
(614) 469-0333 TTY
www.cscc.edu

CUYAHOGA COMMUNITY COLLEGE
Western Campus
11000 Pleasant Valley Rd
Parma, OH 44130
(216) 987-5096 V/TTY
(216) 987-5612 Fax
www.tri-c.cc.oh.us

KENT STATE UNIVERSITY
405 White Hall
Kent, OH 44242-0001
(330) 672-4450 V/TTY
(330) 672-2512 Fax
www.kent.edu

OHIO SCHOOL FOR THE DEAF
Dept of Interpreting and Sign Language Resources
500 Morse Rd
Columbus, OH 43214
(614) 995-1566 V/TTY
(614) 995-1567 Fax
eduterp@osd.ode.state.oh.us

SINCLAIR COMMUNITY COLLEGE
444 W Third St
Dayton, OH 45402
(937) 512-2722 V/TTY
(937) 512-5222 Fax
www.sinclair.edu

UNIVERSITY OF AKRON
Division of Public Service Technology
Polskyís 161
Akron, OH 44325
(330) 972-8317
(330) 972-5476 Fax
www.uakron.edu
leah6@uakron.edu

OKLAHOMA

EAST CENTRAL UNIVERSITY
Couseling/Services to the Deaf
Ada, OK 74820
(405) 332-8000 ext. 578
www.ecok.edu

OKLAHOMA STATE UNIVERISTY - OKC
900 N Portland
Oklahoma City, OK 73107
(405) 945-3288 V/TTY
(405) 945-9101 Fax
www.osuokc.edu

TULSA COMMUNITY COLLEGE
3727 E Apache
Tulsa, OK 74115-3151
(918) 595-7450 V/TTY
(918) 595-7447 Fax
www.tulsacc.edu

OREGON

PORTLAND COMMUNITY COLLEGE
Interpreter Training Program
PO Box 19000
Portland, OR 97280-0990
(503) 977-4672
www.pcc.edu

WESTERN OREGON UNIVERSITY
Regional Resource Center on Deafness
345 N Monmouth Ave.
Monmouth, OR 97361
(503) 838-8444 V/TTY
(503) 838-8228 Fax
www.wou.edu/rrcd

PENNSYLVANIA

BLOOMSBURG UNIVERSITY
Navy Hall #226-D
Bloomsburg, PA 17815
(570) 389-4076
(570) 389-3980 TTY
www.bloomu.edu

COMMUNITY COLLEGE OF ALLEGHENY
COUNTY
North Campus
8701 Perry Hwy
Pittsburgh, PA 15237-5372
(412) 369-4172
(412) 369-3624 Fax
www.ccac.edu

COMMUNITY COLLEGE OF PHILADELPHIA
1700 Spring Garden
Philadelphia, PA 19130
(814) 886-6378
(814) 886-2978 Fax
(814) 886-5533 TTY
www/ccp.cc.pa.us

MOUNT ALOYSIUS COLLEGE
7373 Admiral Peary Highway
Cresson, PA 16630
(814) 886-6378
(814) 886-2978 Fax
(814) 886-5533 TTY
www.mtaloy.edu

PUERTO RICO

SORDOS DE PR, INC.
P O Box 362665
San Juan, PR 00936-2665
(787) 622-1768
(787) 781-4661 Fax
earr@rforest.net

SOUTH CAROLINA

SPARTANBURG TECHNICAL COLLEGE
Interpreter Training Program
PO Box 4386
Spartanburg, SC 29305-4386
(864) 591-3714
(864) 591-3946 Fax
www.stcsc.edu/itp

SOUTH DAKOTA

SOUTHEAST TECHNICAL INSTITUTE
2320 N Career Ave
Sioux Falls, SD 57107-1302
(605) 367-8459
(605) 367-6108 Fax
www.southeasttech.com

TENNESSEE

CHATTANOOGA STATE TECHNICAL COMMU-
NITY COLLEGE
4501 Amnicola Highway
Chattanooga, TN 37406-1097
(423) 697-4415
(423) 697-2467 Fax
www.chattanoogastate.edu

MARYVILLE COLLEGE
502 E. Lamar Alexander Pkwy
Maryville, TN 37804-5904
(865) 981-8148
(865) 981-8010 Fax
(865) 981-8149 TTY
www.maryvillecollege.edu

NASHVILLE STATE TECHNICAL INSTITUTE
120 White Bridge Rd
Nashville, TN 37209
(615) 353-3033
(615) 353-3756 Fax
www.nsti.tec.tn.us

TENNESSEE TEMPLE UNIVERSITY
1815 Union Ave
Chattanooga, TN 37404
(423) 493-4326
(423) 493-4497 Fax
www.tntemple.edu

UNIVERSITY OF TENNESSEE
Claxton Addition 102
Knoxville, TN 37996
(865) 974-8495
(865) 974-8674 Fax
http://sunsite.utk.edu/cod/eitp/index.html

TEXAS

AUSTIN COMMUNITY COLLEGE
1212 Rio Grande
Austin, TX 78701
(512) 223-3205
(512) 223-3406 Fax
(512) 223-3052 TTY
www.austincc.edu

COLLIN COUNTY COMMUNITY COLLEGE
DISTRICT
2800 East Spring Creek Parkway
Plano, TX 75074
(972) 881-5152
(972) 881-5629 Fax
(972) 881-5138 TTY
www.ccccd.edu/cs/his/signlang.html

DEL MAR COLLEGE
Interpreter for the Deaf Program
101 Baldwin
Corpus Christi, TX 78404
(361) 698-1318
(361) 698-1598 Fax
www.delmar.edu

EASTFIELD COLLEGE
3737 Motley Dr
Mesquite, TX 75150-2033
(972) 860-7161 V/TTY
(972) 860-8342 Fax
www.efc.dcccd.edu

EL PASO COMMUNITY COLLEGE
PO Box 20500
El Paso, TX 79998
(915) 831-2432 V/TTY
(915) 831-2095 Fax
www.epcc.edu/community/nmip/
welcome.html

HOUSTON COMMUNITY COLLEGE – CEN-
TRAL
1301 Alabama, Rm 101N
Houston, TX 77004
(713) 718-6846
(713) 718-6883 Fax
www.hccs.cc.tx.us

McLENNAN COMMUNITY COLLEGE
1400 College Dr.
Waco, TX 76708
(254) 299-8733
(254) 299-8747 Fax
www.mclennan.edu/departments/intr/

NORTH HARRIS COLLEGE
2700 W. W. Thorne - A 160 C
Houston, TX 77073
(281) 618-5535
(281) 618-7103 Fax
(281) 618-5519 TTY
www.northharriscollege.com

SAN ANTONIO COLLEGE
1300 San Pedro Avenue/NTC 005
San Antonio, TX 78212-4299
(210) 733-2071
(210) 733-2074 Fax
(210) 733-2072 TTY
www.accd.edu

SOUTHWEST COLLEGIATE INSTITUTE FOR
THE DEAF
3200 Ave C
Big Spring, TX 79720
(915) 264-3700 V/TTY
(915) 264-3707 Fax
www.hc.cc.tx.us/swcid/danny1/homedc.htm

TARRANT COUNTY COLLEGE
4801 Marine Creek Pkwy
Fort Worth, TX 76179
(817) 515-7762 V/TTY
(817) 515-7039 Fax
www.web.tccd.net

TYLER JUNIOR COLLEGE
PO Box 9020
Tyler, TX 75711
(903) 510-2774 V/TTY
www.tyler.cc.tx.us

U.S. VIRGIN ISLANDS

UNIVERSITY OF THE VIRGIN ISLANDS
#2 John Brewer Bay
St. Thomas, USVI 00802
(340) 693-1322
(340) 693-1325 Fax
www.uvi.edu
yhabtes@uvi.edu

UTAH

SALT LAKE COMMUNITY COLLEGE
Dept of ASL/Interpreting
4600 S Redwood Rd
PO Box 30808
Salt Lake City, UT 84130
(801) 957-4929 V/TTY
(801) 957-4853 Fax
www.slcc.edu

VIRGINIA

J. SARGEANT REYNOLDS COMMUNITY COLLEGE
PO Box 85622
Richmond, VA 23285
(804) 750-1999
(804) 225-2153 Fax
www.jsr.cc.va.us

NEW RIVER COMMUNITY COLLEGE
PO Box 1127
Dublin, VA 24084
(540) 674-3600 V/TTY
(540) 674-3642 Fax
www.nr.cc.va.us

TIDEWATER COMMUNITY COLLEGE
ASL/Interpreter Education Program
1428 Cedar Rd
Chesapeake, VA 23322
(757) 822-5015
(757) 822-5155 Fax
(757) 822-5018 TTY
www.tc.cc.va.us/programs/curr/career

WASHINGTON

AMERICAN SIGN LANGUAGE & INTERPRETING SCHOOL OF SEATTLE (ASLIS)
PO Box 31468
Seattle, WA 98103
(206) 860-3503 V/TTY
(206) 860-9255 Fax
www.aslis.org

SPOKANE FALLS COMMUNITY COLLEGE
West 3410 Ft Wright Dr
MS 3190
Spokane, WA 99224-5288
(509) 533-3730 V/TTY
(509) 533-4143 Fax
www.sfcc.spokane.cc.wa.us

WEST VIRGINIA

FAIRMONT STATE COMMUNITY AND TECHNICAL COLLEGE
Interpreter Training Program
School of Language and Literature
1201 Locust Ave.
Fairmont, WV 26554
(304) 367-4252
(304) 367-4893 Fax
(304) 367-4022 TTY
www.fscwv.edu

WISCONSIN

FOX VALLEY TECHNICAL COLLEGE
1825 N Bluemound Dr
PO Box 2277
Appleton, WI 54912-2277
(920) 996-2820
(920) 831-4314 Fax
(920) 996-2820 TTY
www.fvtc.edu

MILWAUKEE AREA TECHNICAL COLLEGE
700 W State St
Milwaukee, WI 53233
(414) 297-6784
(414) 297-7990 Fax
(414) 297-8407 TTY
www.milwaukee.tec.wi.us

NORTHCENTRAL TECHNICAL COLLEGE
1000 W. Campus Drive
Wausau, WI 54401
(715) 675-3331
(715) 675-0918 Fax
(715) 675-6341 TTY
www.ntc.edu/programs/eitp

UNIVERSITY OF WISCONSIN - MILWAUKEE
PO Box 413 END 610
Milwaukee, WI 53201
(414) 229-5258
(414) 229-5300 Fax
www.uwm.edu/Dept/EXED/itp.htm

WYOMING

SHERIDAN COLLEGE
Educational Interpreting Program
3059 Coffeen Ave
PO Box 1500
Sheridan, WY 82801-1500
(307) 674-6446 ext.6231 V/TTY
(307) 674-4293 Fax
www.sc.whecn.edu

Information obtained via RID with permission

American Sign Language-English Interpreter Preparation Programs
CANADA

ALBERTA

GRANT MacEWAN COLLEGE
Interpreter Training Program
Millwoods Campus
7319 - 29 Avenue
Edmonton, Alberta T5J 2P2
(403) 497-4067
(403) 497-4084 Fax
(403) 497-4068 TTY
www.gmcc.ab.ca

BRITISH COLUMBIA

DOUGLAS COLLEGE
P.O. Box 2503
700 Royal Avenue
New Westminster, B.C. V 3L 5B2
(604) 527-5131
(604) 527-5095 Fax
(604) 527-5553 TTY
www.douglas.bc.ca/sli

MANITOBA

RED RIVER COLLEGE
2055 Notre Dame Avenue, # D104
Winnipeg, Manitoba R3H 0J9
(204) 632-2467
(204) 632-2135 TTY
www.rrc.mb.ca/home.htm

NOVA SCOTIA

NOVA SCOTIA COMMUNITY COLLEGE
Halifax Campus
1825 Bell Road
Halifax, N.S. B3H 2Z4
(902) 491-4624
(902) 491-4711 Fax
(902) 491-4625 TTY
www.nscc.ns.ca

ONTARIO

CAMBRIAN COLLEGE
1400 Barrydowne Rd.
Sudbury, Ontario P3A 3V8
(705) 566-8101
www.cambrianc.on.ca

GEORGE BROWN COLLEGE
P.O. Box 1015
Toronto, Ontario M5T 2T9
(416) 415-2333
(416) 415-2695 Fax
www.gbrownc.on.ca

ST. CLAIR COLLEGE
2000 Talbot Road West
Windsor, Ontario M9A 6S4
(519) 972-2711
(519) 972-2700
(519) 966-0053 TTY
www.stclairc.on.ca

Reprinted with permission from RID

BACHELOR DEGREE PROGRAMS

ARKANSAS

UNIVERSITY OF ARKANSAS AT LITTLE ROCK
2801 S. University Avenue
Little Rock, AR 72204-1099
(501) 569-3169 V/TTY
(501) 569-8129 Fax
www.ualr.edu/~rehdept/int-ed/front_page.htm

ARIZONA

UNIVERISITY OF ARIZONA
Interpreter Training Program
Deaf Studies Program
College of Education
Tucson, AZ 85721
(520) 621-5208 V/TTY
(520) 621-3821 Fax
www.arizona.edu

CALIFORNIA

CALIFORNIA STATE UNIVERSITY AT NORTHRIDGE
Deaf Studies Major
18111 Nordhoff St
Northridge, CA 91330-8265
(818) 667-5116
(818) 677-5717 Fax
(818) 677-4973 TTY
www.csun.edu/~sch_educ/dfst/df

FLORIDA

UNIVERSITY OF SOUTH FLORIDA
4202 East Fowler Ave
PCD 1017
Tampa, FL 33620
(813) 974-9788 V/TTY
(813) 974-0822 Fax
www.cas.usf.edu/csd/index.htm

ILLINOIS

COLUMBIA COLLEGE CHICAGO
600 S Michigan Ave
Chicago, IL 60605
(312) 344-7837
(312) 344-8055 Fax
(312) 344-8499 TTY
www.colum.edu

IDAHO

COLLEGE OF SOUTHERN IDAHO
315 Falls Ave PO Box 1238
Twin Falls, ID 83303-1238
(208) 733-9554 ext.2181
www.csi.edu

IDAHO STATE UNIVERSITY
Campus Box 8116
Pocatello, ID 83209
(208) 282-4350 V/TTY
(208) 282-4571 Fax
www.isu.edu

INDIANA

BETHEL COLLEGE
ASL/English Interpreter Training Prgm.
1001 W McKinley Ave
Mishawaka, IN 46545
(219) 257-7615 V/TTY
www.bethelcollege.edu

GOSHEN COLLEGE
1700 South Main St
Goshen, IN 46526
(219) 535-7382
www.goshen.edu

INDIANA UNIVERSITY PURDUE UNIVERSITY INDIANAPOLIS (IUPUI)
425 University Boulevard
Indianapolis, IN 46202
(317) 274-8930 V/TTY
(317) 278-1287 Fax
www.iupui.edu/~interprt

KENTUCKY

EASTERN KENTUCKY UNIVERSITY
245 Wallace Bldg.
Richmond, KY 40475
(606) 622-4442
(606) 622-4398 Fax
www.eku.edu

MAINE

UNIVERSITY OF SOUTHERN MAINE
68 High St
Portland, ME 04101
(207) 780-5955
(207) 780-5940 Fax
(207) 780-5933 TTY
www.usm.maine.edu/lin

MASSACHUSETTS

NORTHEASTERN UNIVERSITY
400 Meserve Hall
360 Huntington Ave
Boston, MA 02115
(617) 373-3064
(617) 373-3065 Fax
(617) 373-3067 TTY
www.asl.neu.edu

MICHIGAN

MADONNA UNIVERSITY
36600 Schoolcraft Rd.
Livonia, MI 48150
(734) 432-5617 V/TTY
(734) 432-5393 Fax
ww2.munet.edu/rust2/default.htm

MINNESOTA

COLLEGE OF ST. CATHERINE
Interpreting Program
601 25th Ave South
Minneapolis, MN 55454
(651) 690-7862 V/TTY
(651) 690-7849 Fax
www.stkate.edu

MISSOURI

WILLIAM WOODS UNIVERSITY
One University Avenue
Fulton, MO 65251-1098
(573) 592-1123 V
(573) 592-1139 Fax
(573) 592-1140 TTY
www.williamwoods.edu

NEW HAMPSHIRE

UNIVERSITY OF NEW HAMPSHIRE
Sign Language Interpreting Program
400 Commercial St
Manchaster, NH 03101
(603) 641-4143
(603) 641-4303 Fax
(603) 662-4511 TTY
www.unh.edu

NEW MEXICO

UNIVERSITY OF NEW MEXICO
Department of Linguistics Humanities
Building #112
Albuquerque, NM 87131
(505) 277-0928 V/TTY
(505) 277-1754 Fax
www.unm.edu/~sign/
sign@unm.edu

NEW YORK

NATIONAL TECHNICAL INSTITUTE FOR THE DEAF (NTID)
52 Lomb Memorial Dr.
LBJ Building
Rochester, NY 14623-5604
(716) 475-6431 V/TTY
(716) 475-6500 Fax
www.ntidweb.rit.edu

NORTH CAROLINA

GARDNER WEBB UNIVERSITY
110 South Main St.
Boiling Springs, NC 28017
(704) 406-4418
(704) 406-4329 Fax
(704) 406-2371 TTY
www.gardner-webb.edu

UNIVERSITY OF NORTH CAROLINA - GREENSBORO
Interpreter Training Program
316 Ferguson Bldg
Box 26171
Greensboro, NC 27402-6171
(336) 334-3772 V/TTY
(336) 334-4617 Fax
www.uncg.edu

OHIO

KENT STATE UNIVERSITY
405 White Hall
Kent, OH 44242-0001
(330) 672-4450 V/TTY
(330) 672-2512 Fax
www.kent.edu

OREGON

WESTERN OREGON UNIVERSITY
Regional Resource Center on Deafness
345 N Monmouth Ave.
Monmouth, OR 97361
(503) 838-8444 V/TTY
(503) 838-8228 Fax
www.wou.edu/rrcd

PENNSYLVANIA

BLOOMSBURG UNIVERSITY
Navy Hall #226-D
Bloomsburg, PA 17815
(570) 389-4076
(570) 389-3980 TTY
www.bloomu.edu

MOUNT ALOYSIUS COLLEGE
7373 Admiral Peary Highway
Cresson, PA 16630
(814) 886-6378
(814) 886-2978 Fax
(814) 886-5533 TTY
www.mtaloy.edu

TENNESSEE

MARYVILLE COLLEGE
502 E Lamar Alexander Pkwy
Maryville, TN 37804-5904
(865) 981-8148
(865) 981-8010 Fax
(865) 981-8149 TTY
www.maryvillecollege.edu

TENNESSEE TEMPLE UNIVERSITY
1815 Union Ave.
Chattanooga, TN 37404
(423) 493-4326
(423) 493-4497 Fax
www.tntemple.edu

UNIVERSITY OF TENNESSEE
Claxton Addition 102
Knoxville, TN 37996
(865) 974-8495
(865) 974-8674 Fax
http://sunsite.utk.edu/cod/eitp/index.html

WISCONSIN

UNIVERSITY OF WISCONSIN - MILWAUKEE
PO Box 413 END 610
Milwaukee, WI 53201
(414) 229-5258
(414) 229-5300 Fax
www.uwm.edu/Dept/EXED/itp.htm

Information obtained via RID with permission

GRADUATE LEVEL PROGRAMS

DISTRICT OF COLUMBIA

GALLAUDET UNIVERSITY
800 Florida Ave NE
Washington, DC 20002
(202) 651-5450 V/TTY
(202) 651-5741 Fax
www.depts.gallaudet.edu/asl/pages/interpretation.htm

INDIANA

INDIANA UNIVERSITY PURDUE UNIVERSITY INDIANAPOLIS
(IUPUI)
425 University Boulevard
Indianapolis, IN 46202
(317) 274-8930 V/TTY
(317) 278-1287 Fax
www.iupui.edu/~interprt

OHIO

KENT STATE UNIVERSITY
405 White Hall
Kent, OH 44242-0001
(330) 672-4450 V/TTY
(330) 672-2512 Fax
www.kent.edu

Information obtained via RID with permission

Annual Membership Application

Fiscal Year 2004 (July 1, 2003 - June 30, 2004)

Registry of Interpreters for the Deaf
333 Commerce Street
Alexandria, VA 22314
703/838-0030 (V) 703/838-0459 (TTY), 703/838-0454 FAX
membership@rid.org • www.rid.org

Member-Get-A-Member Campaign
I was referred by:
_____

❑ Deaf ❑ Deaf-Blind ❑ Hard-of-Hearing ❑ Hearing | ❑ Female ❑ Male

Check All That Apply:
❑ African American/Black ❑ Asian American/Pacific Islander ❑ Euro-American/White
❑ Hispanic/Latino(a) ❑ American Indian/Alaskan Native ❑ Other _____

Confidential Information:
❑ Home Phone ❑ Work Phone ❑ Address
❑ Fax ❑ E-mail

Mr. Mrs. Ms. Dr. _____

Address: _____ Apt. _____

City: _____ State: _____ Zip: _____

Phone(s): _____
   Home: V TTY B   Work: V TTY B   Fax:

E-mail: _____

CODE OF ETHICS:
By joining RID, a member agrees to adhere to the RID Code of Ethics. The Ethical Practices System applies to current individual members who are providing interpreting services and not to organizations or non-practitioners.

Would you like to be listed in the Membership Directory as a freelance interpreter? ❑ YES ❑ NO

List any RID Affiliate Chapter(s) that you belong to:
(Voting members must be a member of an affiliate chapter) _____

MEMBERSHIP CATEGORIES

Are You an NAD Member? ❑ YES ❑ NO

❑ **Certified*** — $115 (1 Year)
Individuals holding **current** — $225 (2 Years - Save $5!)
RID certification. — $335 (3 Years - Save $10!)

Senior Citizen Discount* — $67 (1 Year)
55 years of age or older. — $129 (2 Years - Save $5!)
Must attach a copy of an I.D. — $191 (3 Years - Save $10!)
if not already submitted.

❑ **Certified: Inactive** — $24 (1 Year)
Contact Membership Services for details.

❑ **Certified: Retired** — $24 (1 Year)
Formerly certified individuals who have retired from interpreting or transliterating. Must be 55 years of age or older. Must attach a photocopy of an I.D.

❑ **Student** — $25 (1 Year)
For students currently enrolled at least part-time in an interpreter training program. **Must attach current copy of class schedule or current letter from coordinator/instructor to application.** Does not include eligibility to vote.

❑ **Trial** — $15 (1 Year)
Receive a subscription to *VIEWS* as a one year introduction to RID. No other benefits or member discounts apply.

❑ **Associate** — $85 (1 Year)
Individuals engaged in interpreting — $165 (2 Years - Save $5!)
or transliterating but not holding RID — $245 (3 Years - Save $10!)
certification. Eligible to participate in the Associate Continuing Education Tracking Program (ACET) **Add $15**

Senior Citizen Discount — $45 (1 Year)
55 years of age or older. — $85 (2 Years - Save $5!)
Must attach a copy of an I.D. — $125 (3 Years - Save $10!)
if not already submitted.

❑ **Organizational** — $150 (1 Year)
Organizations and agencies that support RID's purposes and activities.
   ❑ Interpreter service agency
   ❑ Interpreter training program
   ❑ Other

❑ **Supporting** — $24 (1 Year)
Individuals who support RID **but are not engaged in interpreting**. Does not include eligibility to vote or reduced testing fees.

*****IMPORTANT:** Certified members must satisfy Certification Maintenance Program (CMP) requirements to maintain Certified status.

SPECIAL INTEREST GROUPS - Activities of SIGs are determined and carried out by the SIG leadership. You must be an RID member to join a SIG.

❑ Deaf Caucus - $10.00 ❑ Educational Interpreters and Transliterators - $ 5.00 ❑ Hearing Interpreters with Deaf Parents - $ 10.00
❑ Interpreter Service Managers - $ 5.00 ❑ Interpreters and Transliterators of Color - $ 5.00 ❑ Interpreters for the Deaf-Blind - $10.00
❑ Lesbian and Gay Interpreters and Transliterators - $10.00

PRORATED MEMBERSHIP DUES
*****FOR NEW MEMBERS ONLY*****
Prorated membership dues are available only to **NEW** members joining the organization after the first quarter of our fiscal year. See the chart below to determine if pro-rated dues apply.

If You Join Between:	4/1-9/30	10/1-12/31	1/1-3/31
CATEGORY:			
Associate	$85.00	$63.75	$42.50
Student	$25.00	$18.75	$12.50
Supporting	$24.00	$18.00	$12.00
Organizational	$150.00	$112.50	$75.00
Trial	$15.00	$11.25	$7.50

PAYMENT METHOD ❑ MC ❑ VISA ❑ Disc. ❑ AmEx ❑ Ck#_____ ❑ Money Order
Card#: _____ Exp. Date: _____
Signature: _____

PAYMENT INFORMATION

Membership Dues and Fees	$_____
Late Fee - Add $9.50 (Certified members renewing after 7/31/03)	$_____
ACET (Associate members only-optional)	$_____
Special Interest Group (optional)	$_____
Tax Deductible Contribution (optional)	$_____
TOTAL Enclosed (U.S. Dollars Only)	$_____

SAMPLE

NAD Certified Interpreter Special Membership Application

Fiscal Year 2004 (July 1, 2003 - June 30, 2004)

Use this form for NAD Level III, IV and V certification maintenance.

Registry of Interpreters for the Deaf
333 Commerce Street
Alexandria, VA 22314
703/838-0030 (V) 703/838-0459 (TTY), 703/838-0454 FAX
membership@rid.org • www.rid.org

❑ Deaf ❑ Deaf-Blind ❑ Hard-of-Hearing ❑ Hearing | ❑ Female ❑ Male
Check All That Apply:
❑ African American/Black ❑ Asian American/Pacific Islander ❑ Euro-American/White
❑ Hispanic/Latino(a) ❑ American Indian/Alaskan Native ❑ Other _____

Mr. Mrs. Ms. Dr. _____

Address: _____ Apt. _____

City: _____ State: _____ Zip: _____

Phone(s): _____
　　　Home: V TTY B　　　Work: V TTY B　　　Fax:

E-mail: _____

Confidential Information:
❑ Home Phone ❑ Work Phone ❑ Address
❑ Fax ❑ E-mail

CODE OF ETHICS:
By joining RID, you agree to adhere to the RID Code of Ethics and the NAD Code of Ethics. The Ethical Practices System applies to current individual members who are providing interpreting services and not to organizations or non-practitioners.

Would you like to be listed in the Membership Directory as a freelance interpreter? ❑ YES ❑ NO

List any RID Affiliate Chapter(s) that you belong to: **(Voting members must be a member of an affiliate chapter)** _____

NAD CERTIFICATION LEVEL AWARDED _____ (Level III, IV, or V)

Please Check One:

❑ **Certified* (NAD)**
For individuals holding **current NAD certification only.**

NOTE: Current RID Associate members holding NAD certification may change to the Certified category by selecting this option.

$85 (valid through 6/30/04)
Includes RID and NAD membership**, with associated benefits and privileges.

❑ **Certified* (NAD and RID)**
For individuals holding **current NAD and RID certification.**

$35 (valid through 6/30/04)
Includes NAD membership** only, with associated benefits and privileges. Those holding RID certification must renew their RID membership separately.

Return form to:
Registry of Interpreters for the Deaf
333 Commerce Street
Alexandria, VA 22314
703/838-0454 FAX

* Certified members must keep their annual membership current and satisfy Certification Maintenance Program (CMP) requirements to maintain Certified status.

** For individuals who already hold NAD membership, the number of months remaining will be extended accordingly, beyond 6/30/04.

SPECIAL INTEREST GROUPS - Activities of SIGs are determined and carried out by the SIG leadership. You must be an RID member to join a SIG.

❑ Deaf Caucus - $10.00 ❑ Educational Interpreters and Transliterators - $ 5.00 ❑ Hearing Interpreters with Deaf Parents - $ 10.00
❑ Interpreter Service Managers - $ 5.00 ❑ Interpreters and Transliterators of Color - $ 5.00 ❑ Interpreters for the Deaf-Blind - $10.00
❑ Lesbian and Gay Interpreters and Transliterators - $10.00

PAYMENT METHOD

❑ MC ❑ VISA ❑ Disc. ❑ AmEx ❑ Ck#_____ ❑ Money Order

Card#: _____

Exp. Date: _____

Signature: _____

PAYMENT INFORMATION

Membership Dues and Fees　　　　　　$_____

Special Interest Group (optional)　　　$_____

Tax Deductible Contribution (optional)　$_____
Contribution for: ❑ NAD ❑ RID
(all contributions will be acknowledged in writing)

TOTAL Enclosed (U.S. Dollars Only)　　$_____

EXPLANATION OF CERTIFICATES (RID)

The certificates described below are an indication that the interpreter or transliterator was assessed by a group of professional peers according to a nationally recognized standard of minimum competence. The individual's performance was deemed to meet or exceed this national standard.

RID Certificates are recognized as valid certificates provided the interpreter/transliterator meets all requirements of membership including participation in the Certification Maintenance Program. All interpreters and transliterators are required to adhere to the RID Code of Ethics governing ethical behavior within the profession. Violations of the Code of Ethics could result in a complaint filed against the interpreter/transliterator through the RID Ethical Practices System.

The RID National Testing System (NTS) strives to maintain adherence to nationally recognized testing industry standards of validity, reliability and equity. As a result, an independent psychometrician (test development expert) is retained by RID and oversees test development and revision processes. RID maintains affiliation with the National Organization for Competency Assurance (NOCA), the entity that sets national criteria for validity, reliability and fairness in testing and credentialing.

CI (CERTIFICATE OF INTERPRETATION)

Holders of this certificate are recognized as fully certified in Interpretation and have demonstrated the ability to interpret between American Sign Language (ASL) and spoken English in both sign-to-voice and voice-to-sign. The interpreter's ability to transliterate is not considered in this certification. Holders of the CI are recommended for a broad range of interpretation assignments. This test is currently available.

CT (CERTIFICATE OF TRANSLITERATION)

Holders of this certificate are recognized as fully certified in Transliteration and have demonstrated the ability to transliterate between English-based sign language and spoken English in both sign-to-voice and voice-to-sign. The transliterator's ability to interpret is not considered in this certification. Holders of the CT are recommended for a broad range of transliteration assignments. This test is currently available.

CI AND CT (CERTIFICATE OF INTERPRETATION AND CERTIFICATE OF TRANSLITERATION)

Holders of both full certificates (as listed above) have demonstrated competence in both interpretation and transliteration and have the same flexibility of job acceptance as holders of the CSC listed below. Holders of the CI and CT are recommended for a broad range of interpretation and transliteration assignments.

CLIP (Conditional Legal Interpreting Permit) NO LONGER VALID – EXPIRED DECEMBER, 1999. The CLIP is no longer offered.

CLIP-R (CONDITIONAL LEGAL INTERPRETING PERMIT-RELAY)

Holders of this conditional permit have completed an RID recognized training program designed for interpreters and transliterators who work in legal settings and who are also Deaf or hard-of-hearing. Generalist certification for

Interpreters/transliterators who are Deaf or hard-of-hearing (RSC, CDI-P, or CDI) is required prior to enrollment in the training program. This permit is valid until one year after the Specialist Certificate: Legal written and performance test for Deaf interpreters is available nationally. CLIP-R holders must take and pass the new legal certification examination in order to maintain certification in the specialized area of interpreting in legal settings. Holders of this conditional permit are recommended for a broad range of assignments in the legal setting. The CLIP-R is still offered.

CDI-P (Certified Deaf Interpreter-Provisional) NO LONGER VALID. The CDI-P is no longer offered.

CDI (CERTIFIED DEAF INTERPRETER)

Holders of this certification are interpreters who are Deaf or hard-of-hearing and who have demonstrated a minimum of one year experience working as an interpreter, completion of at least 8 hours of training on the RID Code of Ethics, and 8 hours of training in general interpretation as it relates to the interpreter who is Deaf or hard-of-hearing and have passed a comprehensive combination written and performance test. Holders of this certificate are recommended for a broad range of assignments where an interpreter who is Deaf or hard-of-hearing would be beneficial.

CSC (Comprehensive Skills Certificate)

Holders of this full certificate have demonstrated the ability to interpret between American Sign Language and spoken English and to transliterate between spoken English and a English-based sign language. The CSC examination was offered until 1987. Holders of this certificate are recommended for a broad range of interpreting and transliterating assignments. This test is no longer offered.

MCSC (Master Comprehensive Skills Certificate)

The MCSC examination was designed with the intent of testing for a higher standard of performance than the CSC. Holders of this certificate were required to hold the CSC prior to taking this exam. Holders of this certificate are recommended for a broad range of interpreting and transliterating assignments. This certificate is no longer offered.

RSC (Reverse Skills Certificate)

Holders of this full certificate demonstrated the ability to interpret between American Sign Language and English-based sign language or transliterate between spoken English and a signed code for English. Holders of this certificate are Deaf or hard-of-hearing and interpretation/transliteration is rendered in American Sign Language, spoken English, a signed code for English or written English. Holders of the RSC are recommended for a broad range of interpreting assignments where the use of an interpreter who is Deaf or hard-of-hearing would be beneficial. This certificate is no longer offered. People interested in this area will apply for the CDI-P and/or take the CDI exam.

SC:L (Specialist Certificate: Legal)

Holders of this specialist certificate have demonstrated specialized knowledge of legal settings and greater familiarity with language used in the legal system. Generalist certification and documented training and experience is required prior to sitting for this exam. Holders of the SC:L are recommended for a broad range of assignments in the legal setting. This test is currently available.

Prov. SC:L (Provisional Specialist Certificate: Legal) **NO LONGER VALID. EXPIRED DECEMBER, 1999.** Prov. SC:L is no longer offered.

SC:PA (SPECIALIST CERTIFICATE: PERFORMING ARTS)

Holders of this certificate were required to hold RID generalist certification (CSC) prior to sitting for this examination and have demonstrated specialized knowledge in performing arts interpretation. Holders of this certificate are recommended for a broad range of assignments in the performing arts setting. The SC:PA is no longer offered.

OTC (ORAL TRANSLITERATION CERTIFICATE)

Holders of this generalist certificate have demonstrated ability to transliterate a spoken message from a person who hears to a person who is deaf or hard-of-hearing and the ability to understand and repeat the message and intent of the speech and mouth movements of the person who is deaf or hard-of-hearing. This test is currently available.

OIC:C (ORAL INTERPRETING CERTIFICATE: COMPREHENSIVE)

Holders of this generalist certificate demonstrated the ability to transliterate a spoken message from a person who hears to a person who is deaf or hard-of-hearing and the ability to understand and repeat the message and intent of the speech and mouth movements of the person who is deaf or hard-of-hearing. This certification is no longer offered. Individuals wishing oral certification should take the OTC exam noted above.

OIC:S/V (ORAL INTERPRETING CERTIFICATE: SPOKEN TO VISIBLE)

Holders of this partial certificate demonstrated the ability to transliterate a spoken message from a person who hears to a person who is deaf or hard-of-hearing. This individual received scores on the OIC:C examination which prevented the awarding of full OIC:C certification. The OIC:S/V is no longer offered. Individuals wishing oral certification should take the OTC exam noted above.

OIC:V/S (ORAL INTERPRETING CERTIFICATE: VISIBLE TO SPOKEN)

Holders of this partial certificate demonstrated ability to understand the speech and silent mouth movements of a person who is deaf or hard-of-hearing and to repeat the message for a hearing person. This individual received scores on the OIC:C examination which prevented the awarding of full OIC:C certification. The OIC:V/S is no longer offered. Individuals wishing oral certification should take the OTC exam noted above.

IC/TC (INTERPRETATION CERTIFICATE/TRANSLITERATION CERTIFICATE)

Holders of this partial certificate demonstrated ability to transliterate between English and a signed code for English and the ability to interpret between American Sign Language and spoken English. This individual received scores on the CSC examination which prevented the awarding of full CSC certification. The IC/TC is no longer offered.

IC (INTERPRETATION CERTIFICATE)

Holder of this partial certificate demonstrated ability to interpret between American Sign Language and spoken English. This individual received scores on the CSC examination which prevented the awarding of full CSC certification or partial IC/TC certification. The IC was formerly known as the Expressive Interpreting Certificate (EIC). The IC is no longer offered.

TC (TRANSLITERATION CERTIFICATE)

Holders of this partial certificate demonstrated the ability to transliterate between spoken English and a signed code for English. This individual received scores on the CSC examination which prevented the awarding of full CSC certification or IC/TC certification. The TC was formerly known as the Expressive Transliterating Certificate (ETC). The TC is no longer offered.

Approved and printed with permission from RID

2004 NATIONAL TESTING SYSTEM COMPUTER-BASED TESTING APPLICATION
GENERALIST WRITTEN TEST

THIS APPLICATION IS FOR THE GENERALIST WRITTEN TEST ONLY AND DOES NOT INCLUDE THE OTC, SC:L, OR CDI WRITTEN TESTS.

Name: _____
(Last)   (First)   (M.I.)

SSN: _____ Memb.#: _____
(Social Security Number)   (RID Membership Number)

Address: _____
(Street)   (Apt. #)

_____
(City)   (State)   (Zip)

Phone: _____ V TTY Both _____ V TTY Both
(Home)   (Work)

Pager: _____ E-Mail: _____

Cell Phone: _____

NOTE: All Information is mandatory except pager, cell phone, and RID member number for non-members.

Are you an RID member in good standing? ☐ YES ☐ NO
If yes, which? ☐ Certified ☐ Associate ☐ Student

If you have a disability or need that requires a special accommodation, please describe below. Official verification of the need for the accommodation MUST accompany this application.

_____
_____
_____
_____
_____
_____

Test	Item	Member	Non-Member	Payment
Written	Test Fee (includes $40 non-refundable application fee)	$240.00	$295.00	
	Retake Fee (includes $40 non-refundable application fee)	$180.00	$275.00	
			TOTAL amount enclosed (U.S.)	

IMPORTANT

- Applications will be accepted through March 5, 2004. No applications for this test will be accepted after March 5, 2004.

- CERTIFICATE OF INTERPRETATION/CERTIFICATE OF TRANSLITERATION TESTS (CI and CT) - After this administration, the Generalist Written Test will no longer be offered. CI and CT generalist performance tests can be taken only by candidates for certification (individuals who have already passed the Generalist Written Test or who are currently RID certified members in good standing of the national RID). Member fees do not apply to supporting members.

IMPORTANT: Please read the following statement and description of the RID tests. All applicants must sign this acknowledgement that they have read and will abide by the following agreement.

I understand and agree that all materials developed and used in the test that I am applying to take are the copyrighted property of the Registry of Interpreters for the Deaf, Inc. (RID), which is a not-for-profit organization; that the test and test results are likewise the property of RID and are not to be shared, duplicated or disseminated in any fashion; that such are not diagnostic in nature and can be used for no purpose other than as intended by RID; and that the scores and method of grading cannot be reviewed by anyone (myself included) except by those authorized by RID to evaluate and/or grade.

I have read and understand the conditions and requirements placed on me by RID in taking the test applied for and do agree to abide by all of these and the rules for taking the test as set out by RID. I hold harmless RID, its officers, agents, and employees from any and all liability, except intentional wrongdoing, in the offering, taking, grading, and reporting of these tests. I understand and agree with the above statements.

Signed:_____ Date: _____
(REQUIRED) By signing this, I certify that I am 18 or older.

RID shall not discriminate in matters of certification testing or membership on the basis of age, color, creed, disability, ethnicity, hearing status, national origin, race, religion, gender or sexual orientation.

Payment Information

IMPORTANT: RID must receive payment in full before you will be eligible to take the test.

You may fax or mail your application.

Money Order or Check # _____

☐ VISA ☐ Master Card ☐ AmEx ☐ Discover

Card # _____

Expiration Date _____

Signature _____

Send Application, Fees, and any Supporting Documentation to:

**RID, Inc.
333 Commerce Street
Alexandria, VA 22314
(703) 838-0454 Fax**

RID NATIONAL TESTING SYSTEM COMPREHENSIVE APPLICATION 2003

Please check the box of the test for which you are applying. Please use a separate form for each test application.

CI AND CT	OTC	SC:L	CDI
❑ CI Perf. ❑ CT Perf.	❑ Written ❑ Perf.	❑ Written ❑ Perf.	❑ Written ❑ Written ❑ Perf. English ASL
PLEASE SEE BACK OF FORM FOR NOTES ON THIS TEST.	PLEASE SEE BACK OF FORM FOR SUGGESTED REQUIREMENTS.	PLEASE SEE BACK OF FORM FOR ELIGIBILITY REQUIREMENTS.	PLEASE SEE BACK OF FORM FOR ELIGIBILITY REQUIREMENTS.

Name: _____
(Last)   (First)   (M.I.)

SSN: _____ Memb.#: _____
(Social Security/Insurance Number)   (RID Membership Number)

Address: _____
(Street)   (Apt. #)

_____
(City)   (State)   (Zip)

Phone: _____ V TTY Both _____ V TTY Both
(Home)   (Work)

Pager: _____ E-Mail: _____

Have you passed the appropriate written test? ❑ YES ❑ NO
If yes, when?_____

Are you an RID member in good standing? ❑ YES ❑ NO
If yes, which? ❑ Certified ❑ Associate ❑ Student

Do you maintain other RID certification? ❑ YES ❑ NO
If yes, which? _____

Test location/date preference(s)?
Date: _____ Site Code _____
Site Name: _____

Do you have a disability which requires accommodations?
❑ NO If yes, what is the specific accommodation requested?

Physician's verification of need for reasonable accommodation must accompany this application.

Test	Item	Member	Non-Member	Payment
Written	Application ($30 non-refundable)/Test Fee	$140.00	$195.00	
	Retake Fee	$80.00	$105.00	
Performance	Application ($30 non-refundable)/Test Fee	$225.00	$310.00	
	Retake Fee	$195.00	$280.00	
			Subtotal	
			TOTAL amount enclosed (U.S.)	

IMPORTANT

- You must pass the appropriate written test before you can apply for that certification's performance test.
- Application deadline is eight weeks in advance of any testing date. Applications received after the deadline will be applied toward the next published test date at the requested site, or if you are testing at a supersite, you must call them directly to schedule testing.
- RID is not responsible for any incorrectly checked boxes.

Due to the nature of performance-based testing, generally four candidates are tested per day. Candidate applications are prioritized on a first-come, first-served basis. Applicants who decline a performance test opportunity will be placed on the waiting list for the next published test in their preferred location.

IMPORTANT: Please read the following statement and description of the RID tests. All applicants must sign this acknowledgement that they have read and will abide by the following agreement.

I understand and agree that all materials developed and used in the test that I am applying to take are the copyrighted property of the Registry of Interpreters for the Deaf, Inc. (RID), which is a not-for-profit organization; that the test and test results are likewise the property of RID and are not to be shared, duplicated or disseminated in any fashion; that such are not diagnostic in nature and can be used for no purpose other than as intended by RID; and that the scores and method of grading cannot be reviewed by anyone (myself included) except by those authorized by RID to evaluate and/or grade.

I have read and understand the conditions and requirements placed on me by RID in taking the test applied for and do agree to abide by all of these and the rules for taking the test as set out by RID. I hold harmless RID, its officers, agents, and employees from any and all liability, except intentional wrongdoing, in the offering, taking, grading, and reporting of these tests. I understand and agree with the above statements.

Signed:_____ Date: _____
(REQUIRED) By signing this I certify that I am 18 or older.

RID shall not discriminate in matters of certification testing or membership on the basis of age, color, creed, disability, ethnicity, hearing status, national origin, race, religion, gender or sexual orientation.

Payment Information

IMPORTANT: RID must receive payment in full before you will be eligible to take the test.

Money Order or Check # _____

❑ VISA ❑ Master Card ❑ AmEx ❑ Discover

Card # _____

_____

Expiration Date _____

Signature _____

Send Application, Fees, and Supporting Documentation to:
RID, Inc.
333 Commerce Street
Alexandria, VA 22314
(703) 838-0454 Fax

REV 7/10/03

APPLICATION INSTRUCTIONS AND ELIGIBILITY INFORMATION

Please make sure that the application is completely filled out and signed. Send application, fees, and all required supporting documentation to: RID, Inc., 333 Commerce Street, Alexandria, VA 22314, (703) 838-0454 Fax. RID is not able to take applications over the phone, by e-mail, or by Internet at this time.

CERTIFICATE OF INTERPRETATION/CERTIFICATE OF TRANSLITERATION TESTS (CI and CT)

The generalist written test will no longer be administered. CI and CT generalist performance tests can be taken only by candidates for certification (individuals who have already passed the generalist written test or who are currently certified members in good standing of the national RID). Member fees do not apply to supporting members.

ORAL TRANSLITERATION CERTIFICATE TEST (OTC)

Oral performance tests can be taken only by individuals who have passed the OTC written test. Member fees do not apply to supporting members. Applicants for the OTC examination are strongly encouraged, but not mandated, to satisfy all of the recommended criteria in at least one of the following categories:

Category #1: Successful completion of at least 50 hours of education specifically in the area of oral transliterating (e.g. oral transliterating workshops) and completion of at least 50 hours of documented experience (supervised or unsupervised) in oral transliterating;

Category #2: Successful completion of an Associate degree (in any field), successful completion of at least 35 hours of education specifically in the area of oral transliterating, and at least 50 hours of experience (supervised or unsupervised) in oral transliterating;

Category #3: Successful completion of an Associate degree in interpreting, successful completion of at least 25 hours of education specifically in the area of oral transliterating, (credit bearing education, e.g. college course work, or non-credit bearing education, e.g. workshops), and at least 50 hours of experience (supervised or unsupervised) in oral transliterating;

Category #4: Possess any valid RID Certification and demonstrate successful completion of at least 25 hours of education specifically in the area of oral transliterating, and at least 50 hours of experience (supervised or unsupervised) in oral transliterating.

SPECIALIST CERTIFICATE: LEGAL TEST (SC:L)

Applicants for the SC:L written examination must attach all appropriate documentation showing eligibility to sit for the written examination and be a member in good standing. Applicants are not considered registered until all eligibility documentation and fees have been processed by the National Office. SC:L performance tests can only be taken by individuals who have passed the SC:L written test.

Category #1: Possess valid CSC, CI and CT, or MCSC. Successful completion of BA or BS in any field or AA in interpreting. Five years general interpreting experience (post-RID Certification) strongly recommended. Documentation of at least 50 hours of legal interpreting experience/or mentoring, and 30 hours of formal legal training.

Category #2: Possess valid CSC, CI and CT, or MCSC. Successful completion of AA in any field. Five years general interpreting experience (post-RID Certification) strongly recommended. Documentation of at least 75 hours of legal interpreting experience and 50 hours of formal legal training.

Category #3: Possess valid CSC, CI and CT, or MCSC. Five years general interpreting experience (post-RID Certification) strongly recommended. Documentation of at least 100 hours of legal interpreting experience and 70 hours of formal legal training.

Category #4: Possess current SC:L (Do not need to re-take the test, but are invited to do so.)

Documentation of legal interpreting experience can be a formal letter from the court clerk or from the interpreter service agency. Documentation of training can be transcripts, certificate(s) of attendance, or a formal letter from the instructor verifying your attendance and stating the training date, location, duration, and topics covered. Mentoring must be with an interpreter who holds any valid RID certification.

CERTIFIED DEAF INTERPRETER TEST (CDI)

The CDI performance test can be taken only by candidates for certification (individuals who have passed the CDI written test). Member fees do not apply to supporting members.

Candidate applications are prioritized on a first-come, first-served basis. Applicants who decline a performance test opportunity will be placed on the waiting list for the next published test in their preferred location.

Eligibility Requirements: An individual interested in taking the CDI Written Exam must satisfy all of the eligibility criteria. Applicants for the CDI Written Exam must attach appropriate documentation showing eligibility to sit for the test and are not considered registered until all eligibility documentation and fees have been processed by the National Office.

1. Verification that applicant is deaf or hard-of-hearing. Physician's or audiologist's verification of deafness required. The applicant is responsible for providing this documentation with the application.

2. Verification of having completed at least 8 hours of training on the RID Code of Ethics (documentation must indicate date(s), location(s), and duration of training).

3. Verification of having completed at least 8 hours of training on the role and function of a Deaf interpreter (documentation must indicate date(s), location(s), and duration of training).

Training documentation may be in the form of course transcripts, letter(s) of verification signed by the person teaching the training session(s), certificate(s)/letter(s) of completion, or other valid documentation, and must be attached to the application.

RID, Inc. is hereby authorized to verify documentation sent by me and may contact my health care providers concerning any information I have sent RID pertaining to the nature and extent of my hearing loss. My health care providers are authorized to provide RID, Inc. all information pertaining to me regarding treatment, examination, testing or care pertaining to my hearing loss.

Signed:_____ Date: / /

(SIGNATURE FOR CDI TEST APPLICANTS ONLY)

CERTIFICATION MAINTENANCE PROGRAM (CMP) (RID)

OVERVIEW OF THE CMP

The CMP is the vehicle through which the continued skill development of certified interpreters is encouraged and monitored. Certification maintenance is a way for practitioners to maintain their skill levels, keep up with developments in the interpreting field, and assure consumers that a certified interpreter means quality interpreting services.

RID's Certification Maintenance Program began operation on July 1, 1994 and relies on RID Approved Sponsors to provide appropriate educational activities for participants. These activities can be group activities, such as workshops, lectures, or conferences or independent study activities, such as mentoring and self-study. Organizations, agencies, affiliate chapters and individuals seeking to be Approved Sponsors must complete an application process developed by the Professional Development Committee (PDC). Sponsors are monitored regularly to ensure that their activities are of high quality.

Like many educational and other professional agencies, RID requires participants to earn a specific number of continuing education units (CEUs). The CEU is a nationally recognized unit of measurement for activities that meet established criteria for increasing knowledge and competency. One CEU is equal to ten (10) contact hours of participation in an organized continuing education experience, the experience of which is based on responsible sponsorship, capable direction, and qualified instruction.

CYCLE TIMELINES

December 31, 1999 marked the end of the first Certification Maintenance Program cycle for more than 1,900 interpreters. Completing their first cycle requirements of 9 CEUs, this group of 1,900+ interpreters began their second cycle time line on January 1, 2000 and will have four years (December 31, 2003) to complete a required 8 CEUs-6 of which must be in the Professional Studies category.

Certified Deaf Interpreters who received certification prior to July 1, 1996 had their first cycle end on December 31, 2000 and are expected to complete the required 9 CEUs by that date. This group began their second cycle time line on January 1, 2001 and will have four years (December 31, 2004) to complete a required 8 CEUs-6 of which must be in the Professional Studies category.

Those interpreters who were certified July 1, 1995 through June 30, 1996 had their first certification maintenance program cycle extended to December 31, 2000 and were expected to earn 8 CEUs by that date (6 CEUs of which must be in the Professional Studies category).

Those interpreters who were certified July 1, 1996 through June 30, 1997 have had their first certification maintenance program cycle extended to December 31, 2001 and are expected to earn 8 CEUs by that date (6 CEUs of which must be in the Professional Studies category).

Those interpreters who were certified July 1, 1997 through June 30, 1998 have had their first certification maintenance program cycle extended to December 31, 2002 and are expected to earn 8 CEUs by that date (6 CEUs of which must be in the Professional Studies category).

Those interpreters who were certified July 1, 1998 through June 30, 1999 have had their first certification maintenance program cycle extended to December 31, 2003 and are expected to earn 8 CEUs by that date (6 CEUs of which must be in the Professional Studies category).

Those interpreters who will be certified between July 1, 1999 through June 30, 2000 will be expected to earn 8 CEUs by December 31, 2004 (6 CEUs of which must be in the Professional Studies category).

After an interpreter's first cycle is completed, every cycle thereafter will begin on January 1 and run for four calendar years.

Who Participates?

Every RID certified interpreter must participate in the CMP. If you are a newly certified interpreter, you can wait until the start of the next fiscal year (July 1) to join the CMP. However, you may elect to join immediately upon being certified in order to start earning CEUs.

What are the Requirements?

The certified interpreter must earn 8.0 CEUs (80 hours) in a cycle. These eight CEUs are divided into two Content Areas: Professional Studies and General Studies.

Professional Studies - A minimum of 6 CEUs must be related to either 1) Linguistic and Cultural Studies which includes the study of any language or linguistic system, and the study of any specific culture, 2) Theoretical and Experiential Studies which includes the process of interpreting and transliterating theory and skill building activities, 3) Specialization Studies which includes specialized aspects of interpreting used in settings such as the legal, medical, mental health, and substance abuse recovery fields.

General Studies - This content area includes 1) Human Service and Leadership Studies which include topics such as leadership skills, public relations, public speaking, and community resources, and 2) General knowledge studies which include areas less obviously related to the field of interpreting and transliteration, with studies that are educationally beneficial to the participant.

How To Earn CEUs

Participants must work with an RID-Approved Sponsor to earn CEU credits. An updated listing of Approved Sponsors is available on RID's Fax-on-Demand at 800-711-3691, on the RID Web Site, and in the February 2002 issue of the VIEWS

publication. When considering a workshop check the brochure or flyer for the RID CMP and a statement that reads "This organization is an RID Sponsor approved activity".

Activities That Earn CEUs

There are three means for earning CEUs:

1. RID Approved Sponsor initiated activities such as workshops, short courses, conferences, silent weekends.

2. Participant-Initiated activities such as academic coursework, in-service workshops, attending workshops or conferences of other organizations.

3. Independent Study activities such as home study with videos, research or literature reviews, study groups, acting as a mentor or mentoree, curriculum/workshop development, teaching a workshop for the first time.

How to earn CEUs for a workshop given by an Approved Sponsor

Earning CEUs when an RID Approved Sponsor conducts the workshop is a simple process. Sign up for the workshop. When you attend, sign your name on the sign-in sheet marked, "RID Certification Maintenance Program – Certified Interpreters Only Sign Here." Be sure to have your RID Membership Number available. The membership number can be found in the lower right hand corner of your membership card.

How To Earn CEUs For An Activity Not Offered By An Approved Sponsor

1. For many of the activities listed above, you may set up an Independent Study with an RID Sponsor. Each Independent Study Plan is limited to 2.0 CEUs. You must establish the Independent Study before you begin the activity. The following steps detail the procedure to earn CEUs through the Independent Study process:

    a. Decide the activity for which you want to earn CEUs.

    b. Contact an Approved Sponsor who processes Independent Studies and discuss your ideas. Find out the type of documentation required and the number of CEUs that you can earn. You will be asked to respond in writing to the following questions:

        (1) What do I want to do? Briefly describe the activity you will complete for CEUs.

        (2) Why do I want to do it? Personal needs? Professional growth? Skill enhancement in a specific area? Increased general knowledge? Remaining current in the field?

        (3) What are my specific goals? Keep your goals measurable, observable, tangible!

        (4) How will I accomplish my goals? Briefly describe your action plan.

        (5) How will I show my sponsor what I learned? Describe your evaluation process.

        (6) How many CEUs is it worth?

    c. The Sponsor will sign and approve the Plan. You may now begin work on the activity (any work done before this point cannot earn CEUs). It is important to document your time and efforts while you work on your activity.

    d. At the completion of the activity, send the Sponsor your report, documentation, and other information outlined in the Activity Plan. The Sponsor will review the documentation to ensure that it meets the standards and goals agreed upon in the Activity Plan.

e. The Sponsor will fill out the Independent Study Activity Report and send all required paperwork to the National Office to be added to your record.

2. Another avenue for earning CEUs not offered by an RID Approved Sponsor is through Academic Coursework. The procedure is simple and requires contact with an RID Approved Sponsor for filing the paperwork for the course. Once your academic transcript is finalized, you must submit a copy to the RID Approved Sponsor in order to attain CEU credits. If the course is offered during a semester, the number of CEUs equals 1.5 per credit (ie. a 3 credit course = 4.5 CEUS). If the course is offered during a quarter, the number of CEUs equals 1 per credit (i.e. a 3 credit course = 3 CEUs.) You must earn a grade of a C or better to receive CEUs. The course must have been taken during the participant's current CMP cycle. Paperwork may be filed anytime during that current cycle.

3. The third alternative for earning CEUs not offered by an RID Approved Sponsor is by selecting the activity you wish to participate in and contacting an RID Approved Sponsor to "sponsor" you and enable you to earn CEUs. Paperwork documentation prior to the activity must be completed by you and the RID Sponsor (the paperwork is entitled Participant Initiated Non RID Activity) and documentation support is usually required.

Reprinted with permission from RID

ASSOCIATE CONTINUING EDUCATION TRACKING PROGRAM (ACET) (RID)

OVERVIEW OF THE ACET

RID's Associate Continuing Education Tracking program relies on RID Approved Sponsors to provide appropriate educational activities for participants. These activities can be group activities, such as workshops, lectures, or conferences or independent study activities, such as mentoring and self-study. Organizations, agencies, affiliate chapters and individuals seeking to be Approved Sponsors must complete an application process developed by the Professional Development Committee (PDC). Sponsors are monitored regularly to ensure that their activities are of high quality.

Used by many educational and other professional agencies, the CEU is a nationally recognized unit of measurement for activities that meet established criteria for increasing knowledge and competency. One CEU is equal to ten (10) contact hours of participation in an organized continuing education experience, the experience of which is based on responsible sponsorship, capable direction, and qualified instruction.

WHO PARTICIPATES?

Any RID associate interpreter may join the ACET program. Tracking of CEUs begins once the $15 ACET fee is received for the fiscal year (July 1 - June 30). The ACET program is designed to track and document your continuing education for the fiscal year. An annual transcript of your activities and CEUs is then printed and sent to you.

HOW TO EARN CEUs

Participants must work with an RID-Approved Sponsor to earn CEU credits. An updated listing of Approved Sponsors is available on RID's Fax-on-Demand at 800-711-3691, on the RID Web Site, in the October 98 issue of the VIEWS publication or at the National Office. When considering a workshop or academic course, check the brochure or flyer for the RID CMP and a statement that reads "This organization is an RID Sponsor approved activity."

ACTIVITIES THAT EARN CEUS

There are three means for earning CEUs:

1. RID Approved Sponsor initiated activities such as workshops, short courses, conferences, silent weekends.

2. Participant-Initiated activities such as academic coursework, in-service workshops, attending workshops or conferences of other organizations.

3. Independent Study activities such as home study with videos, research or literature reviews, study groups, acting as a mentor or mentoree, curriculum/workshop development, teaching a workshop for the first time.

HOW TO EARN CEUS FOR A WORKSHOP GIVEN BY AN APPROVED SPONSOR

Earning CEUs when an RID Approved Sponsor conducts the workshop is a simple process. Sign up for the workshop. When you attend, sign your name on the sign-in sheet marked, "RID Associate Continuing Education Tracking (ACET) Program - ACET Members Only Sign Here." The RID Sponsor submits the completed sign-in sheet to the National Office and the National Office will credit the activity to your record.

HOW TO EARN CEUS FOR AN ACTIVITY NOT OFFERED BY AN APPROVED SPONSOR

1. For many of the activities listed above, you may set up an Independent Study with an RID Sponsor. Each Independent Study Plan is limited to 2.0 CEUs. You must establish the Independent Study before you begin the activity. The following steps detail the procedure to earn CEUs through the Independent Study process: Decide the activity for which you want to earn CEUs. Contact an Approved Sponsor who processes Independent Studies and discuss your ideas. Find out the type of documentation required and the number of CEUs that you can earn. You will be asked to respond in writing to the following questions:

   a. What do I want to do? Briefly describe the activity you will complete for CEUs.

   b. Why do I want to do it? Personal needs? Professional growth? Skill enhancement in a specific area? Increased general knowledge? Remaining current in the field?

    c. What are my specific goals? Keep your goals measurable, observable, tangible!

    d. How will I accomplish my goals? Briefly describe your action plan.

    e. How will I show my sponsor what I learned? Describe your evaluation process.

    f. How many CEUs is it worth? The Sponsor will sign and approve the Plan. You may now begin work on the activity (any work done before this point cannot earn CEUs). It is important to document your time and efforts while you work on your activity. At the completion of the activity, send the Sponsor your report, documentation, and other information outlined in the Activity Plan. The Sponsor will review the documentation to ensure that it meets the standards and goals agreed upon in the Activity Plan. The sponsor will fill out the Independent Study Activity Report and send all required paperwork to the National Office to be added to your record.

2. Another avenue for earning CEUs not offered by an RID Approved Sponsor is through Academic Coursework. The procedure is simple and requires contact with an RID Approved Sponsor for filing the paperwork for the course. Once your academic transcript is finalized, you must submit a copy to the RID Approved Sponsor in order to attain CEU credits. If the course is offered during a semester, the number of CEUs equals 1.5 per credit (ie. a 3 credit course = 4.5 CEUS). If the course is offered during a quarter, the number of CEUs equals 1 per credit (i.e. a 3 credit course = 3 CEUs.) You must earn a grade of a C or better to receive CEUs.

3. The third alternative for earning CEUs not offered by an RID Approved Sponsor is by selecting the activity you wish to participate in and contacting an RID approved Sponsor to "sponsor" you and enable you to earn CEUs. Paperwork documentation prior to the activity must be completed by you and the RID Sponsor (the paperwork is entitled Participant Initiated Non RID activity) and documentation support is usually required.

Reprinted with permission from RID

APPROVED CMP AND ACET SPONSORS

(Partial listing: Contact RID for current and complete listings)

REGION I

CONNECTICUT
Family Services Woodfield
77 Glenstone
Vernon, CT 06066
Audrey Silva
(860) 798-0815
aslaudrey@aol.com

MAINE
Maine RID
29 Manter Street
Cape Elizabeth, ME 04107
Ann Swope
(207) 799-4868
acswope@aol.com

MASSACCHUSETTS
Boston U. Ctr. for Interpreter
Ed.
Office of Disability Services
19 Deerfield Street
Boston, MA 02215
Laurie Shaffer
(617) 353-6882
(617) 353-9646 (fax)

Kellie Mills Stewart*
1 Purcell Drive
Chelmsford, MA 01824
(617) 496-3720
(617) 495-0815 (fax)
KStewart@fas.havard.edu

Northeastern University ASL
Program
Interpreter Education Project
405 Meserve Hall
Boston, MA 02115
Diana Doucette
(617) 373-2463
(617) 373-3065 (fax)
ddoucett@lynx.dac.neu.edu

Massachusetts RID
567 Tremont St. #28
Boston, MA 02118
Jim Lipsky
(617) 267-5188 (V/fax)
JSL567@aol.com

Southeast Mentorship Project
P.O. Box 388
East Taunton, MA 02718
Russell Ross
(508) 822-2279
(508) 822-1087 (fax)

NEW HAMPSHIRE
New Hampshire RID*
23 Dwindell Drive
Concord, NH 03301
Julia Barnwell-Emley
(603) 244-7736 (V/TTY)
Emley23@mediaone.com

NEW JERSEY
New Jersey RID*
800 Chews Landing, Apt. 3F
Lindenwold, NJ 08021
Roseanne Schatek
(856) 627-2030
(856) 627-0826 (fax)
rose-99@msn.com

NEW YORK
CUNY Consortium Interpreter
Educational Project
LaGuardia Community College,
Interpreter Education Projects
31-10 Thompson Ave.
Room C-239
Long Island City, NY 11101
Jo Ann Kranis
(718) 482-5313
(718) 609-2005 (fax)
JoannK@lagcc.cuny.edu

Deaf & Hard of Hearing
Interpreting Serv., Inc.
1076 Jackson Ave.
Long Island, NY 11101
Joshua Finkle
(718) 433-1092
(718) 392-3576 (fax)
jfinkle33@aol.com

Deaf Wellness Center
University of Rochester
300 Crittenden Blvd.
Rochester, NY 14642
(585) 275-8572
rdean@rochester.rr.com

Gennessee Valley RID*
Univ. Rochester Medical
Center
601 Elmwood Ave.
Box 602
Rochester, NY 14642
Kathy Miraglia
(716) 275-4778
(716) 461-5275 (fax)
kathy_miraglia@urmc.rochester.edu

Interpretek*
1200 A Scottsville Rd.
Suite 130
Rochester, NY 14624
Michael Rizzolo
(585) 235-7500
(585) 235-7882 (fax)
mrizzolo@rpa.net

Mill Neck Interpreter Services
1025 Old Country Road
Suite 402C
Westbury, NY 11590
Judith Rackovitch
(516) 512-6222 (V/TTY)
(516) 512-6336 (fax)
judirocks10@aol.com
Monroe #1 BOCES /

Western Regional Professional
Dev. Site for Ed. Interpreters
15 Linden Park
Rochester, NY 14625
(716) 249-7013
(716) 218-6266 (fax)

NTID*
Dept. of ASL & Interpreting Ed
52 Lomb Memorial Dr.
LBJ Buliding
Rochester, NY 14623
(716) 475-6431
(716) 475-6500 (fax)
RXPNSS@rit.edu

NTID
Dept. of Interpreting Services
Rochester Inst. of Tech.
97 Lomb Memorial Dr.
Bldg. 14-1568
Rochester, NY 14623
Jo Ellen Clark
(585) 475-6316
(585) 475-7526 (fax)
jocdis@vmsmail.rit.edu

New York City Board of Ed.
22 E St., Rm. 304
New York, NY 10016
Beth Prevor
(212) 689-4020
BethPrevor@aol.com

New York City Metro RID*
P.O. Box 1632 # 1D
New York, NY 10025
Debbie Matthews

Professional Interpreter &
Sign Language Consultants
333 Frantone Lane
Loudonville, NY 12211
Karen Lefebvre
(518) 459-4518
Klefebvr@localnet.com

Sign Language Resources*
533 Rock Cut Road
Walden, NY 12586
Mary Darragh MacLean
(845) 566-7951
(845) 271-7471 (fax)

Theatre Development Fund-
Signing for the Theatre
1501 Broadway
Suite 2110
New York, NY 10036
Laura Klein
(212) 221-0885 x252
(212) 768-1563 (fax)
laurak@tdf.org

PENNSYLVANIA

Deaf-Hearing Communication
Centre Inc.*
630 Fairview Road
Suite 100
Swarthmore, PA 19081
Maria Elia
(610) 604-0452
(610) 534-4942 (fax)
mariaelia@nni.com

Feed Your Head, Inc.*
P.O. Box 703
Lansdowne, PA 19050
Don Rubel
(609) 371-2770

Pennsylvania RID
2413 Richey Street
Williamsport, PA 17701
Stephanie Ellison
(570) 320-0111
StephanieEllisonCMP@yahoo
.com

REGION II

ALABAMA
Alabama RID*
JCCD-ES
5950 Monticello Drive
Montgomery, AL 36117
Deb Walker
(334) 244-8090
dwalker@jccd.org

DISTRICT OF COLUMBIA
Capitol Community Institute*
1720 Minnesota Ave., SE
Washington, D.C. 20020
Sandra Matthews
(202) 889-3995
(202) 889-6312 (fax)
omeccorp1@aol.com

Gallaudet University
College for Continuing Ed.
Washington, D.C. 20002
Beverly Hollrah
(202) 651-6056
(202) 651-6019 (fax)
beverly.hollrah@gallaudet.edu

National Alliance of Black
Interpreters (NAOBI)
P.O. Box 30071
Washington, D.C. 20030
Catherine Robinson-Willett
(240) 463-6551
NAOBIDC@yahoo.com

FLORIDA
Access Through Sign
Language
P.O. Box 570289
Orlando, FL 32857
Emilia Lorenti
(407) 382-3823
(407) 382-0999 (TTY)
(407) 382-0683 (fax)
info@AccessASL.com

American Sign Lang. Srvs.,
Inc.*
1310 North Main Street
Kissimmee, FL 34744
Angela Roth
(407) 518-7900
(407) 518-7903 (fax)
ASLService@aol.com

Florida RID
P.O. Box 423142
Kissimmee, FL 34742
George Costa, Jr.
(407) 344-8723
(407) 344-8733 (fax)
GCJrFRID@cs.com

Alysse Lemery Rasmussen*
407 S 12th Street
Leesburg, FL 34748
(352) 365-1793
(352) 365-1466 (fax)
TeachASLInfo@aol.com

St. Petersburg Junior College*
2465 Drew St.
Clearwater, FL 32095
Sammie Elser
(727) 791-2759
(727) 791-2638 (fax)
elsers@email.spjc.cc.fl.us

GEORGIA
Georgia Parimeter College*
Interpreter Training Program
555 North Indian Creek Dr.
Clarkston, GA 30021
Christine Smith
(404) 299-4360
(404) 299-4364 (fax)
csmith@gpc.peachnet.edu

North American Mission
Board*
Southern Baptist Convention
4200 North Point Pkwy.
Alpharetta, GA 330202
Rodney Webb
(770) 410-6230

(770) 410-6012 (fax)
RWEBB@NAMB.NET

MARYLAND
Birnbaum Interpreting Services
8555 16th Street
Suite 300
Silver Spring, MD 20910
Sarah Yates
(301) 587-8885
(301) 565-0366 (fax)
Sly44444@aol.com

Interpreting Training Resources
10724 Liberty Road
Frederick, MD 21701
Janice Martin
(301) 898-4249
(301) 898-0391 (fax)
ITRmartin@aol.com

Potomac Chapter RID*
12336 LaPlata Street
Silver Spring, MD 20904
Carol Tipton
(301) 572-7528
(301) 572-2030 (fax)
carol_tipton@hotmail.com

Professional Interpreter Exchange*
9101 Cherry Lane
Suite 104-105
Laurel, MD 20708
Jennifer Parsons
(301) 725-3402 x14
(301) 725-3412 (fax)
jen@pieinc.com

Sign Language Associates*
11160 Veirs Mill Road
Ste. 506
Silver Spring, MD 20910
Janet Bailey
(301) 946-9710
(301) 946-9685 (fax)
Jlbailey@signlanguage.com

NORTH CAROLINA
Gardner-Webb University*
ASL Studies Program
Boiling Springs, NC 28017
Mary High
(704) 406-4418
(704) 406-3508 (fax)
mhigh@gardner-webb.edu

Interpreters, Inc.*
P.O. Box 604
Wake Forest, NC 27588
Kathy Beetham
(919) 570-8686
iinc@interpretersinc.com

North Carolina RID*
1511 Duke Valentine Wynne Rd.
Louisburg, NC 27549
Connie Jo Hutchinson
(919) 496-4214
conniejo71@mindspring.com

SOUTH CAROLINA
South Carolina RID*
145 Lynn Road
Spartanburg, SC 29306
Steve Fitzmaurice
(864) 573-1075 (V/TTY)
(864) 573-1075 (fax)
canucks@bellsouth.net

TENNESSEE
Tennessee RID*
2838 Cansler Dr.
Maryville, TN 37801
Beth Foreman
(423) 681-8294
(423) 681-7548 (fax)
bethforeman@sprintmail.com

VIRGINIA
Virginia RID*
8802 Lawndell Road
Richmond, VA 23229
Allison Weippert
(804) 290-0600
ALFranger@aol.com

REGION III

ILLINOIS

Anixter Ctr. Training Institute
2032 North Clybourn
Chicago, IL 60614
Beverly Otey
(773) 929-8200 x214
(773) 929-3779 (TTY)
(773) 929-3244 (fax)
botey@anixter.org

CAIRS*
36 S. Wabash Street
Suite 1100
Chicago, IL 60603
Cherly Yallen
(312) 895-4300
(312) 895-4320 (TTY)
(312) 895-4313 (fax)
cairs1@aol.com

Illinois RID*
13757 S. Kendall
Plainfield, IL 60544
Leslie Jeziorski
(815) 886-2686
CMP@ilrid.org

Waubonsee Community
College*
Route 47 at Waubonsee Dr.
Sugar Grove, IL 60554
Dr. William Marzano
(630) 801-7900
(630) 896-1054 (TTY)
(630) 892-4668 (fax)
wmarzano@mail.wcc.cc.il.us

INDIANA

Deaf and Hard of Hearing Srvs
P.O. Box 7083
Indianapolis, IN 46207
Jerry Cooper
(317) 232-1143
(317) 233-1566 (fax)

Deaf Connection
4101 Howard Street
Hobart, IN 46342
(219) 945-1653
deafConnection@aol.com

Indiana RID*
305 Beacon Point Lane
Fortville, IN 46040
Carrie Westhoelter
(317) 485-0337
icridcmp@hotmail.com

KENTUCKY

Kentucky RID*
7308 Cardinal Road
Crestwood, KY 40014
Tammy Cantrell
(502) 852-4519
(502) 852-1542 (fax)
tscant01@louisville.edu

MICHIGAN

Division on Deafness*
Family Independence Agency
320 North Washington Square
Lansing, MI 48909
Maureen Wallace
(517) 334-8000
(517) 334-6622 (TTY)
(517) 334-6637 (fax)
wallacem2@state.mi.us

Madonna University
College of Continuing &
Professional Studies-
Sign Language Studies
36600 Schoolcraft Rd.
Livonia, MI 48150
Teresa Quattlander
(734) 432-5616
(734) 432-5393 (fax)
quattla@smtp.munet.edu

Sign Lines*
4785 Clintonville Rd.
Clarkston, MI 48346
Kim Willett
(248) 674-5018
signlines@aol.com

MINNESOTA

Dynamic Communications,
Inc.*
6517 Hunter Rd.
Corcoran, MN 55340
Pam Nygren
(763) 478-8963
(763) 478-3093 (fax)
info@aslis.com

Minnesota RID*
6418 Hokah Drive
Lino Lakes, MN 55014
Mary Hoglund
(651) 486-9925
hoglundmc@yahoo.com

SLICES*
14649 Hanover Lane
Apple Valley, MN 55124
Richard Laurion
(612) 827-1885
(952) 953-6043 (fax)
richard@slicesweb.com

OHIO

Hallenross and Associates,
LLC*
585 Binns Blvd.
Columbus, OH 43204
Linda Ross
(614) 296-8937
hallenross@aol.com

Mt. Carmel Health System
St. Ann's Hospital Emergency
Care Ctr
500 Cleveland Ave.
Westerville, OH 43081
Betsy Wood
(614) 898-8871
(614) 898-8850 (fax)

Ohio RID*
6005 Whiteacre Rd.
Toledo, OH 43615
Nancy Hazlett
(419) 841-1987
(419) 343-9321
nancy.hazlett@sev.org

WISCONSIN
Professional Interpreting
Enterprise
6510 W. Layton Ave.
Suite 2
Greenfield, WI 53220
Stephanie Kerkvliet
(414) 282-8115
(414) 282-8117 (fax)
PIELLC@EXEPC.com

Northcentral Technical College
1000 W. Campus Dr.
Wausau, WI 54401
Margaret Holt
(715) 675-3331
(715) 675-6341 (TTY)
(715) 675-0918 (fax)
Holt@ntc.edu

Wisconsin RID
UW – Milwaukee
PO Box 413
Enderis 6th Fl.
Milwaukee, WI 53211
Beth Urquhart
(414) 229-3975
(414) 229-5500 (fax)
bethu@uwm.edu

REGION IV

ARKANSAS
Arkansas RID*
P.O. Box 46511
Little Rock, AR 72214
Myra Taff-Watson
(501) 569-3169
(501) 569-8129 (fax)
mgtaffwatson@uair.edu

CANADA
AVLIC
#9-5708-208th St.
Langley, BC
Canada, V3A 8L4
Barb Mykle-Hotzon
(604) 530-0810
(604) 530-0867 (fax)
bmykle@telus.net

COLORADO
Advanced Seminars, Inc.*
11938 E. Arizona Avenue
Aurora, CO 80012
Anna Witter-Merithew
(303) 750-0250 (V/TTY)
Awitterrmer@home.com

Distance Opportunities for
Interpreter Training Ctr.*
FRCC, Lowry Campus
Bldg. 758
1059 Alton Way - Box 7
Denver, CO 80030
Deborah Nathanson
(303) 365-7678 (TTY)
(303) 365-7677 (fax)
Deborah.Nathanson@frontran
ge.edu

LOUISIANA
The Betty and Leonard
Phillips Deaf Action Ctr.
601 Jordan Street
Shreveport, LA 71101
Cara Hagee-Johnston
(318) 425-7781 x208
(318) 226-1299 (fax)
cjohnston@deafaction.org

Daniel D. Burch*
10632 Ferncliff Ave.
Baton Rouge, LA 70815
(225) 273-3396
slsi@bellsouth.net

Deaf Action Center of
Greater New Orleans
1000 Howard Ave.
New Orleans, LA 70113
Shari Bernius
(504) 523-3755
(504) 525-6729 (fax)
SHARIANN59@aol.com

Louisiana RID*
P.O. Box 979
Oberlin, LA 70655
Ann Reed
(318) 639-4747

MISSOURI
St. Louis Chapter of RID*
P.O. Box 50341
St. Louis, MO 63105
Leanne Helmrich
(314) 781-4707
nofxpez@juno.com

St. Louis Comm. College
(Florissant Valley)*
3400 Pershall Road
Communication North
St. Louis, MO 63135
Mary Luebke
(314) 595-4470
(314) 595-2080 (fax)
mluebke@stlcc.edu

Signs of Development*
P.O. Box 1288
Maryland Heights, MO 63043
(314) 739-9936
Lynne@signs-of-
development.org

Special School District*
Deaf Programs
12110 Clayton Rd.
St. Louis, MO 63131
(314) 989-8342 x6553
(314) 989-8504 (fax)
gshearburn@sssd.k12.mo.us

NEBRASKA
Nebraska Commission f/t
Deaf & Hard of Hearing*
4600 Valley Road
Suite.420
Lincoln, NE 68510
Jennifer Taylor
(402) 595-3991
(402) 471-3067 (fax)

NEW MEXICO
New Mexico RID*
78 Aeby Lane
Espanola, NM 87532
Laura Murphy
(505) 747-2816
murphy@espanola.com

University of New Mexico*
Student Support Services
2021 Mesa Vista Hall
Albuquerque, NM 87131
Bonnie Smith
505-277-3506
505-277-3510 (fax)
bonniels@unm.edu

OKLAHOMA
Oklahoma RID*
OSU Interpreter Training Prgm
900 North Portland Ave.
Oklahoma City, OK 73107
Joni Bice
(405) 945-3288
(405) 945-9131 (fax)
bice@osuokc.edu

TEXAS
Collin County Comm. College*
2800 East Spring Creek Pkwy
Plano, TX 75074
Henry Whalen
(972) 881-5152
(972) 881-5138 (TTY)
(972) 881-5629 (fax)
hwhalen@ccccd.edu

El Paso Community College*
Sign Lang/Interp. Prep Prgm
P.O. Box 20500
El Paso, TX 79998
Mary Mooney
(915) 831-2432
(915) 831-2725 (fax)
nmip@epcc.edu

Goodrich Center for the Deaf
2500 Liscomb St.
Fort Worth, TX 76110
Michael Bothell
(817) 926-5305
(817) 921-9528 (fax)
michaelb@goodrichcenter.com

Houston Comm College
Central*
1301 Alabama
J.B. Whiteley Bldg, Rm. 101
Houston, TX 77004
Shirley Pacetti
(713) 718-6846
(713) 718-6883 (fax)
pacetti@hccc.cc.tx.us

San Antonio College ITP*
1300 San Pedro Ave.
NTC 005A
San Antonio, TX 78212
Lauri Metcalf
(210) 733-2071
(210) 733-2074 (fax)
laumetca@accdvm.accd.edu

Texas Society RID
1325 Memory Lane
Dallas, TX 75217
Chris Grooms
(214) 398-0962
(214) 969-5592 (fax)
mis2301@airmail.net

REGION V

ARIZONA
University of Arizona
Disability Resource Ctr.
1540 East Second St.
Tucson, AZ 85721
Barbara Borich
(520) 621-5176
(520) 621-9423 (fax)
bborich@email.arizona.edu

CALIFORNIA
Angela Funke Koetz
47613 Mardia St.
Freemont, CA 94539
(510) 438-9836
(510) 440-8344 (fax)
AFKASL@aol.com

Communique*
856 Fourth St.
Santa Rosa, CA 95404
Luisa Grossi
(707) 546-6869 (V/TTY)
(707) 546-1770 (fax)
luisa@cqterps.com

El Camino College*
16007 Crenshaw Blvd
Torrance, CA 90506
Susan Marron
(310) 660-6754
(310) 660-3922 (fax)
smarron@elcamino.cc.ca.us

Hands On Sign Language
Services*
P.O. Box 418
Auburn, CA 95604
Vicki Darden
(800) 900-9478
(800) 900-9479 (TTY)
(888) 9000-9477 (fax)
vdarden@hovrs.com

National Ctr on Deafness
CSUN
18111 Nordhoff St.
Northridge, CA 91330
Lauren Kinast
(818) 677-7045
(818) 677-7192 (fax)
daphne.craft@csun.edu

Northern California RID
P.O. Box 3228
Fremont, CA 94539
(510) 839-0171
(510) 834-4889 (fax)
philiplab@earthlink.com

S.E.E. Center f/t Advancement of Deaf Children
P. O. Box 1181
Los Alamitos, CA 90720
(562) 430-1467
(562) 795-6614 (fax)

Sign Lang. Interp. Services*
3942 Terra Vista Way
Sacramento, CA 95821
Roseanne DeVlaming
(916) 483-4751
(916) 487-8177 (fax)
info@signinterpreting.com

Southern California RID*
5017 Canoga Ave.
Woodland Hills, CA 91364
Ila Sachs
(818) 347-6923
isachs@vcccd.net

Treehouse Video LLC
P. O. Box 14934
San Francisco, CA 94114
(415) 861-5810
(415) 861-0827 (fax)
dan@treehousevideo.com

HAWAII
Hawaii RID*
P.O. Box 2416
Honolulu, HI 96804
Valerie Miehlstein
(808) 732-4622
(808) 739-5464 (fax)

OREGON
Oregon RID*
C/O P-S Squared, Inc.
10568 SE Washington St.
Portland, OR 97214
Michele Paoletti-Schelp
(503) 236-3656
(503) 236-2826 (TTY)
(503) 236-3262 (fax)
michele@p-ssquared.com

Region X Interpreter Education
Center, RRCD
Western Oregon University
345 N. Monmouth Ave.
Monmouth, OR 97361
Julie Simon
(503) 838-8731
(503) 838-8039 (TTY)
(503) 838-8228 (fax)
simonjh@wou.edu

Sign Enhancers, Inc.*
10568 SE Washington St.
Portland, OR 97216
Johann Paoletti-Schelp
(503) 257-4777 (V)
(503) 257-4778 (fax/TTY)
Johann@SignEnhancers.com

UTAH
UTRID*
65 W Columbia Dr.
Midvale, UT 84047
Kelli Sundell
(801) 561-4203
KSSUNDELL@aol.com

WASHINGTON
Patricia (Trix) Bruce*
Trix's ASL Workshop
1429-1 Ave. D PMB
Snohomish, WA 98290
asl.workshop@verizon.net

Sign On: A Sign Language*
Interpreting Resource
6041 California Ave. SW
Seattle, WA 98136
(206) 632-7100
(206) 632-0405 (fax)
terps@signonasl.com

Washington State RID*
330 Stanwood Bryant Rd.
Arlington, WA 98223
Katrina Jarman
(206) 409-4896
kjarman@aol.com

*Denotes Sponsor of
Independent Studies

Reprinted with permission from RID

RID AFFILIATE CHAPTERS AND REGIONS

The Affiliate Chapters of RID are divided into five regions, covering all fifty states, the District of Columbia, Puerto Rico, and a number of provinces in Canada. In addition, many states also have local chapters of RID.

Region Representatives are elected to the Board of Directors for a period of two years. These Region Representatives work not only on the broad issues affecting the entire profession, but also work closely with the Presidents and members of state and local chapters on issues special to their areas. The Region Representatives provide detailed reports of the plethora of activities in their regions in the VIEWS newsletter each month.

REGION I
Connecticut, Delaware, Maine, Massachusetts, New Hampshire, New Jersey, New York, Pennsylvania, Rhode Island, Vermont, West Virginia

REGION II
Alabama, District of Columbia, Florida, Georgia, Maryland, Mississippi, North Carolina, Puerto Rico, South Carolina, Tennessee, Virginia, Virgin Islands

REGION III
Illinois, Indiana, Kentucky, Michigan, Minnesota, Ohio, Wisconsin

REGION IV
Arkansas, Colorado, Iowa, Kansas, Louisiana, Missouri, Montana, Nebraska, New Mexico, North Dakota, Oklahoma, South Dakota, Texas, Wyoming

CANADA: Alberta, Manitoba, Saskatchewan

REGION V
Alaska, Arizona, California, Hawaii, Idaho, Nevada, Oregon, Utah, Washington

CANADA: British Columbia

Reprinted with permission from RID

NATIONAL ASSOCIATION OF THE DEAF

814 Thayer Avenue, Silver Spring, MD 20910-4500
301-587-1789 TTY, 301-587-1788 Voice, 301-587-1791 FAX
Headquarters: NADinfo@nad.org, Membership: NADmember@nad.org
World Wide Web: www.nad.org

Individual Membership Application

Individual Membership Categories
(Please check appropriate box)

❑	Regular	$40
❑	Senior (60+)	$25
❑	Student	$25
	(copy of full-time student ID required)	
❑	International	$60
	(US funds only)	

Additional Membership Options

American Sign Language Teachers Association (ASLTA)

(NAD membership required; see membership options above)

❑	Individual	$25

Sections
(NAD membership required)

❑	Library Friends Section	$ 5
❑	Senior Citizens Section	$ 5
❑	Interpreters Section	$ 5

Contributions Welcome

We welcome your contributions of any level!

Donors contributing $25 or more at one time will receive recognition in *NADmag* and Annual Report as well as written acknowledgment of their contribution. Contact the NAD Headquarters for more details about contribution options.

❑ **Yes!** Here is my contribution $_____

The NAD is a 501(c)(3) non-profit organization; all contributions are tax deductible to the extent allowed by law.

Please print clearly:

_____
First   Middle   Last Name

_____
Street Address

_____
City   State   Zip+4

_____
Daytime Phone   TTY/Voice/Both

_____
Daytime FAX

_____
Evening Phone   TTY/Voice/Both

_____
Evening FAX

_____
Email Address

Total Membership and Contribution $_____
*(Please check appropriate boxes in left column
and write in total amount above)*

Two Easy Ways to Pay!

❑ FAX this form with your credit card payment to the NAD at 301-587-1791.

❑ Mail this form with your check (payable to NAD) or credit card payment.

  ❑ Visa   ❑ MasterCard

Expiration Date: ____/____

_____
Account Number

_____
Signature

Mail to : National Association of the Deaf
Membership Department
814 Thayer Avenue
Silver Spring, MD 20910-4500

NATIONAL ASSOCIATION OF THE DEAF CERTIFICATIONS

ASSESSMENT LEVELS

There are five assessment levels, Level I (Novice I), Level II (Novice II), Level III (Generalist), Level IV (Advanced), and Level V (Master), which are explained below. Important Note: Candidates who attain Levels III, IV, and V receive certification (certificate, suitable for framing, and wallet-sized certificate) along with their profile/graph.

Candidates who attain Levels I and II receive the profile/graph sheet, but are not certified as interpreters.

NON-CERTIFIED ASSESSMENT LEVELS:

Level I (Novice I): The individual who attains this level possesses good voice-to-sign skills but may not know the appropriate sign for everything needed. Also, the individual possesses minimal sign-to-voice skills and may fingerspell more than necessary, demonstrate considerable lag time, and delete considerably in order to keep up.

Level II (Novice II): The individual who attains this level possesses good voice-to-sign skills and fingerspells less than those who possess Novice I skills. The individual possesses fair sign-to-voice skills, may lag behind farther than is comfortable, and delete more than is acceptable.

CERTIFIED ASSESSMENT LEVELS:

Level III (Generalist): The individual who attains this level possesses above average voice-to-sign skills, and good sign-to-voice skills, and demonstrates the interpreting skill necessary for some situations.

Level IV (Advanced): The individual who attains this level possesses excellent voice-to-sign skills and above average sign-to-voice skills, and demonstrates the interpreting skill necessary for most situations.

Level V (Master): The individual who attains this level possesses superior voice-to-sign skills and excellent sign-to-voice skills, and demonstrates the interpreting skill necessary for just about all situations.

Reprinted with permission from NAD

NCI Test Question Development

By Scott Bublitz, Ph.D., CASTLE Worldwide

Writing, Reviewing, Referencing, and Validating the NCI Written Examination

After completing the National Council on Interpreting (NCI) content outline as described in the previous article, the next step in test development is to write items that determine whether or not a candidate possesses sufficient knowledge and skills to be a competent interpreter. The purpose of this article is to describe the process involved in writing, reviewing, referencing, and validating the NCI examination. There are three different components of the test that candidates must take to achieve certification. They are:

1. A written, 150-item multiple-choice test;
2. An interview test containing in-depth questions assessing decision making; and
3. A performance test involving several scenarios in which the candidate demonstrates proficiency in interpreting.

This article will focus on the development of the multiple-choice section of the test. Future articles will discuss the interview and performance sections, respectively.

Development of the Multiple-Choice Examination

NCI retained CASTLE Worldwide, Inc. (CASTLE) of Research Triangle Park, North Carolina to assist in the development of the written section of the test. Each question on the test is designed to assist in making correct pass/fail decisions. The closed-book examination contains 150 multiple-choice questions related to the 12 tasks defined in the NCI content outline. These tasks were validated in March 2002 by a role delineation survey that was sent to 1,000 qualified practitioners in the field of interpreting.

How Were Test Questions Prepared?

Every step in the development of the NCI Certification Examination involves individuals who have documented expertise in interpreting. These individuals represent the best talents in the profession and have been carefully selected for their ability to ensure a quality examination.

Questions developed for use on the examination must meet rigorous requirements designed to ensure validity and fairness for all candidates. The requirements are based on the belief that knowledgeable interpreters should be involved in all phases of question writing and review, and that repeated analysis of the questions ensures their quality.

• All questions were written by distinguished content experts in the field of interpreting.

• The content experts received training on how to write appropriate questions with features that are consistent with best practices. The training enabled the content experts to avoid unintended barriers to the performance of knowledgeable candidates for certification, as well as unintended clues to individuals who do not possess the knowledge being tested.

• The training also prepared content experts to write questions at three different cognitive levels: Knowledge, Application, and Analysis. Questions at the knowledge level require candidates to recall a specific piece of information. Knowledge level questions involve little more than bringing to mind the appropriate material stored in memory. Questions at the application level typically pose a situation that interpreters may reasonably experience in performing their responsibilities. Interpreters must apply their knowledge of facts and procedures in order to solve questions at this level. The analysis level requires interpreters to demonstrate their understanding of both the knowledge and the relationship among facts, principles, methods, and procedures. To answer questions at this level, interpreters must break the material into its component parts so that the organizational structure may be understood.

• All questions were reviewed and revised by expert interpreters other than the item writer. One purpose of the revision is to ensure that questions target the knowledge and skill areas more effectively. Another purpose is to remove any unintended cues that would allow unknowledgeable candidates to answer a question correctly. Other revisions eliminated ambiguity or other potential problems with questions.

• A CASTLE psychometrician reviewed the questions with the content experts and suggested modifications to ensure they conform to accepted item construction standards.

• Every question was referenced to an appropriate publication in the field of interpreting. Appropriate publications included textbooks, manuals, standards, and guidelines of various types. Referencing provides evidence that questions are current, valid, and correct as written.

• In March 2002, each question was evaluated again for importance, criticality, and relevance to the field of interpreting. When there was agreement that questions assess important, critical, and relevant knowledge and skill areas, they were then added to the item bank for possible use on the test.

• Each question was linked through a classification system to the NCI content outline. By linking questions, NCI ensured that the test reflects the practice of interpreters in a consistent and representative manner.

Summary

The test development and review process involves an application of the NCI content outline, as well as question writing, referencing, and validation. After administering the test, analyses will be conducted to demonstrate that questions perform their intended function. The test development process, along with the statistical analysis of questions, ensures the quality of the NCI Certification Examination and the validity of competency decisions made using the test. ∎

Overview of the NCI Performance and Interview Examinations

By Scott Bublitz, Ph.D., CASTLE Worldwide

Introduction

Many examinations have been developed to assess minimum competence of entry-level workers in their professions. These examinations are called certification examinations. The validity of a certification examination involves the demonstration of at least two major qualities. First, the content of the examination must be job related. The job relatedness of the examination is determined by conducting an in-depth analysis of the profession, or a job analysis study, to define the knowledge, skills, and abilities required of the entry-level professional. Second, the examination should cover areas where lack of knowledge could cause harm to the public. Harm may be physical, emotional, or financial. These qualities make up some of the defining characteristics of what is called the content validity of the examination.

Under the direction of CASTLE Worldwide, the procedures NCI will apply to develop the certified interpreter examination will ensure content validity and reliability. CASTLE applies strict standards to the examination development, administration, and scoring processes. The standards CASTLE applies are derived from:

- *The Revised Joint Technical Standards for Educational and Psychological Testing*, published by the American Psychological Association (1999);
- *Uniform Guidelines on Employee Selection Procedures*, developed by the Equal Employment Opportunity Commission;
- *Standards for Accreditation of National Certification Organizations*, developed by the National Commission for Certifying Agencies;
- *The Guidelines for Non-Written Examinations*, developed by the National Commission for Certifying Agencies (1991); and
- A review of the published literature on psychometric and legal

standards for certification/licensure tests.

In order to assess the required knowledge and skills of the competent interpreter, the NCI examination will include three components: written multiple choice, performance, and interview. This article will discuss the performance and interview sections of the NCI examination.

Purpose of the Performance Examination

The purpose of a performance examination is to assess the skills of interpreting in a real-world situation. Performance examinations have many advantages. They tap skills and aspects of job performance that cannot be measured in other ways. They are generally viewed by examinees as "fair" because of the similarity and clear connection between test items and competence on the job. They weed out candidates who "know what to do, but can't do it" (National Commission for Certifying Agencies, 1991). However, performance examinations present many challenges if improperly developed.

The performance examination must cover a more restricted topical area because examinees must respond to a limited number of prompts covering specific practice scenarios in a limited time frame. The test presents unique challenges in development (Loyd, Engelhard, and Crocker, 1996). The raters must be highly-skilled professionals to make qualified judgments about the candidate's performance and must be trained to score the test in a consistent manner.

Purpose of the Interview Examination

The purpose of NCI's interview examination will be to assess the candidate's ability to respond in scenarios related to ethical decision-making, attitude and cultural competence of interpreters. Since attitude itself is difficult

to measure, attitude and cultural competence will be measured through the evaluation of high-level decision-making.

The committee has developed real-world scenarios from a variety of settings. They consist of one-on-one situations, small group, large group and professional development situations. They are directly linked to the tenets of the Code of Ethics being developed for the NCI from the existing NAD and RID Codes of Ethics. The joint NAD-RID Code of Ethics Review Committee is working on this project.

The interview examination also falls into the performance or practical assessment category. The interview examination is subject to the same development issues as the performance examination. The scope of the content covered in the examination is limited, raters must be highly skilled and trained, and the scoring is more involved when compared to a written multiple-choice examination.

Developing the Performance and Interview Examinations

The skills assessed in each performance and interview prompt will be drawn directly from NCI's job analysis study. The performance and interview development committees will develop the components of each prompt using instructional worksheets/templates.

Each performance and interview prompt is reviewed, edited, and approved for technical accuracy by the full development committee. The prompt is then reviewed for psychometric integrity and grammatical correctness. Next, the full development committee validates the prompt. The committee rates the prompt according to its importance, criticality, and relevance to the NCI-certified interpreter. The prompt is also evaluated according to the following guidelines:

1. The prompt statement leads the candidate to apply the skills necessary for the required response.

2. Sufficient information is available in the prompt for the candidate to provide the required response.

3. All inconsistencies in the prompt have been rectified.

4. The scoring criteria cover all the

necessary steps to perform the technique or skill.

5. The scoring criteria are in the proper sequence.

6. Each scoring criterion focuses the rater's attention on a different aspect of performance. (i.e., each scoring criterion is mutually exclusive.)

7. Each scoring criterion asks the rater to assess a single aspect of performance.

8. The rater will interpret the scoring criteria in the intended manner.

9. The candidate's performance is not affected by his/her regional or ethnic background.

10. The scoring criteria are supported by published references (at least two).

After developing and validating the performance and interview prompts, content experts identify scoring scales or anchors, which will be used as the standard for scoring the performance and interview prompts. The panel of experts also validates the scoring scales used to assess the candidates according to their importance, criticality, and relevance to the certified interpreter. Using this validation data, the committee develops model responses for each prompt. Finally, the panel will establish a criterion-referenced passing score for each prompt.

Objectivity of Scoring Procedures

The many facets of competent performance on a complex task introduce the possibility that raters may view a candidate's performance differently. If two raters who evaluate the same candidate do not provide the same rating, the test's reliability is reduced. The test's validity also suffers because the candidate's score is affected by something other than his or her performance – it is affected by the rater which happened to be assigned. The resulting measurement error impedes the ability of the test to serve the purposes for which it was intended; i.e., in order to be judged valid, a test must first be judged reliable.

There are many ways to reduce the subjectivity in scoring practical examinations and increase the consistency across raters. The NCI development committees will adhere to the following requirements during determination of the scoring criteria.

- Each scoring criterion must be singular and clear.
- A correct response to the prompt must be accurately defined as agreed upon by the content experts and documented in appropriate published references.
- In addition, the set of scoring criteria for each prompt must fully cover the skills to be assessed by the prompt.

The scoring criteria for the NCI performance and interview prompts are clearly linked to protection of the public. Content experts will rate each scoring criterion according to its importance, criticality, and relevance to the certified interpreter. These ratings are the basis for scoring weights assigned to each scoring anchor. Clear and detailed documentation of the rationale for the scoring anchor and the weighting scheme have been developed. By following the guidelines described above, NCI has ensured the reliability and validity of its certification program. ∎

Reprinted with permission from RID

Performance Test Procedures

There have been questions regarding the procedures for processing a performance testing application for the candidate and a performance testing date for the sites. This is offered to clarify that process.

Persons passing the RID written test will have five years from the date on their test results notification letter to take and pass the performance portion of the test.

It is recommended that candidates submit their applications as soon as they are ready to take the performance portion of the test, as the list of testing slots at Regional Testing Centers (RTCs) is prioritized by the date the completed applications are received by RID. Indicating a specific testing site and date on your application does not guarantee that you will automatically be approved for the testing slot you desire.

The process for testing at an RTC is as follows:
- Before the testing deadline, all applications for persons wanting to test must be **received** by RID. You may only apply for the performance portion of the test if you have already passed the written portion of the same test.
- 8 weeks before testing date - Application deadline.
- 7 weeks before testing date – Final receipt letters are sent.
- 6 weeks before testing date - Testing date acceptance letters are sent to candidates who have identified that site.
- 4 weeks before testing date - Candidate response deadline--we gather all responses by phone, fax, e-mail and post.
- 2-3 weeks before testing date - Final test confirmation letters and directions to the site are sent to candidates.
- 1-3 weeks before testing date - Testing materials are sent to the site.
- Testing date.

The process for supersites is very different than for RTCs. It goes as follows:
- Before the testing deadline, all applications for persons wanting to test must be **received** by RID. You may only apply for the performance portion of the test if you have already passed the written portion of the same test.
- 8 weeks before testing date - Application deadline.
- 7 weeks before testing date –Receipt letters are sent.
- 6 weeks before testing date – Once a candidate has their receipt letter they may call a supersite directly to arrange for testing date.

(All of the above can take place more than 8 weeks before a testing date—and at many of the busier supersites it is recommended to do so.)

- 5-6 weeks before testing date - Supersite coordinator/LTA contacts RID to confirm the eligibility of the candidates who have reserved a testing date with them.
- 3-5 weeks before testing date - Final test confirmation letters and directions to the site are sent (often e-mailed) to candidates **by the supersite.**
- Testing date.

As you can see, the supersite option offers much greater flexibility in scheduling for both the site and the candidate. Calling to schedule a test at supersites, however, is **not** an "on-demand" operation. More correctly stated, it is testing by appointment and is dependent on the availability of the supersite schedule.

The goal for completing the rating of your examination is 90 days from the date of testing. During certain times of the year, (i.e., in the summer and fall, when many more candidates test and less raters are available) that goal may be exceeded periodically.

If a colleague who tested at the same time and location as you receives their results before you, there is no cause for alarm. It simply means that your tape was in all likelihood sent to a different group of raters and will be processed in accordance with that group's timeline. The National Office has been formulating a method by which members could confidentially track their rating progress on-line. Please check the RID website for the most current information regarding this proposed system.

In order to allow the NTS staff to work as efficiently as possible, please do not call the National Office for the results of your performance test until at least three months have transpired.

Everyone in the NTS greatly appreciates the work done by site coordinators and LTAs who often work sacrificially in order to make testing available for their colleagues.

NAD-RID NATIONAL INTERPRETER CERTIFICATION KNOWLEDGE (WRITTEN) TEST APPLICATION

THIS APPLICATION IS NOT FOR THE NAD-RID NATIONAL INTERPRETER CERTIFICATION (NIC) PERFORMANCE TEST. THE NAD-RID NIC PERFORMANCE TEST IS SCHEDULED TO BEGIN IN MID-2005.

Name: _____
(Last)   (First)   (M.I.)

SSN: _____ Memb.#: _____
(Social Security Number)   (RID Membership Number)

Address: _____
(Street)   (Apt. #)

_____
(City)   (State)   (Zip)

Phone: _____ V TTY Both _____ V TTY Both
(Home)   (Work)

Pager: _____ E-Mail: _____

Cell Phone: _____

NOTE: All Information is mandatory except pager, cell phone, and RID member number for non-members.

PLEASE CHOOSE ONE METHOD OF TESTING

☐ **Computer-Based Testing**
- Offered at over 400 sites nationwide
- Testing retakes allowed every 3 months
- Results available immediately at test site
- On-demand test scheduling through CASTLE testing
- Application deadline 4 weeks before test date

☐ **Pencil and Paper Test**
- Offered at 50 sites nationwide
- Testing retakes allowed every 6 months
- Results available 10 business days after receipt of test from site
- Test offered on the first Saturday of June and December
- Application deadline 8 weeks before test date

Test	Item	Member	Non-Member	Payment
NIC Written - Computer Based (INTRODUCTORY PRICE)	Test Fee (includes $40 non-refundable application fee)	$225.00	$325.00	
	Retake Fee (includes $40 non-refundable application fee)	$175.00	$275.00	
NIC Written - Pencil and Paper	Test Fee (includes $40 non-refundable application fee)	$175.00	$275.00	
	Retake Fee (includes $40 non-refundable application fee)	$125.00	$225.00	

TOTAL amount enclosed (U.S.)

☞ In order to receive the member rate you MUST be a member in good standing and include your member number above.

Do you maintain other RID certification? ☐ YES ☐ NO
If yes, which? _____

Test location/date preference(s)? For Pencil and Paper Test Only.
Date: _____ Site Code _____
Site Name: _____

If you have a disability or need that requires a special accommodation, please describe below. Official verification of the need for the accommodation MUST accompany this application.

_____

Payment Information

IMPORTANT: RID must receive payment in full before you will be eligible to take the test. You may fax or mail your application.

Money Order or Check # _____

☐ VISA ☐ Master Card ☐ AmEx ☐ Discover

Card # _____

Expiration Date _____

Signature _____

Send Application, Fees, and any Supporting Documentation to:
RID, Inc.
333 Commerce Street
Alexandria, VA 22314
(703) 838-0454 Fax

IMPORTANT: Please read the following statement and description of the RID tests. All applicants must sign this acknowledgement that they have read and will abide by the following agreement.

I understand and agree that all materials developed and used in the test that I am applying to take are the copyrighted property of the Registry of Interpreters for the Deaf, Inc. (RID), which is a not-for-profit organization; that the test and test results are likewise the property of RID and are not to be shared, duplicated or disseminated in any fashion; that such are not diagnostic in nature and can be used for no purpose other than as intended by RID; and that the scores and method of grading cannot be reviewed by anyone (myself included) except by those authorized by RID to evaluate and/or grade.

I have read and understand the conditions and requirements placed on me by RID in taking the test applied for and do agree to abide by all of these and the rules for taking the test as set out by RID. I hold harmless RID, its officers, agents, and employees from any and all liability, except intentional wrongdoing, in the offering, taking, grading, and reporting of these tests. I understand and agree with the above statements.

Signed: _____ Date: _____
(REQUIRED) By signing this, I certify that I am 18 or older.

RID shall not discriminate in matters of certification testing or membership on the basis of age, color, creed, disability, ethnicity, hearing status, national origin, race, religion, gender or sexual orientation.

REV 2/13/04

NAD-RID National Interpreter Certification (NIC) Knowledge Examination
Suggested Reference Materials

What follows is a list of suggested references that may be helpful as you prepare for the NAD-RID National Interpreter Certification Knowledge (written) Examination. This list does not attempt to include all acceptable references, nor is it suggested that the examinations questions are necessarily based on all of these references. RID does not intend the list to imply endorsement of these specific references and reserves the right to update this list as needed.

For a more comprehensive listing of articles related to the field of interpretation and deafness, you may wish to refer to: *An Annotated Bibliography on Interpretation*, compiled by Carol Patrie and Julie Mertz, Gallaudet University, 1997.

You may access the RID Standard Practice Papers, RID Code of Ethics, and RID Bylaws through the RID website (www.rid.org) or the RID fax-on-demand system by calling 1-800-736-9280.

NAD-RID NIC Suggested Reference Materials
A Place of Their Own: Creating Deaf Community in America, John Vickrey Van Cleve and Barry A. Crouch, Gallaudet University Press, 1989
American Sign Language: A Teacher's Resource Text on Grammar and Culture, Baker-Shenk and Cokely, Gallaudet University Press, 1980
Best Practices in Educational Interpreting, Seal, Allyn & Bacon Publishers, 1998
Deaf Plus – A Multicultural Perspective, Christensen, Dawn Sign Press, 2000
Encounters with Reality, Cartwright, RID Press, 1999
Excerpt from a lecture given by George Veditz in 1913 titled "Preservation of the Sign Language." with translation by Carol Padden. Padden and Humphries, 1988
"Exploring Ethics: A Case for Revising the Code of Ethics," Cokeley, 2000 Journal of Interpretation, RID Publications, 2000
Interpreting: An Introduction, Frishberg, RID Publications, 1990
Interpreting: The Art of Cross Cultural Mediation, Proceedings of the 1985 RID Convention, Marina McIntire, Editor. RID Publications, 1986
Linguistics of American Sign Language, Valli and Lucas, Gallaudet University Press, 1995
National Multicultural Interpreter Project (NMIP) Curriculum, TIEM Project web site, NMIP, El Paso Community College, 2000
Reading Between the Signs: A Practical Approach to Cultural Adjustment, Mindess, RID Publications, 1999
Reading Between the Signs: Intercultural Communication for Sign Language Interpreters, Mindess, Intercultural Press, 1999
RID Code of Ethics, RID Publications
RID Standard Practice Papers, RID Publications
RID Bylaws, RID Publications
Sign Language Interpreting: Exploring Its Art and Science; Stewart, Schein, and Cartwright; Allyn & Bacon Publishers, 1998
So You Want To Be An Interpreter, 3rd Edition, Humphrey and Alcorn, H&H Publishers, 2001
Transliterating: Show me the English, Kelly, RID Press, 2001

AMERICANS WITH DISABILITIES ACT (ADA) HANDBOOK INFORMATION

Below is a reproduction of the "Introduction" page to the **ADA Handbook:**

Introduction

The *ADA Handbook* represents one part of the overall effort by the Equal Opportunity Commission (EEOC) and the Department of Justice (DOJ) to provide information and assistance on the ADA to people with disabilities, businesses, and the affected public. It is intended to serve as a basic resource document on the ADA, EEOC and DOJ are scheduled to publish ADA technical assistance manuals, containing more specific information on how to comply with the law, in early 1992. Further technical assistance will be provided through training, videotapes, information hotlines, media outreach, speaking presentations, and other publications. EEOC has responsibility for providing technical assistance for title I, dealing with employment. DOJ has responsibility for providing technical assistance for titles II and III, addressing public services and public accommodations, respectively. Many businesses with 15 or more employees will be covered by both title I and title III of the Act.

The *Handbook* contains annotated regulations for titles, I, II, and III, resources for obtaining additional assistance, and an appendix which contains supplementary information related to the implementation of the ADA.

Duplication of all or parts of the *Handbook* is encouraged.

This document is available in the following alternate formats:
> Braille
> Large Print
> Audiotape
> Electronic file on computer disk and electronic bulletin board
> (202) 514 - 6193

To order additional copies of this document call:
> At EEOC:
> 800 - 669 - EEOC (Voice)
> 800 - 800 - 3302 (TDD)

> At DOJ:
> (202) 514 - 0301 (Voice)
> (202) 514 - 0383 (TDD)

Websites for additional information:
> http://www.eeoc.gov
> http://www.usdoj.gov

INDEX

A

ABEDATA, 203

Academic transcripts, 51

Accented speech, 106

Accountants, 60

Acoustics, 97

ADARA, 204

Agencies, 42

    interpreting for, 75–76

AIDS-related interpreting, 74–75

ALABAMA

    Approved CMP and ACT Sponsors, 292

    Associate, Certification, and Continuing Education Programs, 251

    Bachelor's Degree Programs, 265

    birth certification location information, 153

    state tax contact information, 190

    Workers' Compensation Administrators, 229

ALASKA

    birth certification location information, 153

    state tax contact information, 190

    Workers' Compensation Administrators, 229

ALBERTA

    American Sign Language-English Interpreter Preparation Programs, 264

    Workers' Compensation Administrators, 248

ALCOHOLICS ANONYMOUS (AA)

    Preamble, 195

    Serenity Prayer, 195

    terminology, 104–105

    Twelve Steps, 196

    Twelve Traditions, 197

Alexander Graham Bell Association for the Deaf, 204

American Academy of Audiology (AAA), 204–205

American Academy of Otolaryngology-Head and Neck Surgery, 205

American Association of the Deaf-Blind, 205

American Hearing Research Foundation, 206

American Samoa, Workers' Compensation Administrators, 247

American Society for Deaf Children (ASDC), 206

American Speech-Language-Hearing Association (ASHA), 206

American Tinnitus Association (ATA), 207

Americans with Disabilities Act (ADA) Handbook, 307

Anti-Trust Act, 31

Application for federal employment — SF 171, 146–150

    general information page, 150

    optional application for federal employment —OF 612, 151–152

Approved CMP and ACT Sponsors, 291–296

ARIZONA

    Approved CMP and ACT Sponsors, 296

    Associate, Certification, and Continuing Education Programs, 251

    Bachelor's Degree Programs, 265

    birth certification location information, 153

    state tax contact information, 190

    Workers' Compensation Administrators, 229

ARKANSAS

    Approved CMP and ACT Sponsors, 295

    Associate, Certification, and Continuing Education Programs, 251

    birth certification location information, 153

    state tax contact information, 190

    Workers' Compensation Administrators, 229

Arkansas Rehabilitation Research and Training Center for Persons Who are Deaf and Hard of Hearing, 207

Assignment intake information, 46, 56, 185

    forms for, 55–56

Association of Late-Deafened Adults (ALDA), 207

Atlanta Region, Workers' Compensation Administrators, 228

Attire, 99, 101–102, 112, 131–133

Attitude, 113–114

Auditory-Verbal International, 208

B

BEGINNINGS for Parents of Hearing Impaired Children, 208

Better Hearing Institute (BHI), 208–209

Billing and filing, 57–59

    invoices, 58

    sample invoice, 59

Birth certificate, 44

    location information, 153–164

Blending in, 103

Booking form, 141

Workers' Compensation Administrators, 229

Boston Subregion, Workers' Compensation Administrators, 227

Boys Town National Research Hospital, 209

BRITISH COLUMBIA

    American Sign Language-English Interpreter Preparation Programs, 264

    Workers' Compensation Administrators, 248

Budgeting your time, 122

Business cards, 41, 45

Business interpreting, 76–78

C

CALIFORNIA

    Approved CMP and ACT Sponsors, 296–297

    Associate, Certification, and Continuing Education Programs, 251–252

    Bachelor's Degree Programs, 265

    birth certification location information, 154

    state tax contact information, 190

    Workers' Compensation Administrators, 230

Canada. *See also* individual provinces

    Approved CMP and ACT Sponsors, 295

Captioned Media Program (CMP), 209

Carpal tunnel syndrome (CTS), 118–120, 199

Certificate of Interpretation (CI), 29, 275–276

Certificate of Transliteration (CT), 29, 275–276

Certified Deaf Interpreter (CDI), 29, 276

Charitable contributions, 135–138

Chicago Region, Workers' Compensation Administrators, 228

Children of Deaf Adults (CODA's), 26

Chiropractic adjustments, 119

CISS International Committee of Sports for the Deaf, 217

Cochlear Implant Association, Inc. (CIAI), 210

Code of Ethics, xix, xxi following, 111–112

COLORADO
Approved CMP and ACT Sponsors, 295

Associate, Certification, and Continuing Education Programs, 252

birth certification location information, 154

state tax contact information, 190

Workers' Compensation Administrators, 230–231

Community service interpreting, 78–79

Comprehensive Skills Certificate (CSC), 277

Conditional Legal Interpreting Permit-Relay (CLIP-R), 276

Conference booking form, 141

Conference of Educational Administrators of Schools and Programs for the Deaf, 210

CONNECTICUT
Approved CMP and ACT Sponsors, 291

Associate, Certification, and Continuing Education Programs, 252

birth certification location information, 154

state tax contact information, 190

Workers' Compensation Administrators, 231

Continuing Education Units (CEUs), 29

Contributions, 136

Convention booking form, 141

Corporate interpreting, 76–78

Council of American Instructors of the Deaf, 211

Course training record form, 142

Courtroom culture, 90

D

Dallas Region, Workers' Compensation Administrators, 228

Deaf-blind interpreting, 79–81

Deaf Children's Literacy Project, 219–220

Deafness and Communicative Disorders Branch, 211

Deafness Research Foundation, 211

Definitions of an interpreter, 23–25

translation/translator, 25

transliteration/transliterator, 25

what some D/deaf customers view us as, 24

what some hearing customers view us as, 23

what some interpreters think of themselves as, 24

what we are asked to do, 23

what we are called, 23

DELAWARE
birth certification location information, 154

state tax contact information, 190

Workers' Compensation Administrators, 231

Denver Region, Workers' Compensation Administrators, 228

Describing tasks, 81

Directory of National Organizations of and for Deaf and Hard of Hearing People, 203–220

Disability insurance, 65

DISTRICT OF COLUMBIA
Approved CMP and ACT Sponsors, 292

Associate, Certification, and Continuing Education Programs, 253

birth certification location information, 155

state tax contact information, 190

Workers' Compensation Administrators, 231

Donations sample worksheet, 200

E

The Ear Foundation, 212

Educational/academic interpreting, 82–83

Emergency essentials sheet, 194

Emergency interpreting, 84–86

"911" situations, 85–86

public emergency situations, 84–85

Emerson, Ralph Waldo, xiii

Employee evaluations, 88

Episcopal Conference of the Deaf, 212

Errors and omissions insurance, 66

Estimated Quarterly Taxes worksheet, 187

Ethical issues, 112. See also Code of Ethics

Ethnicity concerns, 123

F

Federal jobs, 43

OF 612 optional application form, 151–152

applying for a federal government position, 43

brochure on applying for, 144–145

SF 171 application form, 146–150

Financial planning, 66–67

Fingerspelling, 80

FLORIDA
Approved CMP and ACT Sponsors, 292–293

Associate, Certification, and Continuing Education Programs, 253

Bachelor's Degree Programs, 265

birth certification location information, 155

state tax contact information, 190

Workers' Compensation Administrators, 231–232

G

Gallaudet University, 212

Alumni Association, 212

GEORGIA
Approved CMP and ACT Sponsors, 293

Associate, Certification, and Continuing Education Programs, 253

birth certification location information, 155

state tax contact information, 190

Workers' Compensation Administrators, 232

Getting started, 39–69

assignment intake forms, 55–56

billing and filing, 57–59

business cards, 41, 45

federal government interpreting positions, 43

financial planning, 66–67

getting organized, 45–46

getting out there, 41–42

identification, 43–45

planning for today/planning for tomorrow, 63–66

resumes, 46–53

taxes, 60–62

"tool kit" for interpreters, 67–69

travel/mileage records, 57

Giving back to the community, 135–138

Government interpreting position, 86–87

Guam, Workers' Compensation Administrators, 247

Guiding tasks, 81

H

Hand care, 120, 198

Harassment, 124–127

HAWAII
Approved CMP and ACT Sponsors, 297
Associate, Certification, and Continuing Education Programs, 253
birth certification location information, 155
state tax contact information, 190
Workers' Compensation Administrators, 232

Health hazards, 92

Health insurance, 63–64

Hear Now, 213–214

Hearing Education and Awareness for Rockers- H.E.A.R., 213–214

Heath Resource Center, 214

Helen Keller National Center for Deaf-Blind Youths and Adults, 214

Hepatitis shots, 92–93

History of interpreting, 26

Home address, 44–45, 126

House Ear Institute, 215

Hughes, Virginia, xv

I

IDAHO
Associate, Certification, and Continuing Education Programs, 254
Bachelor's Degree Programs, 266
birth certification location information, 156
state tax contact information, 190
Workers' Compensation Administrators, 232–233

Identification, 43–45
birth certificate, 44
passport, 44–45
social security number, 44

ILLINOIS
Approved CMP and ACT Sponsors, 294
Associate, Certification, and Continuing Education Programs, 254

Bachelor's Degree Programs, 266
birth certification location information, 156
state tax contact information, 190
Workers' Compensation Administrators, 233

Independent Retirement Accounts (IRAs), 67

INDIANA
Approved CMP and ACT Sponsors, 294
Associate, Certification, and Continuing Education Programs, 254
Bachelor's Degree Programs, 266
birth certification location information, 156
state tax contact information, 190
Workers' Compensation Administrators, 233

Intake information, 46, 185

Intern (unpaid) work, 50–51

Internal Revenue Service (IRS), 60
centers for, 188–189

International Catholic Deaf Association, 215

International Hearing Society, 215

Interpretation Certificate (IC), 279

Interpreter profile, 27–28
education, 27
employment settings, 27–28
job functions, 27
services provided, 28
years experience, 27

Interpreting situations, 71–104
agency or "staff" interpreting, 75–76
AIDS-related interpreting, 74–75
business/corporate interpreting, 76–78
community services interpreting, 78–80
deaf-blind interpreting, 79–81

educational/academic interpreting, 82–83
emergency interpreting, 84–86
government interpreting position, 86–89
legal interpreting, 85, 89–91
medical interpreting, 85, 91–93
mental health interpreting, 94–95
platform/performing arts interpreting, 96–97
religious interpreting, 98–99
social interpreting, 101–103
spiritual/metaphysical/ "alternative" interpreting, 99–101
support groups interpreting, 103–105
technical interpreting, 105–106
video relay service (VRS), 106–108

Introduction to interpreting, 23–37

Invoices, 58–57

IOWA
Associate, Certification, and Continuing Education Programs, 255
birth certification location information, 157
state tax contact information, 190
Workers' Compensation Administrators, 233

J

Jewish Deaf Congress, 216

John Tracy Clinic (JTC), 216

Junior National Association of the Deaf, 216–210

Just Say "No," 123–125

K

KANSAS
Associate, Certification, and Continuing Education Programs, 255

birth certification location information, 157
state tax contact information, 190
Workers' Compensation Administrators, 228, 233–234

Keller, Helen, xiii

KENTUCKY
Approved CMP and ACT Sponsors, 294
Bachelor's Degree Programs, 267
birth certification location information, 157
state tax contact information, 191
Workers' Compensation Administrators, 234

L

Labrador, Workers' Compensation Administrators, 249

League for the Hard of Hearing, 217

Legal-ese, 90

Legal interpreting, 85, 89–90

Life insurance, 66

Lifestyles issues, 124

Louisiana
Approved CMP and ACT Sponsors, 295
Associate, Certification, and Continuing Education Programs, 255
birth certification location information, 157
state tax contact information, 191
Workers' Compensation Administrators, 234

M

MAINE
Approved CMP and ACT Sponsors, 291
Bachelor's Degree Programs, 267
birth certification location information, 158
state tax contact information, 191
Workers' Compensation Administrators, 235

MANITOBA
American Sign Language-English Interpreter Preparation Programs, 264
Workers' Compensation Administrators, 248

MARYLAND
Approved CMP and ACT Sponsors, 293
Associate, Certification, and Continuing Education Programs, 255
birth certification location information, 158
state tax contact information, 191
Workers' Compensation Administrators, 235

MASSACHUSETTS
Approved CMP and ACT Sponsors, 291
Associate, Certification, and Continuing Education Programs, 255
Bachelor's Degree Programs, 267
birth certification location information, 158
state tax contact information, 191
Workers' Compensation Administrators, 235

Master Comprehensive Skills Certificate (MCSC), 277

Mastery, not perfection, 114

The Media Access Group at WGBH, 217

Medical interpreting, 85, 91–93

Mental health interpreting, 94–95

MICHIGAN
Approved CMP and ACT Sponsors, 294
Associate, Certification, and Continuing Education Programs, 256
Bachelor's Degree Programs, 267
birth certification location information, 158–159
state tax contact information, 191

Workers' Compensation Administrators, 235–236

MINNESOTA
Approved CMP and ACT Sponsors, 294
Associate, Certification, and Continuing Education Programs, 256
Bachelor's Degree Programs, 268
birth certification location information, 159
state tax contact information, 191
Workers' Compensation Administrators, 236

Miranda warning, 90

MISSISSIPPI
Associate, Certification, and Continuing Education Programs, 256
birth certification location information, 159
state tax contact information, 191
Workers' Compensation Administrators, 237

MISSOURI
Approved CMP and ACT Sponsors, 295
Associate, Certification, and Continuing Education Programs, 256
Bachelor's Degree Programs, 268
birth certification location information, 159–160
state tax contact information, 191
Workers' Compensation Administrators, 237

MONTANA
birth certification location information, 160
state tax contact information, 191
Workers' Compensation Administrators, 237–238

Mutual cancellation policy, 36

N

National Association of School Psychologists (NASP), 217–218

National Association of the Deaf (NAD), 30, 218
assessment, 300
certified assessment levels, 300
Individual Membership Application (sample), 299
Interpreter Code of Ethics, xxi
NAD Certifications, 300
NAD/RID Joint Certification Maintenance Program, 31
NAD/RID National Interpreter Certification (NIC) Knowledge Examination Suggested Reference Materials, 305
NAD/RID National Interpreter Certification Knowledge (Written) Test Application, 304
non-certified assessment levels, 300

National Black Deaf Advocates, 218

National Captioning Institute, 218–219

National Catholic Office of the Deaf, 219

National Center for Accessible Media (NCAM), 219

National Council on Interpreting (NCI), 31–32

National Cued Speech Association (NCSA), 219–220

National Fraternal Society of the Deaf, 220

National Information Center for Children and Youth with Disabilities (NICHCY), 220

National Information Clearinghouse on Children Who are Deaf-Blind, 220–221

National Institute on Deafness and Other Communication Disorders Information Clearinghouse (NIDCD), 221

National Operations Office, Workers' Compensation Administrators, 228

NATIONAL ORGANIZATIONS OF AND FOR DEAF AND HARD OF HEARING PEOPLE
ABEDATA, 203
ADARA, 204
Alexander Graham Bell Association for the Deaf, 204
American Academy of Audiology (AAA), 204–205
American Academy of Otolaryngology-Head and Neck Surgery, 205
American Association of the Deaf-Blind, 205
American Hearing Research Foundation, 206
American Society for Deaf Children (ASDC), 206
American Speech-Language-Hearing Association (ASHA), 206
American Tinnitus Association (ATA), 207
Arkansas Rehabilitation Research and Training Center for Persons Who are Deaf and Hard of Hearing, 207
Association of Late-Deafened Adults (ALDA), 207
Auditory-Verbal International, 208
BEGINNINGS for Parents of Hearing Impaired Children, 208
Better Hearing Institute (BHI), 208–209
Boys Town National Research Hospital, 209
Captioned Media Program (CMP), 209
CISS International Committee of Sports for the Deaf, 217
Cochlear Implant Association, Inc. (CIAI), 210
Conference of Educational Administrators of Schools and Programs for the Deaf, 210
Council of American Instructors of the Deaf, 211

Deaf Children's Literacy Project, 219–220

Deafness and Communicative Disorders Branch, 211

Deafness Research Foundation, 211

The Ear Foundation, 212

Episcopal Conference of the Deaf, 212

Gallaudet University, 212

Gallaudet University Alumni Association, 212

Hear Now, 213–214

Hearing Education and Awareness for Rockers-H.E.A.R., 213–214

Heath Resource Center, 214

Helen Keller National Center for Deaf-Blind Youths and Adults, 214

House Ear Institute, 215

International Catholic Deaf Association, 215

International Hearing Society, 215

Jewish Deaf Congress, 216

John Tracy Clinic (JTC), 216

Junior National Association of the Deaf, 216–217

League for the Hard of Hearing, 217

The Media Access Group at WGBH, 217

National Association of School Psychologists (NASP), 217–218

National Association of the Deaf (NAD), 218

National Black Deaf Advocates, 218

National Captioning Institute, 218–219

National Catholic Office of the Deaf, 219

National Center for Accessible Media (NCAM), 219

National Cued Speech Association (NCSA), 219–220

National Fraternal Society of the Deaf, 220

National Information Center for Children and Youth with Disabilities (NICHCY), 220

National Information Clearinghouse on Children Who are Deaf-Blind, 220–221

National Institute on Deafness and Other Communication Disorders Information Clearinghouse (NIDCD), 221

The National Rehabilitation Information Center, 221

National Technical Institute for the Deaf, 222

The National Theatre of the Deaf, 222

Rainbow Alliance of the Deaf, 223

Registry of Interpreters for the Deaf (RID), 223

Rehabilitation Engineering Research Center on Hearing Enhancement and Assistive Devices (RERC), 223–224

Rehabilitation Research & Training Center for Persons Who are Hard of Hearing or Late Deafened, 224

The SEE Center for the Advancement of Deaf Children, 224

Self Help for Hard of Hearing People, 225

Telecommunications for the Deaf, 225–226

TRIPOD, 225

USA Deaf Sports Federation (USADSF), 226

Vestibular Disorders Association, 226

World Recreation Association of the Deaf, 226

The National Rehabilitation Information Center, 221

National Technical Institute for the Deaf, 222

The National Theatre of the Deaf, 222

Navajo Nation, Workers' Compensation Administrators, 247

NEBRASKA
Approved CMP and ACT Sponsors, 295

Associate, Certification, and Continuing Education Programs, 257

birth certification location information, 160

state tax contact information, 191

Workers' Compensation Administrators, 238

Networking, 41, 143

NEVADA
Associate, Certification, and Continuing Education Programs, 257

birth certification location information, 160

state tax contact information, 191

Workers' Compensation Administrators, 238–239

"New Age" interpreting, 99

New Brunswick, Workers' Compensation Administrators, 248

NEW HAMPSHIRE
Approved CMP and ACT Sponsors, 291

Associate, Certification, and Continuing Education Programs, 257

Bachelor's Degree Programs, 268

birth certification location information, 160

state tax contact information, 191

Workers' Compensation Administrators, 239

NEW JERSEY
Approved CMP and ACT Sponsors, 291

Associate, Certification, and Continuing Education Programs, 257

birth certification location information, 161

state tax contact information, 191

Workers' Compensation Administrators, 239

NEW MEXICO
Approved CMP and ACT Sponsors, 295–296

Associate, Certification, and Continuing Education Programs, 257

Bachelor's Degree Programs, 268

birth certification location information, 161

state tax contact information, 191

Workers' Compensation Administrators, 239

NEW YORK
Approved CMP and ACT Sponsors, 291–292

Associate, Certification, and Continuing Education Programs, 257–258

Bachelor's Degree Programs, 269

birth certification location information, 161

state tax contact information, 191

Workers' Compensation Administrators, 240

New York City, birth certification location information, 161

Newfoundland, Workers' Compensation Administrators, 249

"911" situations, 85–86

NORTH CAROLINA
Approved CMP and ACT Sponsors, 293

Associate, Certification, and Continuing Education Programs, 258

Bachelor's Degree Programs, 269

birth certification location information, 161–162

state tax contact information, 191

Workers' Compensation Administrators, 240

NORTH DAKOTA
Associate, Certification, and Continuing Education Programs, 258

birth certification location information, 162

state tax contact information, 191

Workers' Compensation Administrators, 240

Northeast Region, Workers' Compensation Administrators, 227

Northern Mariana Islands, Workers' Compensation Administrators, 247

Northwest Territories, Workers' Compensation Administrators, 249

NOVA SCOTIA
American Sign Language-English Interpreter Preparation Programs, 264

Workers' Compensation Administrators, 249

O

OHIO
Approved CMP and ACT Sponsors, 294

Associate, Certification, and Continuing Education Programs, 258–259

Bachelor's Degree Programs, 269

birth certification location information, 162

state tax contact information, 191

Workers' Compensation Administrators, 241

OKLAHOMA
Approved CMP and ACT Sponsors, 296

Associate, Certification, and Continuing Education Programs, 259

birth certification location information, 162

state tax contact information, 192

Workers' Compensation Administrators, 241

Oklahoma City bombing, 85

ONTARIO
American Sign Language-English Interpreter Preparation Programs, 264

Workers' Compensation Administrators, 249

Oral Interpreting Certificate: Spoken to Visible (OIC:S/V), 278

Oral Interpreting Certificate: Visible to Spoken (OIC:V/S), 278–279

Oral Interpreting Certificate (OIC:C), 278

Oral Transliteration Certificate (OTC), 29, 278

OREGON
Approved CMP and ACT Sponsors, 297

Associate, Certification, and Continuing Education Programs, 259

Bachelor's Degree Programs, 269

birth certification location information, 162

state tax contact information, 192

Workers' Compensation Administrators, 241–242

Organizations. See National Organizations of and for Deaf and Hard of Hearing People

Organizers, 45–46

P

Partners, 114–117, 133–135
providing replacements, 36, 116–117

Passports, 44–45
application, 174–177

Payment pending file, 57

PENNSYLVANIA
Approved CMP and ACT Sponsors, 292

Associate, Certification, and Continuing Education Programs, 259–260

Bachelor's Degree Programs, 270

birth certification location information, 163

state tax contact information, 192

Workers' Compensation Administrators, 242

Per-hour fee, 36

Personal digital assistance (PDAs), 45–46

Personal safety issues, 94–95, 118–127

Philadelphia Region, Workers' Compensation Administrators, 227

Physical therapy, 119

Planning for today/planning for tomorrow, 63–64
disability insurance, 65
health insurance, 63–64
life insurance, 66
professional liability/errors and omissions insurance, 66
workers' compensation insurance, 64–65

Platform/performing arts interpreting, 96–97

Political views, 124

Post Traumatic Stress Disorder (PTSD), 85

Precautions prior to taking assignments, 114–117

Preparation time, xv, 112–114
getting paid for, 87, 97

Prince Edward Island, Workers' Compensation Administrators, 250

Professional challenges, 109–127
carpal tunnel syndrome/repetitive motion disorder, 118–120, 199
following the Code of Ethics, xix, xxi, 111–112
personal safety considerations, 125–127
preparation, 112–114
stress, 120–122
taking precautions prior to the assignment, 114–117
typical safety precautions, 127
workers' compensation, 117–118

Professional courtesy, 133–135

Professional liability insurance, 66, 90

Professional objective statement, 49

Professional presentation, 131–133

Public emergency situations, 84–85

Publications and Information Dissemination (PID), 222

Puerto Rico, 163
Associate, Certification, and Continuing Education Programs, 260
birth certification location information, 163
Workers' Compensation Administrators, 247

Q

Quarterly taxes, 60–62

Quebec, Workers' Compensation Administrators, 250

R

Rainbow Alliance of the Deaf, 223

References, 48, 51
worksheet for, 184

Registry of Interpreters for the Deaf (RID), 26–30, 41, 223, 251–295
American Sign Language-English Interpreter Preparation Programs, 264
Annual Membership Application (sample), 273
Approved CMP and ACET sponsors, 291–296
Associate Continuing Education Tracking (ACET) Program, 288–290
Bachelor's Degree Programs, 265
Certification Maintenance Program (CMP), 30, 283–287
Code of Ethics, xix
degree requirements for RID test candidates, 29–30
Explanation of Certificates, 29, 275–279
Graduate Degree Programs, 272
interpreter profile, 27–28
mission of, 26
NAD certificate, 274
NAD/RID Joint Certification Maintenance Program, 31

NAD/RID National Interpreter Certification (NIC) Knowledge Examination Suggested Reference Materials, 305

NAD/RID National Interpreter Certification Knowledge (Written) Test Application, 304

National Interpreter Certification, 32

National Testing System Computer-Based Testing Application (sample), 280–281

RID Affiliate Chapters and Regions, 298

RID certification updates, 301

NCI Test Question Development, 301

Overview of the NCI Performance and Interview Examinations, 302

Performance Test Procedures, 304

RID certifications, 28–29

RID Code of Ethics, xix

Rehabilitation Engineering Research Center on Hearing Enhancement and Assistive Devices (RERC), 223–224

Rehabilitation Research & Training Center for Persons Who are Hard of Hearing or Late Deafened, 224

Religious interpreting, 98–97

Religious views, 124

Repetitive motion disorder (RMD), 118–120, 199

Replacements

providing, 36, 115

timing of, 133

Resources, 201–301

Resumes, 46–53

keeping copies of, 54

letters of introduction, 51–53

resume worksheet with explanations, 49–51

sample resume, 48

worksheet for, 182–183

Reverse Skills Certificate (RSC), 277

RHODE ISLAND

birth certification location information, 163

state tax contact information, 192

Workers' Compensation Administrators, 243

S

Salary ranges, 32–37

considerations when developing your fees, 35–37

fee schedule worksheet, 37

San Francisco Region, Workers' Compensation Administrators, 228

Saskatchewan, Workers' Compensation Administrators, 250

Schools and universities, 42

Seattle Region, Workers' Compensation Administrators, 228

The SEE Center for the Advancement of Deaf Children, 224

Self-Employed Pensions (SEPs), 67

Self Help for Hard of Hearing People, 225

Sexual lifestyles issues, 124

SIGN LANGUAGE INTERPRETING exercises for, 198

growth in, xvii–xviii, 82

"Signer-cises," 198

"Slash" positions, 87

Social interpreting, 101–103

SOCIAL SECURITY ADMINISTRATION Application for a Social Security Card, 167–171

Request for Earnings and Benefit Estimate Statement, 172–173

social security number, 44

SOUTH CAROLINA

Approved CMP and ACT Sponsors, 293

Associate, Certification, and Continuing Education Programs, 260

birth certification location information, 163

state tax contact information, 192

Workers' Compensation Administrators, 243

SOUTH DAKOTA

Associate, Certification, and Continuing Education Programs, 260

birth certification location information, 164

state tax contact information, 192

Workers' Compensation Administrators, 243–244

Specialist Certificate: Legal (SC:L), 29, 277

Specialist Certificate: Performing Arts (SC: PA), 278

Spiritual/metaphysical/ "alternative" interpreting, 99–101

"Staff" interpreting, 75–76

Start-up fees, 35

State tax contact information, 190–192

Stress, xi, 113–114, 120–122

budgeting your time, 122

"just say no," 123–125

Substitution work, 42

Support group interpreting, 103–105

T

Tactile interpreting, 80

Taft-Hartley Anti-Trust Act, 31

Taxes, 60–60

sample estimated quarterly taxes worksheet, 62

Teammates, 114–117, 125–132

Technical interpreting, 105–106

Telecommunications for the Deaf, 225–226

TENNESSEE

Approved CMP and ACT Sponsors, 293

Associate, Certification, and Continuing Education Programs, 260

Bachelor's Degree Programs, 270

birth certification location information, 164

state tax contact information, 192

Workers' Compensation Administrators, 244

Tetanus shots, 93

TEXAS

Approved CMP and ACT Sponsors, 296

Associate, Certification, and Continuing Education Programs, 260–261

birth certification location information, 164

state tax contact information, 192

Workers' Compensation Administrators, 244

"Tool kit" for interpreters, 67–69

worksheet for, 193

Transliteration Certificate (TC), 279

Travel/mileage records, 57, 186

TRIPOD, 225

Tuberculosis testing, 93

U

UNITED STATES DEPARTMENT OF STATE Application for Passport by Mail (renewals only), 178–181

Passport Application, 174–177

U.S. Office of Personnel Management (OPM), 43

U.S. Virgin Islands

Associate, Certification, and Continuing Education Programs, 261

birth certification location information, 165

USA Deaf Sports Federation (USADSF), 226

UTAH

Approved CMP and ACT Sponsors, 297

Associate, Certification, and Continuing Education Programs, 262

birth certification location information, 164

state tax contact information, 192

Workers' Compensation Administrators, 244

V

Values concerns, 124

VERMONT

birth certification location information, 165

state tax contact information, 192

Workers' Compensation Administrators, 244–245

Vestibular Disorders Association, 226

Video relay service (VRS), 106–108

VIRGIN ISLANDS

Virgin Islands, Workers' Compensation Administrators, 247

VIRGINIA

Approved CMP and ACT Sponsors, 293

Associate, Certification, and Continuing Education Programs, 262

birth certification location information, 165

state tax contact information, 192

Workers' Compensation Administrators, 245

Vocational rehabilitation office, 41

Volunteering, 135–138

W

WASHINGTON

Approved CMP and ACT Sponsors, 297

Associate, Certification, and Continuing Education Programs, 253, 262–263

birth certification location information, 165

state tax contact information, 192

Workers' Compensation Administrators, 245

WEST VIRGINIA

Associate, Certification, and Continuing Education Programs, 262

birth certification location information, 166

state tax contact information, 192

Workers' Compensation Administrators, 245

Williamson, Marianne, xiii

WISCONSIN

Approved CMP and ACT Sponsors, 295

Associate, Certification, and Continuing Education Programs, 262–263

Bachelor's Degree Programs, 271

birth certification location information, 166

state tax contact information, 192

Workers' Compensation Administrators, 246

Workers' Compensation Administrators Directory, 227–250

Canada, 248–250

other U.S. areas, 247

OWCP Regionals, 227–228

Table of Contents, 227

United States and D.C., 229–247

U.S. Department of Labor, 227

Workers' compensation insurance, 64–65, 117–118

Working with others, 129–138

giving back to the community, 135–138

professional courtesy, 133–135

professional presentation, 131–133

Workshop booking form, 141

World Recreation Association of the Deaf, 226

World Trade Center bombing, 85

WYOMING

Associate, Certification, and Continuing Education Programs, 263

birth certification location information, 166

state tax contact information, 192

Workers' Compensation Administrators, 246

Y

Yukon Territory, Workers' Compensation Administrators, 250

Thank you for purchasing
THE PROFESSIONAL SIGN LANGUAGE INTERPRETER'S HANDBOOK.

DISCLAIMER

Information regarding agencies and programs, approved CMP and ACET sponsors, and Interpreter Training Programs (ITPs) change quite frequently. While glad to provide such information, the author assumes no responsibility for inaccuracies or changes.

We will endeavor to remain current regarding programs and contact information. Information will be updated as it is reported to us.

Please submit updated information to:
Linda@InterpretingInfo.com.
Additions and corrections will be included in the next edition.

Check www.InterpretingInfo.com periodically for downloadable updates.

How to order more copies of
THE PROFESSIONAL SIGN LANGUAGE INTERPRETER'S HANDBOOK

Fax orders: (310) 861-5959. Send this form.

Telephone orders: Call (800) 620-4707. **Have your credit card ready.**
Outside USA call: (310) 364-3938

E-mail orders: Orders@InterpretingInfo.com

Postal orders: Sign Language Interpreting Media (S.L.I.M.)
P.O. Box 491147
Brentwood, CA 90049-4521, USA

Name: _____

Address: _____

_____

City _____ State: _____ Zip: _____

Telephone: _____

Fax number:_____

E-mail address: _____

Number of books:_____ $49.95 each
Sales tax: Please add ($4.12) 8.25 % for each book shipped to California addresses.

Shipping and Handling
USA: $9.00 for first book and $3.00 for each additional book.
(Books will not be delivered to a P.O. box.)
International: Canada $17.00US; Mexico $21.00US; All other countries $27.00US; for each additional book add $10.00US for shipping

ORDER TOTAL: $ _____

Payment: Check ❏   Visa ❏   Mastercard ❏   American Express ❏
Check should be made payable to: **Sign Language Interpreting Media** or **S.L.I.M.**

Card number:_____

Name on card: _____**Exp. date:** _____

Billing address (if different from shipping address)

_____

_____

_____

How to contact the author: Linda@InterpretingInfo.com

For further information and updates, visit our website:
www.InterpretingInfo.com